Palestine

The Prize and Price of Zion

Palestine

The Prize and Price of Zion

Kenneth Cragg

CASSELL

LONDON AND WASHINGTON

Cassell

Wellington House, 125 Strand, London WC2R 0BB

PO Box 605, Herndon, VA 20172

British Library Cataloguing-in-Publication Data
A catalogue record for this book is available from the British Library.

ISBN 0-304-70075-4

See p. 185 for acknowledgements of permissions to quote poetry in Chapter 10.

Cover picture: Palestinian children give new life to discarded household furniture on a
rubbish tip in the Gaza Strip.

Typeset by Keystroke, Jacaranda Lodge, Wolverhampton
Printed and bound in Great Britain by Biddles Ltd, Guildford and King's Lynn

Contents

A short chronology   vi

Preface   xii

 1 Once upon a Gaza Strip   1

 2 The fate of location   17

 3 The cost of inconsequence   35

 4 The prey of ambivalence   51

 5 The anomaly of the holy   71

 6 The victim of the victimized   89

 7 The pawn of friends   108

 8 The politics of realization   127

 9 The odd-handedness of the USA   147

10 The iron in the soul   168

11 'The searchings of Reuben'   186

12 The tests of faiths   204

Name index   226
Subject index   232

A Short Chronology

1862   Publication of Moses Hess's *Rome and Jerusalem*, urging a Jewish 'nation-seeking' in emulation of Italian 'emancipation'.

1876   Accession to the Ottoman Caliphate of Sultan 'Abd al-Hamid II, pledged to a Constitution providing for some liberalization of its Arab provinces – pledges soon rescinded in the notorious tyranny he created, thus setting the dilemma for nascent Arab national feeling of a choice between 'Ottomanism' and 'revolt' as the path to autonomy and self-realization.

1882   Publication of Leo Pinsker's *Auto-Emancipation*, echoing Moses Hess and pioneering Jewish nationalism in response to pogroms across Russia and calling for 'a Jewish state'. Beginning of Jewish immigration to Palestine with political intent (as distinct from the earlier agricultural *Hibbet Zion* or 'Love of Zion', which was innocuous).

1883f.   Forming of Arab secret societies in Beirut and Damascus for liberation from Turkish oppression.

1894   Trial of Alfred Dreyfus, a *cause célèbre* in the stimulation of Zionist self-consciousness and the demand for 'statehood' as the panacea for Jewish burdens and the menace of both anti-Semitism and treacherous 'Gentile' tolerance.

1897   First Zionist Congress in Basle under the charismatic leadership of Theodor Herzl.

1904   Death of Herzl and emergence of Chaim Weizmann in Zionist planning – often in almost 'solo' terms – shaping diverse thinking.

1908   Parliament in Istanbul with a total of 72 Arab representatives, 35 of whom stood for the Lamarkaziyyah Party (non-centralist) pressing for Arab regional autonomy, i.e., 'nationhood' within the Caliphate.

1917   The Balfour Declaration, secured from the British Cabinet by the persuasive skills of Weizmann. It took the form of a Letter from Balfour to Lord Rothschild, expressing the 'favour' with which Great Britain looked on 'the establishment of a national home for the Jewish people in Palestine' without prejudice to 'the civil and religious rights of the existing population'.

1917–18 Success of British advance on Gaza, Jerusalem and Damascus following the Arab Revolt contrived (though against an Islamic caliph) by promise of territorial national independence for the Arabs. The 'liberation' of Palestine brought the final end of 'Ottomanism' as an Arab option.

1919–21 The Versailles Conference and Peace Treaty: refusal of the Mandate over Palestine by the USA and its 'grant' to Britain by the League of Nations, with the task of giving expression to the Balfour Declaration.

1919   The American King–Crane Commission warns of the built-in 'irreconcilables' in the Mandate, anticipating what later tragic exacerbation only too fully proved, though there was (is) no comfort in their prescience.

1920   Haganah formed by Vladimir Jabotinsky to act as a 'Defence Force' giving Zionism, for the first time, a military arm.

1921   Britain appoints Herbert Samuel first High Commissioner for Palestine. Trans-Jordan is separated from the Mandate for Palestine; Samuel appoints Hajj Amin al-Hussaini as Grand Mufti. He proves to be an 'evil counsellor' of Arab tactics. Arabs riot in apprehension of the hidden agenda of the 'Jewish Agency' for immigration and settlement.

1922f. Jewish immigration in *aliyahs*, or 'up-goings', creates the necessary 'presence' in increasing momentum, by purchase and consolidation in scattered units capable of coalescence; the rise of the kibbutzim.

1929   Further Arab riots in protest and bewildered violence; the Mandatory power increasingly besieged by incompatible obligations.

1930   A British 'White Paper' responds by restricting Jewish immigration; the Jewish Agency cries 'foul' and demands the Mandate be read and fulfilled on their terms.

1933f. The rise of Hitler and Nazi Germany and the ground-laying of the Shoah. Zionism will be ever more urgent for Jewish survival.

1936–37 Conference in London. The Peel Commission rules that a Jewish 'National Home' (in state form) is not compatible with Palestinian rights and recommends partition. Neither side agrees.

1939 Outbreak of the Second World War. A 'White Paper' restricts immigration to 75,000 over five years. The exigencies of world war overtake the territory, putting both parties' claims 'on hold'. Zionists seek to participate as a Jewish Brigade. The Grand Mufti opts for Nazi victory and goes to Berlin. Palestinianism on the ground is freed from his malign counsels but remains bitter and confused.

1942 British victory at Alamain in North Africa saves the fledgling Zionist entity from annihilation. The Biltmore debate in New York has the Zionists accepting that Palestine may be partitioned as pragmatic policy, if that has to be the option.

1945 The end of the Second World War, the relative decline of British power and the emergence to world authority of the USA lead to a remitting of the Palestine/Zion problem to the newly-formed United Nations.

1946 UN Commissions and representations move towards the inevitability of partition. Increasingly urgent Jewish flow towards 'haven-Zion'.

1947 The fledgling United Nations, still lacking its due complement of nations, resolves on partition, according 52 per cent to a new state and 48 per cent to a new Palestine, on the basis of consolidating Jewish enclaves amounting – as purchased – to 6 per cent. To take effect on the withdrawal of the Mandatory Power in May 1948. Jerusalem to be an international zone.

1948 Declaration of the new state and its naming as 'Israel'. Palestinians and all Arabs repudiate what they take as the filching of their land.

1948–49 Warfare and two successive 'truces' leave some 80 per cent in Israeli control, during which the UN mediator, Count Bernadotte, is assassinated by the Stern Gang, to preclude any reinstatement of the pre-battles alignment. The perpetrators never punished. Massive emigration of Palestinians into refugee-dom. Consolidating of Jewish influx.

1956   Israeli invasion of Sinai in collusion with Anglo-French conspiracy to unseat 'Abd al-Nasir (Nasser). Israeli aim to secure the southern front against any repeat of the 1948 attack by Egypt. President Eisenhower requires Ben Gurion to withdraw from Sinai.

1965   Embryonic emergence of the Fatah organization, later to develop into the Palestine Liberation Organization, with the aim to recover lost territory and transform world perception of Palestinianism as a 'refugee problem' into a theme of nationhood.

1967   'Abd al-Nasir precipitates a *casus belli* with Israel via a threat to shipping and in a bid for Arab hegemony. An Israeli blitzkrieg frustrates him, despite the entry of Jordan and Syria into the battle. Israel captures Old Jerusalem, enlarges its municipality and proclaims it the 'eternal Jewish capital'; the remaining 20 per cent of mandated Palestine (the 'West Bank', i.e. of the Jordan river) is 'occupied' but not annexed.

1968f. The PLO finds increasing frustration in efforts to put itself 'on the map' by means of raids across the new borders, in face of strong Israeli retaliation and the refusal of Jordan to allow autonomous action for the *feda'in*. Desultory terrorist attacks on international targets.

1970   'Black September': Jordan expels Palestinian resisters after bitter fighting; Jordanian sovereignty impugned by PLO claim for a 'free hand' against Israel. Anwar Sadat becomes President of Egypt on death of 'Abd al-Nasir.

1972   Palestinian terrorists kill Israeli athletes at the Munich Olympics and stain their own cause in desperation at impasse and stalemate over implementation of UN Resolution 242 concerning evacuation by Israel of 'territories occupied' in 1967.

1973   Yom Kippur War: Egypt crosses the Suez Canal and recovers East Bank; withdrawal negotiated after later reverses; cease-fire lines set up in Sinai and Golan.

1974–88 Civil war in Lebanon, precipitated by the tension between Palestinians in arms and the several factions within the country in interpretation of Lebanese identity. Increasing embroilment and frustration, with Syrian intervention and complicity.

1975   United Nations debates the Zionism/racialism issue and resolves that ethnic displacement obtains. Israel, with US backing, decries the racialist reproach. Palestinianism begins to be conceded as an authentic nationalism.

1977 President Sadat's visit to Jerusalem and address to the Knesset, following Menahem Begin's long-thwarted attainment of power.

1978 Initiation of massive emigration of Russian Jews from Soviet Russia into Israel.

1979 The Camp David Accords pledge return (after duly protracted further calculation) of Sinai to Egypt, with a Palestinian autonomy 'linked' to it. Begin has a different reading from that of Carter and Sadat and 'linkage' becomes a 'dead letter'.

1981 Sadat falls victim to an assassin – the price of his *démarche* in 1977.

1982 Israel invades Lebanon in pursuit of 'peace in Galilee'; tragic suffering inflicted on the Lebanese and non-belligerent Palestinians, the armed ones being at length expelled to Tunis or dispersed. Massacres of refugees in the camps of Sabra and Chatila.

1984 US maintains refusal to recognize the PLO as sole representative of the Palestinian people and signs a formal strategic co-operation agreement with Israel.

1985 Israel withdraws from Lebanon, except for buffer zone in the south which becomes a steady source of bitter friction via counter action of Hizballah in defiance of it.

1987 The start of the Intifadah, a Palestinian uprising against Israeli occupation and in assertion of human rights against confiscations, home demolitions and the intensifying misery of an oppressive impasse.

1988 The PLO, seeking to overcome US negation of its legitimacy, resolves to 'recognize the legitimate statehood of Israel' within agreed boundaries still indeterminate – playing, in effect, the ultimate card and finally reversing the decision of 1948 to reject partition. The US remains diplomatically sceptical; Israel charges the PLO with insincerity.

1991 Emergence of the Hamas movement disputing the PLO's mandate and policy – its emergence a product of prolonged frustration.

1991 The Shamir–Likud government finally yields to attend a Peace Conference in Madrid under US auspices after tedious negotiation about which Palestinians were 'appropriate' – resolved under protest by linking them with Jordanians.

1992 Elections in Israel yield a Labour Government under Rabin and Peres. They play a strong hand, exiling a hundred or so Palestinian activists to the snows of Hermon, but a more conciliatory tone emerges on the 'negotiability' of 'land for peace' in some still indeterminate detail.

1993   While 'Madrid' languishes (in Washington), secret and courageous negotiations in Norway bring the Oslo Accords, signed with high ceremony in Washington. They propose a gradualism intended to foster mutual confidence, beginning with cession of Gaza and Jericho to Palestinian authority.

1995–96 Implementation, with some delays, proceeds in six enclaves; arming of Palestinian police; dubious posture on the freezing of settlements of Israelis on the West Bank. Jewish terrorist assassinates Rabin.

1996   Elections proceed for Palestinian Parliament: then Israeli elections which – by the narrowest of margins – return a Likud/Coalition government under Benyamin Netanyahu.

1997   After some disconcerting delay a revised formula is agreed and implemented for the transfer of 80 per cent of the city of Hebron to Palestinian control. Deep anxieties persist about how vulnerable it remains to violent disruption. Other outstanding items of Oslo remain for gradual solution in or before the end of 1998. They have to do with access from Gaza to Jericho, the economic viability of the Palestinian town and rural enclaves, the increasing Jewish settlements, and the place of Jerusalem in the Palestinian identity.

The summer and autumn of 1997 bring increasing frustration, with a simmering explosiveness as delay under Netanyahu reads increasingly like a rescinding of the Oslo Accords. Settlement building on Har Homa ('Mount of slaughter') flouts Oslo and the UN and dismays peace-lovers within Israel by intensifying the signs of adamant confrontation. Shimon Peres is replaced as Leader of the Labour Party. Apprehension has it that the Netanyahu Government has 'a map in mind' that would again truncate Palestinian ground-expression and bury hope of statehood. Palestinian response in a womb of despair?

1998   Israel due to celebrate its jubilee.

Preface

As the chapter headings make clear, this book is concerned with various, inter-locking aspects of a 'Palestine Agonistes' (its first tentative title). It follows that some features of a long story recur in different contexts. It is hoped that readers will understand the reasons when significances repeat themselves from different angles of view.

Books about 'Israel–Palestine' are liable to be out of date before they appear, events moving so ominously. And there are other hazards. Which way, for example, should the land-title run? For 'Palestine–Israel' is equally true and there can be no doubt, historically or emotionally, of the reality of the dual appellation. The land is competitively loved. The Jewish nationalism which, as 'Zionism', claims to retake and renew its Jewishness is matched by a local, native love no less old, no less ardent and no less sold on the necessity of statehood to identity and of territory for statehood. Indeed no small part of the tragedy is that the two aspirations so far reproduce each other, with the disparity contingent on the one-sided perception of covenantal destiny that the mind of Israel prizes.

'Land', then, and 'land-love' are the theme of all else. One might then, ruminatingly, happen on the familiar phrase, 'the lie of the land' and perceive at once a strange irony – a kind of paradox created by entire legitimacy and sinister falsehood. 'The lie of the land' is innocent language to the prospecting engineer or the landscape-gardener. It could readily suit the legend of old Moses, denied entry but surveying from Mount Pisgah the far prospect of the promised territory. There has always been this 'territorial dimension' of Judaism. The pain of exile silenced the 'songs of Zion', when harps hung forlornly on foreign willows. Always in the mind's eye was 'the lie of the loved land', the resident's delight, the exile's yearning.

Topographical detail cherished and savoured how 'the land lay': its stones for iron and its hills for brass, its olive groves and vineyards, its figs and pomegranates, its pastures and streams, its recurring rainfall, its Mediterranean winds. All these might be authentically read as the benison of a tribal lord, the substance of a celestial promise, the *materia divina* of a custodian people come dramatically out of nomadism and bondage into enlandisement and surrogacy for Yahweh, 'Lord of heaven and earth', in earth tenancy and home security, the terms in which Zion perceived its true legitimacy.

Only if we start there does the other sense of 'the lie of the land' emerge, with its burden of an inter-human wrong and the current urgency of the questions Joshua never asked. This dark 'lie of the land' was powerfully identified of old by the Hebrew prophets, by Amos and Isaiah, by Habakkuk and Jeremiah. 'Woe to them that join house to house, who lay field to field till there be no room that they may be placed alone in the midst of the earth.' 'Woe to you, Jerusalem: when will you yet be clean?' 'O Jerusalem, who is there to turn aside and ask how you fare?' Could these voices in their anguished sorrow for 'the lie of the land' be anticipating encroaching 'settlements' on a west bank, the steady attrition of the Arab population of Jerusalem?

It is vital to realize that it is only within the dreamed 'holiness' of a valid Zion that any question arises of its moral quality. If it were only brigandage under no Godward vow, only naked force bound to no covenant, the law of their own will would be their right, the success of their own prowess their sufficient warrant. But, Judaically, it is not so. 'That glory may dwell in our land' was 'the true lie' of it, the vision of a righteousness spelling inclusive benediction. The holy has to be bound over to the ethical or its holiness becomes a conspiracy in wrong. How authenticity obtains is where reckoning belongs. The Zion of the will is mentor of the will to Zion. 'Except the Lord build the house', the psalmist saw its building vain. The Hebrew prophet's verdict on idolatry has the pagan too blind to ask: 'Is there not a lie in my right hand?' 'Is there not a lie in his right land?' might be his question now to an ethic-forfeiting Zionist.

The Book of Joshua may have felt no compunction about the conquest and the elimination of – as Balfour might have phrased it – 'the existing population'. After fifty and more Jewish centuries, twenty Christian ones and fourteen Islamic, it can hardly be so now. Pioneering Zionism always assumed a feasible innocence and, therefore, entailed itself with the

Palestinian demography. Ideals everywhere are liable to ignore their impediments or overlook their obstacles. Zionism often indulged the legend of a waiting vacancy and so darkly prejudiced the fortunes of the existing occupants. Its precarious origins and, by the 1940s, the desperate urgency of its pursuit served to endow its interior mandate with an unequivocal legitimation no scruples need counter and no hesitations obstruct.

Yet another people were present, another identity at stake, another nationalism in birth. Canaanites, Philistines, 'people of the land', had their culture in place, their tillage at work, their ancestry in retrospect. Islam had entrenched itself decisively on 'the rock of Abraham', in a most eloquent symbol of historic irony in terms that made dislodgement the wildest prospect of catastrophic embroilment. That dire *mise-en-scène* apart, the human datum of an occupant reality could only sanely dictate a pattern of compatibility. Compatibility derives verbally – and spiritually – from the same root as compassion.

This book is about the demand of compatibility and the urge to compassion and about the current desperate poverty of both. It is, therefore, also about the Palestinian cost or count of how far these are to seek. Written in the period after the assassination of Prime Minister Rabin and before the election of May 1996, it is hostage to the further march of events and the foreboding they kindle. It may well need an epilogue, publishing being a slow business. Even so, there is point in its concern to address the Palestinian cost of Israel's dramatic recovery of political Zion, a Jewish repopulating of 'territorial dimensions' of its ancient self. For Zion's triumph is Palestine's tribulation, the prize of the one the price in the other.

When John Milton applied the term *Agonistes* to his Hebraic hero Samson, he located him on a Gaza Strip. This writer knew that coast well from a longish sojourn prior to its present tragedy. This forlorn territory provides us with a point of departure into the sorry paradox of enmity and entanglement into which Samson's amours and exploits drew him. For even the fiercest apartheid cannot escape relationships.

From Gaza and its hints and echoes, review has to pass to the several aspects of Palestinian experience. Doing so, it must risk the perennial burden that belongs with all concern for the human cost of Israel – the quick suspicion of a hidden agenda, i.e., a subtle, if latent, anti-Semitism. The risk has to be taken but the suspicion is strenuously denied. It is true that in the soul of Jewry the Shoah constitutes an overwhelming exoneration, *per se*, of any and every dimension of 'rescue' from its tragic horrors, insofar as survivors might find and know it. The conscience of the Hebrew prophets would not approve the invocation of the Shoah as absolving the State of

Israel from all moral concern for its impact on Palestinian sorrows and bereavements, Palestinian culture and story. Rather, retrospect either way, however incommensurate, might be seen to generate a common awareness of the bleak fragility of human life, the vicarious tribulations to which a single humanity is fated by the structured passions and hatreds that humans undergo.

The common property of location is where, leaving a Gaza introit, we have to start. Despite early and tentative vagaries, while Palestine remained within Ottoman control and Theodor Herzl was devising schemes to bargain with the Sublime Porte for a foothold, Palestine it had to be. There was only one 'Holy Land', to fulfil the aspirations of authentic Jewry and to kindle pioneers for the arduous task of braving the odds on the ground or winning over the massively sceptical majority of diaspora Jews still hopeful of genuine 'Gentile' liberties and wary of the implied compromise of nation-seeking elsewhere.

The ill-fortune of Palestinians – those erstwhile 'Philistines' – was this Zionist anomaly of their locale, their occupancy of the coveted territory. Zionist immigration posed no threat to Peru, nor to Mongolia, for history had not bestowed on those lands the mystique of Abraham's foot, nor Moses' Yahweh-summons, nor David's royal realm. 'Host-nation' locale – to use Zionist vocabulary – might be oppressive or broadly feasible, but there was only one territory that could never play 'host', in that it would uniquely spell 'home'. Palestinian history begins its recent saga in that ineluctable fact.

The impetus, ideological and emotional, of the love of the one locale made inexorably for a certain inconsequentiality about the people in place. To be sure, perceptive minds realized that Zion was no vacancy, while the more ardently belligerent perceived a necessary riddance of the unwanted. Pragmatists simply deferred the issue, taxed and distracted by urgent practical matters of acquiring farms, draining swamps, creating a presence and ensuring 'facts'. A persuasion of innocence, not yet – if ever – disproved, was comforting and necessary. *Solvitur ambulando*, had they spoken Latin, would have suited their outlook. The whole enterprise was only precariously 'on the way'. 'Do not ask to see the distant scene', each step suffices for the day.

Similar factors and patterns of mind necessitated a long, if aggravating, ambivalence. Circumspection was vital lest alarm be aroused. Resistance must be allayed, not clumsily aroused. Yet suspicion precisely grows from a sense of the need for it. Uncertain motives motivate the other party more certainly, while perplexities bitterly contending yield only a descending spiral of confusion and embitterment. The story of the British Mandate, locked in its own ill-fated ambiguity, was the most hapless of ventures into the art of fostering 'self-governing' nations. Competitive claimants for this benison could hardly fail to be victimizing each other in the aggravated confusion of their respective ends, but the more frustrated, in the event, was that 'existing population' whose 'civil and religious rights' (only) were not to suffer things 'detrimental'. The Balfour proviso was defeated in the very context of its pledgedness.

Underlying all the foregoing, and hardest of all to appreciate dispassionately, was 'the anomaly of the holy'. Palestine was on the receiving end of a 'mandate' infinitely better sanctioned than the British one. 'The land' was legitimately to be repossessed under a divinely sponsored aegis, disqualifying all ethical caveats and cautions. The Arab mind, in its own ill-advisedness (here to be explored), could never have understood prospectively what, in this mystique, it would be confronting. 'Holiness' was qualified to bestow on pro-Zionist action a sufficient alibi for what, on other counts, might have been morally suspect, a legitimacy that offered absolution to those not minded to interrogate themselves more consciously. That Zionism had many so minded redeems in part its long story. But, in ways too costly and too incorrigible for Palestinian fortunes, its enterprise enjoyed and invoked too far and too harshly the aura of 'divine right'. The question that most presses is the one that stays, namely, in what terms are lands 'held holy'?

Chapters 7 and 8 turn the equation round. Part of the Palestinian trauma was the extent to which Arab neighbours profaned their cause by ill-judgements of policy and chicanery, and how far the Palestinian response to the fates besetting them was lacking in realism, foresight and sagacity. To be sure, such virtues of vision, leadership and self-control would have been hard to come by even for a people more steeled to such demands. In hindsight, it is often argued, the Palestinians could have ensured amply more by a prudent pragmatism than they now struggle forlornly to obtain with so few 'cards' to play. Or perhaps not. But having rejected partitioned statehood and been worsted in battles, they had to emerge against many odds from the status of a pitied refugeedom to that of a credible nationalism, looking not for palliatives but for justice.

In the near-despairing vicissitudes of that effort they were wretchedly 'pawned' to the vagaries or trapped in the jealousies of their fellow Arabs. The inept miscalculations of Egypt's 'Abd al-Nasir played disastrously into Israel's hands, while Jordanian *amour propre* and the chronic fragility of the Lebanon had devastating consequences for the hopes Palestinians themselves tarnished and travestied by ineptness and worse. 'The Politics of Realization' proved a stern and testing school of Palestinian identity. Tribulations are in no way lightened by the discovery of how far they have been self-inflicted – a truth of things which remains beyond all the apologia honesty has to plead.

If one can rightly talk of even-handedness, then odd-handedness is the antonym. To what astonishing lengths did it go on the part of the supposedly fair broker and supreme world-power, the United States. To many an outside observer, it seemed that the Israeli client was manipulating and milking the all-powerful sponsor, so that Zion set the hymn-sheet from which Washington sang. Several factors on the American political stage contributed to this scenario. It was the more remarkable in that solemn Resolutions of the United Nations concerning peace within secure and agreed borders, the non-acquisition or retention of territory by force, the international status of Jerusalem and the return of refugees, were conveniently forgotten or deliberately ignored with the connivance or the negligence of the USA.

All these cumulative factors in the Palestinian *agōn*, as the Greek word would be, had their ultimate register in – to borrow a biblical phrase about the trauma of Joseph in Egypt – 'the iron entering the soul'. The stark physical meaning of the phrase may simply be 'the collar round the captive's neck', but the metaphorical sense is truer still. It is urgent, therefore, to measure the pulse of Palestinian poetry where ultimate things grew articulate and gave utterance to an inward history.

There must be two final chapters. 'The searchings of Reuben' takes warrant from an old biblical narrative to listen-in to the gentler mind of Israel, the kinder heart of Zion, musing on this 'pride and price and prize' of achievement. Those 'searchings' could not fail to prompt a more inclusive testing of religions, the three faiths of the setting and the story and their role in the enmities that fester, and their place in the travail towards peace.

The State of Israel heads towards 'the year of Jubilee' in May 1998, set to celebrate, fifty years on, the historic creation of recovered, political, newly-Davidic Zion. It must be a day of high emotion and exuberant pride. The USA remembers the strange coincidence of its first Jubilee, for, on 4 July 1828, within a few hours of each other, two revered Presidents died – Thomas Jefferson and John Adams. Glad celebration was turned into national mourning. Only chance was to blame. With Israel, is not splendid achievement fraught with inward unease? There is a sharp contention in the bosom of the nation and the political order gives it vexing occasion. There is a grim potential for bitter civil strife, both around the secular/religious divide and also in the contradictions in the very meaning of 'peace'.

The two, confusingly, merge and aggravate. The nation looked, frightened and baffled, into the abyss in November 1995, to know itself capable of Jewish assassination. That dire event had been preceded by verbal vituperation, if not assassination, from elements of the grim resistance of almost half a nation to the projected implications of the Oslo Accords. The nation knew itself tense with bewildering problematics and, by the narrowest of margins in May 1996, opted for what purports to be a steady erosion of the peace measures and reversal of their tentative prospect of Palestinian self-fulfilment in the twin dimensions Zion exemplified as indispensable, namely power and territory.

On that knife-edge electoral decision there ensues a prevarication, a steady de-Palestinianizing of Jerusalem by bureaucratic duress and other means, a deliberate stalling of agreed implementations and, in the impasse thus drawn out, a sustained activity of new Israeli settlements by subsidy and diktat.

Palestinian responses are caught in a hapless dilemma. Hamas- or PFLP-style recourse to violence, however spasmodic and futile, only serves to harden Israeli hearts and provide ground for further stalling. The PLO, as party to Oslo, is virtually in fee to the Israeli Government to maintain security in the townships from which Israeli army and police have conditionally withdrawn. Loyalty in doing so brings no return of fuller implementation; failure only plays into the hands of an Israeli counter-virulence. In that cleft stick the moderate mainstream of Palestinianism is bitterly caught with no assets except withholding compliance – a sequence some Israeli policy-makers would be happy to see. Meanwhile, thanks to the suicide-bombers of the spring of 1996, the enclaves of Palestinian autonomy are ringed with tanks at the ready in a way that never was in the years of Intifadah.

Despair is always the ultimate counterpart of fervent hope: the more authentic and critical the hope, the more *agonistes* the despair. In measure, and at long last, to have seen 'a promised land' in the autumn of 1993 makes the compromise of promise all the more devastating. But it is not only the Palestinian vision that lies forlorn. Zion itself, the dream of an authentic Israel, is critically at the mercy of Zionism. Americans in their first Jubilee grieved for their departed founders – founders who themselves had no cause to grieve. Dying in 1904, still in the strength of his prime, Zion's visionary, Theodor Herzl, had a farewell warning: 'Make no mistakes when I am gone.'

1

Once upon a Gaza Strip

John Milton's *Samson Agonistes* closes with a chorus in the Greek mode, sealing the tragedy of Samson's suicide with the lines,

> Of true experience . . .
> With peace and consolation . . .
> And calm of mind, all passion spent.

It was never so in the Hebraic mode. The Book of Judges is pointedly empty of its usual formula of 'the land having rest' after the feats of its successive heroes, Deborah, Gideon and their peers. A sinister ambivalence prevails. The mighty man's tragic demise amid the massive slaughter of Dagon's worshippers leaves only a legacy of indecision, with those Philistines still in uneasy adjacence and potential menace. Milton needs rewriting.

> Is nothing here for tears, nothing to wring
> And daunt the mind, no puzzle, no dismay
> At what disquiets in a death so dire?
> Gather indeed his kindred and his friends
> With silent obsequy and funeral train
> Home to his father's house.
> Let virgins also thence on sorrow's days
> Visit his tomb with sighs, the while lamenting
> His lot ambiguous in divine employ.[1]

1

There were other protagonists of near-legendary prowess in the long story of Jewry and the land, its promise, its conquest, its tenancy and its forfeiture in exile. Joshua and David are the most renowned. Their legacy is a presence with us. But there is point in opting initially for the symbol of Samson, the native of Dan in the far north[2] who died magnificently at Gaza in the far south. For he is associated intimately with the Philistines in dramatic ways that symbolize so many issues in the Palestinian equation inside the Zionist enterprise of this twentieth century. It was the Philistines whose name was bestowed on the territory west of Jordan from Lebanon to Sinai, though they were a people of the coastal Shephelah and numerous other peoples called it home. It is the Palestinian dimension which still enmeshes Zion in toils of neighbourhood and conflict and, at least for introductory purposes, the saga of Samson's triumph and tragedy may put it suggestively in frame. All parties in its toils are still far from 'peace and consolation, all passion spent'. Milton called Samson 'Agonistes'. The mutual condition we have to explore concerning Palestine–Israel through more than ten decades could be described by the same word.

Some have likened the saga of Samson, the warrior-judge, to the pagan epic of Gilgamesh but nothing Hebraic can well fit into such patterns of heroic tragedy. There is a far deeper irony belonging to the distinctive biblical ethos. Samson is born through a theophany, an annunciation to his nameless mother, the wife of Manoah, a man without a genealogy. For all his sexual drives, Samson remains childless. He is pledged by his mother as *nazir* 'till the day of his death' – a man 'consecrated' to the divine ends of Yahweh, the patron God of Israel. The sign of his being vowed to holy ends is his hair remaining for ever uncut. He is to repudiate wine and every forbidden food.

The last of the 'judges', his story is prefaced by the familiar symbolic 'forty years' of Israel's declension from obedience to Yahweh, though in this instance there is no theme of repentance or appeal to Yahweh, nor after him does the land have rest. Samson is no Pericles. Nevertheless, the Book of Judges presents him as the last in a significant succession linking the conquest under Joshua to the days of Samuel and the rise of the monarchy. Though the strongest and the most renowned of all the Judges, he is also the most disappointing. Manoah, his father, needs some persuading about the authenticity of his wife's pregnancy and, in that context, she asks the pointed question: 'What shall be the judgement of the boy and his work?' (13:12).[3]

She did well to ask. It proved a very dubious one, shot through with the inconclusiveness symbolized, we might say, in Samson's famous 'riddle' about 'the eater' and 'something to eat', 'the strong and the sweet' (14:12–18). His encounters with the Philistines are sharply personal. He seems almost a squanderer of vocation. 'The spirit of Yahweh', it is said, 'rushes upon him', as if matching the impetuous vehemence of his own character. The pagans wrest the clue from his pagan wife, a woman of Timnah, and rightly identify 'the strong and the sweet' with the honey in the lion he has valiantly killed. There may perhaps be a sexual meaning (as Samson – 14:15 – is about to 'enter the bridal chamber'),[4] or should we understand a veiled allusion to things incongruous – 'strong and sweet' being unusually equated – so that Samson 'is' Israel and his *nazir* destiny 'is' Israel's covenant? If the latter, irony is very evident.

For Samson's 'judgeship' is full of incongruities, some of them ritual in character, others elemental. He breaks his *nazir* vow by scooping and eating the honey out of a dead – and thus polluted – carcase and giving it to his parents without disclosing its origin. He makes a weapon of the jawbone of an ass, unclean for a *nazir*-ite even to touch. More importantly, almost the entire cycle of his exploits concerns his own impulses and amours. He marries outside his Hebrew kin, his wooing strongly contrasted with that, for example, which brought Rebekah to Isaac or Rachel to Jacob. There is no betrothal ceremony or family concert. After the prostitute of Gaza, Delilah from 'the wadi of the vines' becomes his paramour. The place name, *nakhal soreq*,[5] may hint at the compromise which in far deeper terms belongs with this liaison. It is almost as if the narrator is unwittingly suggesting how hard it is to be 'dedicated' to divine ends when one is concurrently swayed by personal, or political domestic, intentions. Hints of contemporary Israel are uncanny.

Indeed, some have even wondered who is consecrated to whom in the Yahweh–Samson relation. Certainly Yahweh's purpose is seen to be forever turning on Samson's vagaries, retrieving or overruling or conceding their issue. Samson only seeks Yahweh's glory in terms of his own revenge. It is notable that Samson addresses Yahweh with some disrespect if not temerity, engrossing the divine prescripts, if not the divine glory, in his own passions. In 15:18–19 he demands water when thirsty after his martial feat. The allusion to the smitten rock in the wilderness at Massah and Maribah is plain enough. Now it would seem as if Samson *is* Israel in his own person. He names 'the hill of the jawbone' after his own deeds.

Most of all, beguiled in the lap of Delilah, he consents to the rupture of his 'consecration' and – shaven – forfeits the secret of his strength. When his returning locks remind him of his own destiny he discerns Yahweh's mercy and is kindled to a mighty vengeance on the Philistines. All – as

Milton's Chorus says – is the 'mirror of our fickle state'.[6] It is almost as if the narrator intends to demonstrate all that is inherently ambivalent in the Yahweh–Israel, divine–human, partnership.

So it is supremely in the final denouement of the Samson story. There is a family funeral party, no widow in Israel, no sons and daughters witnessing his burial (16:31). The curtain falls on the 'twenty years' of his judgeship and still the question of the 'men of Judah' in 15:11 reverberates among them:

> Do you not know that the Philistines are our masters? What is this that you have done?

It is true that Samson has taken 'the lords of the Philistines' down with him into Sheol and 'left them years of mourning and lamentation to the sons of Caphtor'. The seeming supremacy of Dagon, the Philistine tribal deity, implied in Samson's capture and blinding and enslavement, is signally disproved. For Dagon's denizens are trapped and slain at the very moment of their exultant triumph and high festival. But the success has all the barrenness of its own ultimate futility. The narrator has no note of ensuing peace and his superb hero is the victim of his own victory: 'Let me die with the Philistines' is his final prayer.

II

There has been scholarly conjecture about the name of *Shamshun*, some assuming an association with 'strength', others finding a link with the sun (*shemesh*) and others suggesting *shem*, 'name', as indicating a notorious prodigy. The narrator, or editor, of Judges has really one 'name', or theme, for all the leaders and vicissitudes he covers, namely that of enmity and conflict *vis-à-vis* 'the people of the land'. 'The hand of our enemies' is the constant story, the 'name of the game', requiring these warrior figures whose feats have gone down in oral celebration to be gathered into a 'history' of confrontation. Israel's jeopardy is linked with neglect of Yahweh or weakness in the proximity of alien worship shrines and foreign peoples. Gideon's exploits are those of a warrior who turns a Canaanite holy place into a shrine for Yahweh. The whole book surveys a cycle of enemy oppression debited to disobedience, rescue and reinstatement. If we see Judges 16:31 as reaching to 1 Samuel, with a medley of intervening stories, the perceptive reader becomes aware of a strange duality until the monarchy emerges beyond the regime of Samuel.

The duality lies in the way tradition remembers and perceives the 'conquest' under Joshua. On the one hand it is said to be complete and entire:

> Joshua took the whole land, fulfilling all the commands the Lord had laid on Moses: he assigned it to Israel, to each tribe its allotted share. Then the land was at peace. (Joshua 11:23)

> Thus the Lord gave Israel all the land which He had sworn to give to their forefathers: they occupied it and they settled in it . . . the Lord delivered all their enemies into their hands. Not a word of all that the Lord had promised the house of Israel went unfulfilled. All came to pass. (Joshua 21:43–45)

Farewelling the assembled tribes (in 23:14), Joshua assures them that 'not one word of what the Lord promised failed to come to pass'. There is at least a narrative assurance of total possession.

Moreover, it is made very clear that prowess, as well as divine fidelity, had brought this total victory. There was, as the narrator sees it, a sort of terror theme. 'The Gibeonites heard how Joshua had dealt with Jericho . . . '(9:3); 'Adoni-Zedek, king of Jerusalem heard what . . . ' (10:1); 'Jabin, king of Hazor heard what . . . ' (11:1). It seems clear that what had happened to Jericho and Ai – and to the miscreant Achan – had fulfilled its purpose by intimidating all and sundry. 'Passing over' and 'passing on' are the refrains of a confident history. Samson and his prodigies, despite their private interests, are part of this same tradition.

Yet, whether in Joshua or Judges, the reader is left with a puzzled mind. Perhaps one should allow for hyperbole and tidy idealism in a narrative written the way the writer wanted it to have been, as unmitigated success and uncompromised right. Yet there is a patent contradiction in what is 'visioned' and what is factual. A Kennizite, Caleb, is promised land by Moses before the entry (Joshua 14:12) and others likewise (17:4). Covenant is made with Rahab, the Jerichoite who harboured the spies, though technically illegal. Judges 1:27–36 deals with tribes who were not dispossessed. The Gibeonites extract agreed survival from Joshua by a subterfuge. 'Anakims' are said to survive in 'Gaza, Gath and Ashdod', 'Geshurites and Maacathites' elsewhere, 'Jebusites' at Jerusalem, 'Canaanites' in Gezer.[7] All these are conceded to be exceptions even by the exuberant compiler of the Book of Joshua. Deuteronomy, however, when its time comes, recapitulates with complete emphasis the duty of radical forcible removal and death of 'the existing population' and their entire displacement by the people of the covenant:

> When the Lord your God brings you into the land which you are about
> to enter and to occupy, when He drives out from before your face
> Hittites, Girgashites, Amorites, Canaanites, Perizzites, Hivites and
> Jebusites – seven nations more numerous and more powerful than you –
> and when the Lord delivers them into your power so that you overcome
> them, you must exterminate them. (Deut 7:1–2)

Later, Deuteronomy 20:10ff. directs that the people of towns that surrender
are to become corvée-style labourers, while those that resist undergo siege
and when defeated are to have all their males slain and the women and
children and all chattels taken as plunder.

It is this insistent presupposition of enmity and confrontation that the
biblical narrative adopts through all these writings, sharply reinforced as it
is by the repudiation not only of alien ethnicity but pagan divinity. The
twin elements of rejectionism make a powerful combination of hostility. It
is a strange anomaly that the most notable of the judge-warriors in terms
of sheer physical prowess should have been the most singly differentiated
by his *nazir* status and yet the most thoroughly in the toils of alien attrac-
tions of the flesh. It is an anomaly that enables the narrator to register his
reproaches in the very context of their futility. For there is no doubt, from
Judges 2:17 and 8:27–33, that 'whoring after pagan women' symbolizes
Israel's apostasy from divine vocation.

In this perhaps Samson may be taken as a subtle parable. For it becomes
clear throughout that he is not alone in the liability to contamination. Even
the most resolute apartheid is, even by that very token, incapable of the
desired immunity. Where incompatibility is most firmly decreed, willed
and asserted, a measure of unwilled but actual compatibility occurs despite
the most fervent disavowals. The contacts, not to say the debts, of things
Judaic to things Canaanite and Philistine are everywhere discernible.
Anomalous the Samson saga may be, but it takes an honest place in the
Scripture. There was always more to Philistia for Israelites than 'If you had
not ploughed with my heifer you would not have solved my riddle', and
more too than Delilah and the gates of Gaza.

III

Yet it is always the antipathy that dominates. The Philistines, though
mysteriously not cited among 'the seven nations', are the reprehensible foil
to everything Judaic. They supply their Goliath to make a legend of the
modest and resourceful David, just as they had yielded their negligible
thousands to the strong arm of Samson and his odd weaponry. It is with a

grim nonchalance that the annalist records the great man's feats of slaughter. He blithely goes down to slay thirty Philistines in order to gather booty to bestow on the thirty – 'companions at his nuptials' – who had solved his riddle. Peeved by his father-in-law, he devastates the standing corn of the Philistines, their vineyards and olive groves, setting up a tally of revenge and counter-revenge. He is seen even by some of his own people as a provoker of strife and he resolves the immediate situation by the slaughter of a thousand Philistines. The tally is no doubt a round figure. What adds to the horror is the laconic tones in which the narrator seems more intrigued with the unconventional weapon (a still 'moist' jawbone of an ass) than the appalling litter of corpses.

The Philistines, in turn, are left with much to avenge. Samson, 'eyeless in Gaza at the mill with slaves', has brought nemesis on himself. Doubtless, finally, he is perceived to have won the argument, with the crowded temple of Dagon falling calamitously around him with its retinue of slain – the time's equivalent of a suicide bomb. 'He had judged Israel twenty years', concludes the annal of his fame. It is hard to see what an adequate answer might be to his nameless mother's query 'What shall be the judgement of his work?' If we want battlefields, there are none – only dubious affrays. There is nothing for posterity to cherish save the memory of an amorous adventurer, a practitioner of violence, contributing massively to the melancholy comment with which the Book of Judges ends: 'Every man did that which was right in his own eyes' (21:25). Samson had shown the way.

One puzzling mystery emerges from the Samson chapters, namely how the purposes of Yahweh have somehow to negotiate throughout with the wilfulness and waywardness of the hero himself. There are times when it is necessary to ask who is manipulating whom. 'The spirit of the Lord' is said to 'rush upon' Samson at the points of dramatic but highly impulsive and unsavoury action. We find him 'calling on the Lord' only at two points of urgency, the one when he is thirsty after strenuous slaughter, the other in prayer for strength in the final moment of revenge. The latter is heartfelt enough: 'Only this once, strengthen me, O God'; the former is petulant to the point of rudeness:

> Thou hast given this great deliverance into the hand of Thy servant: and now am I to die of thirst and fall into uncircumcised hands? (15:18)

Yahweh is responsible in either case, but at 'the well of the caller' Samson names the place after himself. Jacob did better at Bethel and Peniel. Samson is never crippled in theophany, for all his auspicious pre-natal promise. In his case even Yahweh condones the violation of ritual prescripts. It is clear that holy matters can be pliable. For one of theophanic genesis, Samson is strangely free with or of Yahweh himself, whose purposes, nevertheless, are somehow conceived to be 'proceeding' under these incongruous auspices. At least scriptural precedent exists in the Samson saga for a near identification of divine will and human vagary or – better – divine sovereignty readily invoked for human idiosyncrasy. John Milton had a more confident sense of divine design in *Samson Agonistes* than the compiler ever warranted in the Book of Judges, where the didactic motif is that these heroic characters represent periodic divine rescue of the people from the punitive interludes of their apostasies.

It may be that to reflect this way is to ignore the primitive context of a time and place when lions and wild asses still abounded in Palestine–Judea, or to forget how the compiler drew on oral tradition and popular tale. But at least the corporate memory thought it had been so and thoroughly approved that it should be. Mentality provided ample room for a comprehension of Yahweh's ways that could graft them on to the likes of Samson, however incongruous the juncture of such root, such stem.

IV

The sharpest legacy of all, however, was that of utter confrontation, of a singular people ranged instinctively against all others and with the frame of divine reference set essentially against all other sacred or sacral aegis, the stakes vested in a thoroughly tribal competition for the same territories and habitations. Samson, in this sense, personifies a whole biblical tradition of inherent incompatibility within the human species – an incompatibility transacted in wars, conflicts and heroes, alternating back and forth and interpreted as the encounter of patron deities, among whom Yahweh is supreme.

Doubtless fortunes on the fields of struggle ebb and flow depending on the strange emergence of champions and leaders or, mysteriously, the moods celestial that preside. But these vicissitudes are only grist to the mill. What has been gained and then forfeited will need to be acquired back again. Present possession will be fraught with apprehension about future loss. For what both, or all, parties know well about the other is that the other emulates their own register of pride over victory or anger over loss. Indeed, the instincts of antagonism are the one common thing they share. What is presently in hand is potentially in forfeit. Hence that haunting biblical phrase about 'every man under his vine and under his fig-tree, and none making them afraid'.[8] For if – as may well be – the vine and the fig-tree were another man's labour and pride, he is unlikely to forget that they once were his. What attack filched, counter-attack can recoup. Confrontation over time means precariousness in time, until there is a *modus vivendi* which, apart from the human rancour, offended deities do not sanction. For both are equally battle-prone.

Compatibility, on the map and in the heart, was hard to come by in the old biblical mentality, given the covenant concept and the 'elected' reading of history in exodus and the land. These have had a strange consequence in the sacred 'sanction' against 'Philistines', and – by long sequence – 'the Palestinians'. For, etymologically, the two names are one and the same. They, with 'the seven nations' usually listed,[9] came to stand as metaphors or symbols for all that is contrary to divine ends. They serve as the *bête noire* of biblical history until we reach the Gospels and Epistles of the New Testament. God having 'his people' means in some sense that he has his enemies. The logic indicates that these will be those 'his people' identify as such. For centuries the moral danger in this equation was seldom recognized. Indeed, psalmists unashamedly indulged it, calling upon Yahweh to 'avenge them' in the midst of the most sublime adoration.

Given the prestige of the Book of Psalms, the instinct has passed directly into Christian spirituality, with the non-Jewish races in the Hebraic story doing duty as figuring the various aspects of sin and evil that are to be forsworn. Thus we find the following in the *Preces Privatae* of Lancelot Andrewes:[10]

Deprecation

Conceit	Amorite
Envy	Hittite
Wrathfulness	Perizzite
Surfeit	Girgashite
Lasciviousness	Hivite
Distractions of this life	Canaanite
Lukewarmness of Accidie	Jebusite.

There would seem to be a destiny of association between 'the seven deadly sins' (not Andrewes' list) and 'the seven tribes' of Palestine – all to be alike 'deprecated'.[11]

This, of course, is hard for the victims to take, the more so when loaded with political factors and carried into the very situations which urgently demand a mutual 'comprecation' or common disavowal of wilful prejudice and sin. It must always be perilous to enjoy a built-in sanction of incrimination, a built-in destiny to vilification. In this respect the Hebraic Scriptures need to be rescued from themselves by the finest instincts of the Hebrew prophets, who knew that *self*-accusation is the primary duty of 'elected' peoples, and by the perception of the New Testament that, if we are minded to deplore the way the world is, we must begin with 'O wretched man that *I* am'.

Samson, alerted from his amorous ways with the cry 'The Philistines be upon thee, Samson', satisfies his lusts where his official enmities belong. The paradox is at once strange and familiar. Resentments resourcefully cohabit with satisfactions. There follows a sort of compound interest. For 'Philistines' perceive a double warrant for hostility – the original otherness and the added insult. To be characterized by others as inimical is to be reinforced in being so. Only the contrary strategy of the indulging party dispelling the denigratory image enables a different image to become known as the true one. We can be 'justified by faith' precisely because we can be vilified by falsehood.

In an odd sort of way, 'Philistine' has become expressive even of merely snobbish prejudice as a synonym for 'tasteless', 'bourgeois', 'mildly despicable'. Even saintly souls descend to it, like Von Hügel writing of 'a sufficient other-worldliness without fanaticism and a sufficient this-worldliness without philistinism'.[12] Or the poet Gerard Manley Hopkins deploring that 'I am a carrion vulture . . . a Philistine of an aggravated specious kind'.[13] The usage is familiar enough in European literature, denoting people preoccupied with the material side of life and complacent with conventional values.

These brandings might be harmless. Those that belonged with territorial and ethnic equations and tensions were virulent. Pride of place as well as fear of change and the patronage of deities all contributed. It was a bitter irony to Jewry that Roman usage made 'Palestina' (or 'Palaestina') the usual term for a land so variously described as Canaan, Israel, Judea, Samaria, Syria and Philistia, signalling final failure in the Jewish Revolt under Bar Kokhba in 132–135 CE. However, Herodotus had called its coastal peoples *Palastinoi* and the land *Palastina* and Josephus followed suit. The Septuagint used *phulistieim* for the inhabitants. It may be that the Roman use was intended to signify the suppression of 'Judea' as a name as well as a fact, just as Hadrian had renamed Jerusalem 'Aelia Capitolina'. If so, that irony in turn may contribute to the countering suppression of 'Palestine' in the vocabulary of some contemporary Israelis.

The Romans by the second Christian century divided Palestina into Prima, Secunda and Tertia, i.e., the west bank and eastern side of the Jordan valley; eastern and central Galilee; and the southern part of trans-Jordan, the Negev and Sinai. By that time the original 'sea-peoples' of the shore-line and the foothills of the Judean highlands had contrived to give their name to the whole territory south of Lebanon, displacing the 'Canaan' that had been current for long centuries. Archaeologists have traced the Philistines' origin from as far as Crete, Cappadocia or perhaps – by its proximity – Egypt.[14] It may well be that they arrived around the time that the Habiru (Hebrews) entered Canaan from the east. Perhaps they were Aegeans fleeing via Cyprus from their ancestral lands and seizing occasion from some weakening of Egyptian power in Canaan.

Their coastline was sharply distinguished from that of the Phoenicians further north by its complete lack – from the Esdraelon area and Carmel to Al-Arish below Gaza – of natural harbours. The Israelite tribes under Joshua, busy with their encounters with Canaanites in the hills and in the north, had little initial occasion with the 'sea-people'. But steadily those ravines and wadis that figure in the story of Samson and in the fortunes of the 'ark of the covenant' drew the hillsmen down towards the greater fertility of the plains and the coastlanders up towards the heights, whether to gain better control of the steeps or to requite the raiders colonizing downwards.

The Book of Joshua, signalling the old age of its hero, merely notes Philistia as territory not yet subdued and refers to 'the five lords' (i.e., cities) of the Philistines: Gaza, Ashdod, Ashkelon, Gath and Ekron (13:2–3). These areas were, therefore, not available for the distribution that Joshua assigned. It is intriguing that the Philistia that eluded his possession was the earliest context of Zionist settlement, not the upper fastnesses above – the reverse of the biblical geo-history. It could be that the puzzle about Dan and the Danites could be resolved by the conjecture that they were in fact a tribe of 'sea-people' taken into an Israelite identity or federation. Genesis 49:16 makes the strange comment that 'Dan will be [prove to be] as strong as any in Israel'. According to Judges 18, when the Danites later migrated to the north (from Zorak and Eshtaol of the Samson story) they showed no compunction about foreign priests and carved images.[15]

However this may be as an instance of interfusion, the prevailing tradition – as heroicized in Samson – was one of bitter hostility. Philistines, like Goliath, are all of them 'uncircumcised'. The epithet becomes almost synonymous with their name. The David saga hinges on this folk-lorist enmity, a dark tradition which still has its echoes in the Zion–Palestine trauma of otherness. One reference in the remarkable Psalm 87, according to one reading, lists 'Philistia, Tyre and Nubia/Egypt' as those whose sons are Jerusalem's natives.[16] Elsewhere, however, Psalms 60:8 and 108:9 are bitterly satirical, with Philistia as the butt of their ridicule. The Book of Amos boldly credits Yahweh with the migration of the Philistines from Caphtor, which Jeremiah 47:4 describes as 'an island', but Amos does not spare their Gaza from the rhetoric of condemnation which skilfully prefaces his denunciation of his own people (1:6–8). Four of the Philistine Pentapolis are mentioned there and two of them in Jeremiah 47:5. The sentiment recurs in Zephaniah 2:5, while Ezekiel 25:16 names them 'Cherithites'. We must assume that the 'Philistines' who figure in the Genesis narratives of the patriarchs are so named either anachronistically or by fusion with the traditional foes of centuries later, as an inclusive term for the 'unchosen'.

There are hints nevertheless that not all was enmity. King Ahaziah, after an injury in his palace, sent down to Ekron to ask a diviner of Baal-Zebub as to his recovery, incurring in the process the wrath of Elisha, who enquired: 'Is there no god in Israel?' (2 Kings 1:2ff.). In another context, Isaiah 2:6 deplores the fact that Israel's towns are 'full of soothsayers speaking like Philistines . . . the children of foreigners are everywhere'. Those foreigners, of course, had more to do than visit oracles, however impressive their reputation in Samaria. One of the border towns of Philistia, Gezer, yields a peasant's calendar of country life from around 1000 BCE:

December/January	Planting grain
February/March	Late planting
April	Hoeing up of flax
May	Harvesting barley
June	Harvest and feasting
July/August	Vine-tending
September	Month of summer fruit
October/November	Two months of olive-harvest

– unless the cycle was interrupted by those raiders from the hills above and the fortunes of battle brought others 'reaping what they had not sown'.[17]

One strange irony of the fates was that Jabna in the Shephelah near the mouth of the Wadi Rubin, a Philistine centre worthy to be numbered with the Pentapolis, became after the fall of Jerusalem in 70 CE the famed rabbinic school of Jewry, the refuge of the Talmudists renewing a spiritual Judea after the loss of the Temple. It was variously known as Jabneel, or Jamnia by the Greeks. Judas Maccabeus burnt the ships at the mole on Jabna's beach, the fires – it is said – being visible even from Jerusalem (2 Macc 12:9). History plays strange tricks on its valiant folk. Judas Maccabeus may have seen himself recapitulating the feats of Samson in the same coast-lands, avenging the opposing feats of Philistines who had penetrated in their heyday as far as Megiddo and Bethshean in the tragic defeat and death of Saul, the first Hebrew monarch. Even so, survivors in a gentler vein, when Roman power had extinguished Maccabean meanings, contrived their scholarly haven in the very bosom of old Philistia.[18]

It is wise to see in the reciprocal hostility between the coastlands and the hill country, via the several wadis leading downward and upward between them and celebrated in the Samson saga, a parable of things necessarily reciprocal in more than rolling battles and intermittent massacres on either side. Hostilities are impossible without contacts and contacts mean a common context. The trauma of territory in contention will concern us further in Chapter 2. One curious instance of a strange 'twinning' between Judea and Philistia has to do with the saga in 1 Samuel of 'the ark of the covenant', the despair of Israel about its capture, the embarrassing experience of the Philistines with its possession and the strange arrangements for its eventual return. Its original shrine in Shiloh had some features of Canaanite ritual. Were there not also common elements of superstition in the terms by which an emblem to one party of divine sponsorship became, to the other, an unnerving piece of property it proved desirable to jettison?

Another fascinating evidence of interplay had to do with an apparent Philistine monopoly of iron tools and weapons – a circumstance starkly contrasted with the balance of weapons between today's Israel and the PLO. According to 1 Samuel 13:19, there were no blacksmiths in the whole of Israel. It would seem that the Philistines had contrived some sort of monopoly of an arms market, or at least that Israelites had to go 'down to Philistia' to sharpen even their agricultural implements. Does this explain why Samson had to rely solely on his hands to slay a lion or that his doughty weapon was an ass's jawbone? It may well be that the Philistine challenge in general underlay the popular plea for a monarchy over Israel, a Ben Gurion-style sense of the crucial reality of weapon procurement. Even the mighty David, in his apprentice years, learned at Ziklag to be a leader of mercenaries for a Philistine king, Achish of Gath (1 Samuel 21 and 27).

When Simon ben Gamaliel II pondered whether to approve the writing of the Torah in the Greek language, he found warrant in words from the benediction of Noah according to Genesis 9:27:

May God enlarge the boundaries of Japheth.
Let him dwell in the tents of Shem.
May Canaan be his slave.

'The tents of Shem' echoes the role of the eastern wilderness in the making of Judea, but their inheritance was to embrace the homesteads above the western sea. For it was these, more than any other, that might qualify the whole as 'a land of milk and honey'. Simon ben Gamaliel's decision conceded that Greek might dwell in the Torah's reaches. For Greece the concession was all the other way, with Torah lifted into the dignity of a higher medium. Such are the prides of cultures, whether rooted in the majesty of wisdom or in the exclusive prestige of covenant. Once they left the wilderness 'the tents of Shem' were never pitched on vacant ground. If not their amours, as with Samson, or their smithies as with Saul, they sought their very habitat with 'people of the land'. The endless necessity of compatibility has forever hinged on the elect paradox of its non-necessity.

V

Was it the theme of the 'uncircumcised' that drew John Milton's Puritan soul to the fascination of Hebraic heroism when he turned his poetic genius to the saga of Samson? Or was it the common bond of tragic blindness he had with his chosen champion of divine ends mysteriously paradoxical? Or did the two impulses coincide through the aegis of covenant and election? Either way, sacred aegis could only obtain under the constraints of human wilfulness and vagary. The 'Agonistes', whether in old Samson or today's Israel, has as much to do with an inner battle as with an outer conflict. The word therefore transfers well as a title for the inner and outer dimensions of Palestinian encounter with the antecedents and achievement of the Zionist State.

'Uncircumcision' may seem a bizarre and antique denominator for present-day *Filastin* but much of the trauma still lies in that subtle, formidable dissociation that Jewish circumcision denotes and defines. Sharp ethnicity, despite the common Semitism, attends stubbornly on Judaic otherness. As a religiously sanctioned differential it waits cripplingly on Israel's self-perception and so on Palestinian destiny.

'Eyeless in Gaza' – since Milton turned the phrase to capture Samson's plight in bitter adversity – could stand as a symbol of all that was precarious and bitter, if never sightless, in Jewish experience of diaspora among the *goyim*. The parts, of course, shift. Samson retrieved his tragedy where it occurred. Philistia was never the arena of the Shoah. He found his redemption only at the price of his own doom, taking his foes with him. His final satisfaction meant a common misery of circumcised and uncircumcised alike.

The supreme task of Zionist redemption is to incorporate into its perceived legitimacy the equal legitimacy of the other 'people of the land'. Samson could only involve his neighbours in a mutual ruin, squandering all his assets in a tragic quarrel. There was, perhaps, an inevitability about his last futility, given the aggravations of his own prowess and the mind-set of his days. The land had no rest. The *Agonistes* now are no less inter-fated.

Let the Samson story recede into the folklore whence it came. Its parable is evident. For Philistia he was both scourge and dilemma. It handled him only to its own undoing. There have been analyses aplenty of the quandaries of Zionism in Israel, fewer of the tribulations these have visited on contemporary Philistia. It seems well to think its recent history an *Agonistes* and to explore its elements with the heart and conscience they deserve, taking care to comprehend no less urgently the yearnings of Zion. For only so can either purpose succeed.

Notes

1 John Milton, *Samson Agonistes*; lines 1721–4 and 1732, 1741–4 are Manoah's final summary:

> Nothing is here for tears, nothing to wail
> Or knock the breast, no weakness, no contempt . . .
> But what may quiet us in a death so noble . . .
> With solemn obsequy and funeral train
> Home to his father's house . . .
> The virgins shall on feastful days
> Visit his tomb with flowers only bewailing
> His lot unfortunate in nuptial choice.

2 The phrase 'the camp of Dan' is uncertain. It may be that tribal locations were fluid and changing so that the northern placing of Dan in tradition was at this point unknown. (See note 15.)

3 There is a clear play on words with *mishpat* (judgement) and *Shafatim* (judges) and an irony in the question between the 'judging' or 'ruling' Samson will fulfil and the verdict that will be passed on it.

4 While 'honey from the lion' is the surface meaning, the sexual context has led some to surmise that what intercourse yields from the strength of the male is 'sweet' in the reception of the female. Both, differently, are 'eaters'. What appears to be 'a' is recognized as 'b', 'a' being Samson and 'b' Israel; 'a' the *nazir* vow and 'b' the covenant between Yahweh and the people.

5 It is not clear how there could be vineyards in a wadi liable to flash floods, or if the place name is meant to signify. Wine-linked or not, Samson should not have been seeking wives and paramours in Philistine territory, and that in defiance of his parents' protest. His lust is as impetuous as a torrent.

6 *Samson Agonistes*, line 164.

7 Cited from Joshua 11:23, 13:13, 15:63 and 16:10.

8 The phrase became almost a description of the Messianic reign. Note Joshua 24:13; Micah 4:4 and Isaiah 65:21–22. Vineyards and fig-trees represent long investments of labour and skill. 'Vineyard' actually became a prophet's metaphor for Israel itself (Isa 5:1–7).

9 The non-inclusion of 'Philistines' among the seven '-ites' is puzzling. Perhaps as sea-peoples they escaped Joshua's attentions while the eastward and northward peoples came into catalogue range.

10 Lancelot Andrewes, *Preces Privatae*, ed. F. E. Brightman (London, 1903), p. 74.

11 'Deprecate': 'to pray against', 'to plead earnestly against', 'to express earnest disapproval of' (OED). Praying *for* enemies is the antonym.

12 Baron Von Hügel, *Eternal Life* (London, 1912), p. 255.

13 Gerard Manley Hopkins, *Journals and Papers*, ed. Humphrey House (1959), p. 107.

14 See N. K. Sanders, *The Sea Peoples: Warriors of the Ancient Mediterranean, 1250–1150 B.C.* (London, 1972), ch. 3.

15 Many obscurities surround the tidy catalogue and location of Israelite tribes. It may well be that the Danuna or Danites are not exceptional in being 'recruited' from non-Exodus peoples of no single territorial continuity.

16 The passage is often read as meaning that all these races have Zion as their 'mother', though there is no parallel to such a thought elsewhere in the Hebrew Scriptures. May it be that these peoples are being called upon to recognize – of Jewish or even Messianic 'princes' – that such are Zion's 'sons'? In that reading the 'universalism' gives way to a rhetorical summons to acknowledge the distinctively Hebraic. Yahweh's 'goodwill' to Zion, announced in the birth of a child, is heralded to the nations. Or is there a reference to a Jewish diaspora among these nations? Or is the meaning that the Lord has those who know Him in these nations, but Zion remains the true mother?

17 See W. F. Albright, 'Palestinian inscriptions' in J. Pritchard (ed.), *Ancient Near-Eastern Texts Relating to the Old Testament* (Princeton, 1955), pp. 330–2.

18 See George Adam Smith, *Historical Geography of the Holy Land* (London, 1966 edn), p. 141.

2
The fate of location

I

Poets in their landscape and novelists in their native Wessex or a Cairene quarter celebrate a partnership that is the very stuff of literature. The New England poet Robert Frost perceived a destiny for the generations of 'pilgrims' to the discovered continent in the call of territory to match the temper of their pioneer ambition. He saw in 'the gift outright' the self-realizing of the settlers responding to its openness. In finding it they found themselves. He did not pause to think of an 'existing population' that might impede a right ambition.[1]

In that central perception of right and destiny there is an uncanny similarity to the Book of Joshua. The disparities, of course, are endless as between Canaanites and Iroquois, Philistines and Mohicans. But there is the same sense of self-validation, of assumed innocence, in the pursuit of manifest destiny, and that destiny married with a land-in-gift, albeit needing to be possessed via dispossession.

Nowhere is an inter-definition of land and people more emphatic and more mythical than in the Hebraic perception of the territory known to others as Canaan or Philistia. Palestine and Palestinians at the initiation of nineteenth-century Zionism in its political form could have had no adequate anticipation of what they would be facing as events unfolded. The sense of radical menace only slowly grew upon them, veiled as it was in ambivalence. Had not Zionism – among Jews themselves – seemed a forlorn and visionary enterprise in an 'enlightened' diaspora? Nor could

Palestinians have envisaged the tragic vindication that Zionism would have in the European enormity of the Nazi Holocaust. Nor, yet again, could they have estimated the incredible hold the new State of Israel would establish on the workings of super-power foreign policy as devised in Washington. Never, one might conclude, had any local patriotism been confronted, in its own modern nascence, with so formidable an array of mystical and tactical odds against which to struggle. The fact that these were sadly compounded by Palestinian counsels and policies does nothing to mitigate the massive dimensions of their adversity.

It falls to Chapters 4, 5 and 6 to take due stock of these. The duty of this one is to explore that basic circumstance from which all else derived, namely the accident of Palestine being the land in question. It had that name, from its 'Philistines', definitively from Roman times. Its Judaic/Israelite story through the climax of the Davidic monarchy and, more briefly, in Maccabean and Hasmonean years put the Palestinian aura into *de facto* eclipse, as did also the tenures of Seleucids, Romans, Byzantines, Islamic Caliphates and finally Ottomans, prior to the emergence of the separate nation-states. There was a nineteenth-century usage by which the entire area from Lebanon down to Gaza was termed 'Syria' – a denominator by which, for example, the historian Arnold Toynbee laid great store.[2] Ottoman administration knew its southern half as the Sanjaq of Jerusalem and its northern half as the Vilayat of Beirut, with a highly artificial border between them running due east from the Jaffa region up into the hills. Israeli theorists may be right in noting that 'Philistia' had never been a political reality since its heyday in the calamitous defeat of Saul on Mount Gilboa in the north-east of its widest realm. The northern kingdom of Israel hardly fared better.

There is something subtle and mysterious about place and presence. Palmyra is a long way from Beersheba. With the Jordan river as an eastern line, Egypt/Sinai to the south and a sharply identified Lebanon to the north, Philistia/Palestine has a verifiable identity on the map and, more insistently, in the consciousness of people-history. Tragically it was also the territory dear to Jewish diaspora and – in the final analysis[3] – the *sine qua non* of Zionist logic and emotion. The conflict resulting from that double situation of Palestinian history and Judaic metahistory[4] has proved the utmost tribulation of geographical circumstance. As Latin might say of Palestinianism, *Ubi est ibi non potest*. There is in Zionism an exilic necessity for the other local party, the paradox of a gathering from out of diaspora and an exodus into one. The Zionism that so inexorably links secure identity with territory means territorial denial to inhabitants who may impede.

There have been endless migrations, displacements, invasions, expropriations and territorial subversions throughout history, but none have been armed with the powerful mystique and divine legitimation that have characterized twentieth-century Zionism in the geographical incidence of an inevitable location. Other chapters will take up the political and tactical aspects. Here, any reckoning with a *Palestina Agonistes* means the measure of its being captive to the Judaic ideology of 'a land for a people and a people for a land' – each ideologically a mutual exclusivity.

II

Scholars believe that the confident emergence of the concept of 'covenant' concerning land and 'election' concerning people belongs with the period of the Deuteronomist in the eighth or seventh century BCE, though refracted back as far as the patriarch Abraham via memory and perception of the saga of the Exodus. There can be no doubt that 'the tribes' shared with other groupings of ethnic identity the sense of patron deities by whose warrant and protection vital land-tenures were sacralized and secured. Thus the narrator in Judges 11:24 credits Chemosh of the Moabites with the bestowal of Moab and warns them off trespass on what Yahweh has granted to Israel. Successful invasion of Canaan under Joshua is perceived as mandated and enabled by Yahweh, the patron of battle array as 'the Lord of Hosts' – a title conspicuous in that book.[5] From such early, unashamedly ethnic sources derives the sublime ethical moralism of the sovereign 'Lord over all', a moral monotheism which, however, never sheds the 'special relationship' with the one people, Israel–Judah.

It is important to realize that long stretches of Jewish thinking have been at odds concerning the meaning and the legitimacy of 'the Chosen People' concept. This has been so, remarkably, even within political Zionism itself.

It seems self-evident that there is nothing exceptional about a near-identity between the 'who' and the 'where' of any human story. Lands and peoples give and receive their very names from each other. There is something elemental and universal about people, place and posterity, about nature, nurture and culture, about tribe, territory and time. Jewry is not, in fact, unique in perceiving this amalgam in divinely sanctioned terms.[6] What is unique has been the tenacity with which the Hebrew mind espoused Yahweh and the reach they still gave to the concept of 'covenant' when its Christian heirs broke it open to 'all believers', not 'born such of the flesh', while retaining the other Testament in which it was enshrined.

Sadly, but no doubt inevitably, it was that different, open fellowship with 'God in Christ' that paradoxically toughened the *sui generis* mentality of Jewry gathering – in a Palestinian refuge – around the Torah and the synagogue after the trauma of the Fall of Jerusalem to the Romans and the forfeiture of the Temple liturgy. That intensification of otherness left its mark on the emerging Christian Scriptures. But the otherness was ultimately self-ensuring, intrinsic to Jewish consciousness via historical memory and the very tragedy of exile. Disallowing the Christian perception of a free and full participation in a faith-community in a Yahweh now perceived in Christ as 'the God of all grace', the Hebrew privacy with that same – and different – Yahweh renewed and fortified itself by the very paradox of bitter and prolonged disjuncture from the fact, and the symbol, of territory.

How it read and bore that paradox through nineteen centuries can only be understood by reference to what land tenure had meant in 'covenant'. 'Land-*in-absentia*' became a spiritual heritage. It was one which required of political Zionism, under Theodor Herzl and beyond, strenuous effort to transform into 'Land-*in-praesentia*'. It did so only by returning to the original vision while disavowing its age-long diaspora truth.[7] We can come intelligently to that strange equation only by appreciating the deep complexity of the Hebrew genius-in-tension around its supreme destiny and knowing it as also the despair and doom of the Palestinians. It remains a doom we might characterize – with a massive proviso – in the words of a recent Christian exponent of 'the land', i.e., 'Nobody has a great name in the history of dislocation'.[8] The proviso is that dogged self-possession in diaspora, Jewish or Palestinian, continues to disprove it.

Yet 'great names', positively, go well with sure territories. In its most adamant terms, Hebraic thinking has it so between Yahweh and themselves. 'Religious Jews', and not religious ones only, opined David Ben Gurion, 'violate the precepts of Judaism and the Torah of Israel by remaining in the diaspora.'[9] The tribes would have done the same by failing to cross over Jordan under Joshua.[10] The developed ideology is that just as 'space' may be sacramentalized on the stage of drama, so 'place' is particularized out of 'space' by election to it and possession in it. The 'wilderness' of transition can even be made symbolic of some kind of incipient chaos from which only tenancy can rescue God's people.[11] The desert, spelling 'non-arrival', could arouse the will to lust for return to Egypt and bondage. Enlandisement was the decisive liberation from slavery.

The sense of being covenanted in this history meant that conquest could be seen as 'no-conquest' but legitimate appropriation in the exact meaning of the word. What is divinely 'gifted' is not crudely 'taken'. Deed is absolved in destiny. Further, there develops a doctrine of the interdependence of place and Torah. Only in the land can Torah be obeyed; only for Torah's sake is land tenanted. Transcendence itself is domesticated and ethnicized, yet somehow does not cease thereby to transcend. Ethnic separatism and land-sanctity are reciprocal. Though the actuality is war and conflict throughout, from entry[12] to the monarchies and beyond, the theory is of a 'land-sabbath' in which Yahweh rules via his people being his people, in a proto-sovereignty. Many prescripts of the Torah are only feasible within the holy borders.

Twentieth-century Zionism moves in the orbit of these perceptions, though with deep tensions and vagaries of interpretation. 'Happy are you, O Israel and the sword of your triumph', sings the eulogist in Deuteronomy 33:29 – terms akin to the militant ardour of political Zion. Other sentiments are more irenic in their cult of 'holiness'. 'Promised land' emphasizes concreteness; righteousness has to be 'earthed', not disparate, visionary and immaterial. Land means cultivation and tenancy spells a very physical reverence in which Yahweh is adored. The very concept of being a 'native' has a spiritual dimension, being more than a physical accident. Birth is incorporated into mystical being *in situ sancto*. 'Holiness' has a kind of historical actuality by virtue of place *per se*,[13] to the extent that 'He who resides outside the land is as if he worships idols'.[14] Rabbi Abraham Heschel has Yahweh saying: 'My people, I am only if you are in history', and 'in history' means the 'visibility' of the Israel that is place for the 'visibility' that is Israel as people.[15] Jewry as faith, Jewry as nation, Jewry as land, are inseparably one. Rabbi Abraham Kook has the point in lyrical prose:

> It is the air of the land of Israel that makes one wise . . . In the impure land of the Gentiles the world of unity is imperceptible and the divided world rules with force . . . The impure soul that is everywhere outside the land of Israel is thus suffused with the stench of idolatry and the Jews there are worshippers of idols . . . The only way in which we may escape the disgrace of idolatry is for the Jewish people to gather in the land of Israel, as it is written [in Leviticus 25:38]: 'To give you Canaan and to be your God'.[16]

It needs little imagination to perceive how this ardent theology of territory poses so formidable an obstacle to any non-Jewish compatibility in terms of mutual tenancy. For some in Zion it spells a total exclusion zone. It requires those so motivated to see boundaries as in no way 'negotiable'. For they are not matters of history but of divine mandate. It makes the very theory of partition obscene. Rabbi Zvi Yehudah Kook, hearing of projected Partition in 1947, asked:

> Where is our Hebron, where is our Shechem and our Jericho? Where? And all of the other side of Jordan – it is ours, every clump of dirt . . . which belongs to the land of God. Is it our right to concede one millimetre of it?[17]

As we must note in another chapter, there were more pragmatic minds, but the sentiment is essentially exclusivist, with any authentic Palestinianism divinely vetoed.

What is mandate to the one must be misery to the other. A passage in one of Amos Oz's novels grimly underlines this separatism – though with a caveat as its end:

> And for what purpose did the Lord, blessed be He, create them [Gentiles]? Why was Ishmael, the *goy*, called Ishmael which means: 'He shall hear the Lord'? Do you know? No? I will tell you. He was called Ishmael so that he could hear what Isaac, his brother and master, ordered him to do. And why was Isaac the Jew called Isaac: i.e. 'He shall laugh'? So that he could laugh at the sight – because the labour of righteous men is done by others.[18]

'Others' may have a shared ancestry and avail for menial needs and services but ideology dispossesses them of the land as never of right.

Sacred particularity may be measured, by contrast, in how the philosopher Hegel perceived the Persian mind-in-empire:

> Persia's unity was conceived in terms of 'the beneficial sun' which shines equally on all, binding the parts into a whole in a purely extrinsic relationship . . . conceived and experienced by the subject as a beneficent one . . . in which the principle of the relation of the part to the whole is grasped as fundamental. The Persian Empire permitted the crystallization and development of individual peoples, such as the Jews.[19]

Indeed, Nehemiah and others had reason to be grateful and the great Cyrus could be seen in Jewish eyes as 'God's anointed' (Isa 45:1). The doctrine of the land, by the mentors we have thus far noted, admits of no 'extrinsic relationship'; that which is Judeo-intrinsic being the only possible one. It seems vain for Palestinians to await some Israeli Cyrus, drawing a different logic from the sun.

III

To have the Palestinian measure of the tragedy inherent in their age-long location, it was vital to have this land-theology clear. For those different Israeli perceptions that have disputed it are in varying degrees hostage to it. Even what remains conceptually indivisible and inalienable can, nevertheless, be pragmatically partitioned or negotiated. So much we will see in later chapters. These pragmatists and strategists might even plead some support from their biblical mentors speaking in other terms than those reviewed, forlorn as any hopes remain of them in Palestinian terms.

Moses, the supreme leader, had died in the wilderness. The sacred Law, though intended for the land, had come outside it during the desert wanderings. Non-enlandisement would remain forever symbolic in the saga of peoplehood itself. Moreover, had not Solomon set a precedent in granting twenty Galilean cities to Hiram, King of Tyre (1 Kings 9:11), in token of the cedar timbers used for the Temple of Yahweh at Jerusalem? Chief Rabbi Schlomo Goren, to be sure, noted the awkward fact and overruled the wisest of Hebrew kings, in denying that he had any relevance to modern Zion in such gratitude.

Far back to Abraham – was his 'right in the land' reconfirmed after he had made peace between Lot's shepherds and his own by agreeing separate allotments of pasturing? Nevertheless Gush Emunim, the Israeli land vigilantes, insist that to return even one strip of it to the Gentiles would 'give control back to the forces of evil'.[20] The 'settlement' at Elon Moreh overlooking Nablus was established in 1979 where tradition had Abraham receiving the famous promise, Nablus being a symbolic centre of Palestinian identity.

Land zealotry is not worried about Israel's 'isolation' if and when the international community reproves or deplores. Let there be 'an ideological chasm between the people of Israel and the nations of the earth', if thus it must be.[21] It is not, on this score, merely that 'security' dictates settlement; it is that settlement is a holy duty that zealots have no liberty to relinquish. 'Normalization' forgoes sanctity: polarization achieves it.

Thus the land debate reverberates throughout Israeli emotion, politics and literature. Its implications will be with us in other chapters. The passions are strongly entrenched, the counsels of conciliation urgent. Professor W. D. Davies, a most careful surveyor of *The Territorial Dimension of Judaism*,[22] concludes that 'the doctrine of the land' is, and always has been, extremely complex. Throughout Jewry there has been 'an undeniable historical diversity'. All that can be meant by concepts of 'return' and 'promise' paradoxically requires counter-philosophies of 'exile' and 'diaspora'. We will need to note this ambivalence further, for its bearing on Palestinian puzzlement, in Chapter 4. Jeremiah, in his famous 'letter to the exiles', enjoined them to settle down in Babylon as a genuine destiny (Jer 29:4–14). Prayer was valid there and did not necessitate the holy soil, though hope of repatriation must continue to be cherished in symbolic time.

That issue of worship and prayer is crucial. For 'the land' in the extra-biblical writings tends to be subsumed into the central city, Jerusalem and the Temple, and – by the same token – territory has the same exclusive character as liturgy does.

And neither sojourner nor alien shall dwell with them any more.[23]

We might say that the practice of worship constitutes in itself the legal right to the land.

In the Jerusalem Talmud, in Kilayyim 7.5, there is a law . . . translated by Lieberman as: 'Though soil cannot be stolen, a man can forfeit his right to this soil by giving up hope of ever regaining it.' The argument is that the people of 'Israel' 'never for a moment gave up hope of regaining the soil of Palestine . . . It is on this foundation that [Jews] now claim that Eretz Israel belongs to them.'[24]

This doctrine might be seen somewhat akin to the Islamic theme of a 'mosque' once 'prayed in' becoming a mosque for ever. Place then becomes as inalienable as worship is indivertible. To abandon that spot of ground then becomes a sort of *shirk*, its being no longer reserved for valid worship.

The parallel is uncanny but can afford little solace to Palestinian sorrows. For a mosque, which may be no larger than a prayer-mat, is never measured in dunams, acres and square miles. Despite the Talmud, 'soil' can indeed be 'stolen', but might not non-Jews also claim that land is not forfeited as long as hope of its regaining is not abandoned? In practical terms that logic can avail Palestinians little, seeing that the principle, in Zionist eyes, is uniquely Jewish.

The entire significance of Jewish diaspora and Jewish debate about its meaning in self-understanding will concern us later. It has often been argued that here, too, there is a hint for the Palestinian soul. Why not embrace your diaspora, accommodate to radical dispossession and, as we Jews have done, develop a self-definition in which land, once a tenacious necessity, can be patiently relinquished? Is not this the solution to which 'the fate' of your 'location' points you? Would not such a resolve be the more amenable in your case than in our Jewish one, seeing that the areas of your dispersion would be your very neighbours, speaking your cherished tongue and comprising the one culture you reverence?

Convenient as it is to Zionist argument, the point has often been made with the idea that no territorial tenacity can ever be of the Hebraic kind. Jewish commendation of this paradigm, however, has always insisted – for its own part – that successful diaspora survival requires its territorial counterpart in a reassuring and unassailable possession by at least 'some of us'. Israel certainly belongs to, and is demanded by, Jews who will never inhabit it even in their dreams. That 'the fate of location' enters powerfully into the historical psyche is evident enough. If it holds for 'Palestine' in Jewish eyes, it cannot be denied to Palestinian eyes.

IV

Cynics have often suggested that the whole 'land' issue is 'theology about a piece of real estate'. There is a sense in which Theodor Herzl, inaugurating political Zionism in the 1890s, did see the land question – initially – in terms of a setting for a state, statehood for a 'nation' (as distinct from habitation for a community) being impossible without an agreed 'piece of earth'. It is said that, deliriously in his last illness in 1904, Herzl was preoccupied with a patch upon the counterpane. How different would have been the fate of Palestine if his original idea of 'somehow–anywhere' had not given way to an 'only Palestine' equation. This passing phase in Herzl's campaign for *Judenstaat* needs to be noted for its wry commentary on the 'location' question. There could be only one 'holy patch', one sacred map.

The question hinges on the basic objective that Herzl had defined. In a seventeenth-century *Tractatus*, the famous philosopher Spinoza had dismissed 'land notions' as dreaming fantasy. This Herzl roundly denied. 'If we will it', he wrote, 'it is not a dream.'[25] But he fully embraced Spinoza's view that Jewish 'chosenness' was a wholly rational and political capacity to maintain itself in sovereignty. 'Eretz' in a non-mystical sense, rather than Eretz Israel mystified, was his concern. He was, in this respect, in line with Pinsker's *Auto-Emancipation*, Moses Hess's *Rome and Jerusalem*, and the historian Graetz's *History of the Jews* in reading Jewish destiny in terms of nineteenth-century European nationhood. *Rome and Jerusalem* was not a theology of ecumenism, nor a treatise on the days of Titus and Hadrian: it had to do with Mazzini and Italian unity and the thrust of the French Revolution.[26]

Herzl, however, eschewed the romanticism of those precursors in a practical assessment of how Jews fared under Gentile sovereignty and anti-Semitism. Jewish experience argued incompatibility with 'Gentile' regimes and society. Jews constituted a 'Gentile' problem. Jews themselves could solve it by abstracting themselves, relieving 'Gentiles' of their indigestible presence and so achieving a double service to both parties in an otherwise provenly intractable situation. There was no abstract nationalism here. Jews were a people *because* the nations excluded them. The idea of identity with nascent Germany, Austria, or other nations by trust in 'the Enlightenment' was both deceptive and futile. Jews must organize to become again a people, constituted by antipathy itself and gaining, even 'buying', recognition in terms avowedly separatist but acquiring international recognition as such. Specificity about 'the land' was not involved. What was requisite was simply place and locale. One cannot be a separate people in perpetual diaspora.

The impulse throughout was the menace otherwise to Jewish continuity and Jewish existence itself. There were several aspects of Herzl's logic that found vindication in attained Zionism. He saw international recognition – indeed gratitude – as vital. Wounded pride and urgent jeopardy fused into one vision to which Herzl gave passionate voice in *Der Judenstaat*, a powerful pamphlet that made no mention of 'holy places' or 'land sanctity'. He wanted what would be a 'neutral land'. Historical associations, of course, weighed in his plans. He practised *gestio negotiorum* among bankers and politicians. He proposed to the Ottoman Sultan that Jewish financing might rescue his imperial finances in exchange for an agreement to colonize in Palestine. Settlements without 'charter', however, he derided as being at the mercy of events and lacking in international 'guarantee'. There must be no risk of repeating, outside Europe, the old European status of 'host nations'. These were to be ended for ever, to their own relief as well as that of Jewry.

By such recognition from 'the powers' – or some of them – the Jewish state might be innocent, an innocuous identity, an entity without an army or, otherwise, a foreign policy. Herzl's foreshadowing here of Israeli 'mindfulness' of world politics was characteristic of the future not only in that sense but also in its being oblivious that there might be, already, another nation in the way. Was the host-nation dilemma escapable?

That question *might* have found possible answer in the notions about Argentina, Kenya, or Uganda ventilated both during Herzl's lifetime and during pre-First World War conjectures around nascent Zionism. The fact that Herzl was ready, even briefly, to entertain them is eloquent commentary on his ruling pragmatism. It is also eloquent of the fate location inevitably held for Palestinians on the receiving end of Zionist inevitability.

Mention of existing populations did not figure in these calculations.

There were, after all, sundry precedents of such oblivious colonization in the Americas, Canada, Australia and New Zealand. Natives did not need to be consulted. Often in the sequel Zionists would wonder at their misfortune in locating their will to dwell with statehood in a location set with a hinterland of self-conscious culture and historical identity over a score and more of centuries, and not in Maori-land or among the tribes of Massachusetts.[27]

The very notions of Argentinian, African or other Zionist alternatives to Palestine were dramatically disowned in the very aberration that entertained them. The details need not detain us. There were deep tensions between the various elements within Western and Eastern European Zionism, deepened by the personality factor in leadership. Herzl wrote:

> I conduct the affairs of the Jews [*sic*] without their mandate, though I remain responsible to them for what I do.[28]

But when it came to allowing the idea of any substitute for Palestine, even in a temporary way, Herzl met sustained antipathy. Weizmann insisted that

> The Jews of Russia were incapable of transferring their longings from the land of their forefathers to any other territory . . . Uganda was even more of a mirage . . . The enormous *practical* significance of this fixation [where the heart of Jewry was fixed], its unique and quite irreplaceable power to awaken the energies of the Jewish people, escaped them [i.e., 'the Westerners'].[29]

Weizmann himself italicized 'practical'. In *Der Judenstaat*, 'Is Palestine or Argentina preferable?' had been a genuine question. In the event it could not remain even rhetorical. Nor were Palestinians allowed, even remotely, to answer it.

It would be clear that Argentina would be a sort of perpetual Goshen. Nor could Jews be satisfied to try to emulate Cecil Rhodes (to whom Herzl appealed) in carving out a kind of Herzliya somewhere. Herzl was accused by ideologues like Ahad Ha-Am of thinking more of physical rescue than of spiritual rebirth, of the alleged bankruptcy of 'emancipation' rather than of creative patience on the ground in vigorous settlement. Nevertheless, Herzl's urgent soliciting of 'the powers', British or other, was an essential tactic which finally rewarded Weizmann with the Balfour Declaration. Despite his wavering over *where*, the vital passion about *whether* and *why* in Herzl's initiation of nineteenth-century Zionism in political terms ensured that the territorial price would be Palestinian. 'The cup might not pass from them.'

V

The implications – as we must see in other chapters – were far more than territorial. Keeping here to the land issue, there is one strange factor that calls for remark. Reference has been made to the 'hinterland' making pure 'colonization' a complex matter. What is surprising, yet also symptomatic, is that geographical location was not meant for geographical or regional participation. Territory on the map was not meant to spell belonging with Arabism; it meant leaping over the centuries back to David and Judas Maccabeus. The land was somehow to be exempted from the centuries. Though 'Arab Christian' is a familiar enough usage, it would sound odd to talk of 'an Arab Jew'.

This paradox of 'place' at once coveted and unwanted, dispensable culturally while indispensable emotionally, entails two factors. The one is the European vintage in the state-making, the other the Western 'givens' in the absorption of Sephardic Jews from the Arab, Ethiopian, Moroccan, Yemeni and other quarters of their long Middle Eastern dispersion.

This studied 'foreignness' of Israel in the region is, of course, actually or potentially modified by factors economic and societal. But it inspires in some observers the unhappy imagery of the unwanted 'transplant' subject to a 'body rejection'. It is, of course, the manner of straightforward imperialisms to trespass where they do not belong for purposes of trade, power rivalry and prestige. Israel, however, sees itself as the 'mother-country' being recreated by its erstwhile colonies of dispersion. That being so, might not the sheer physical contextuality that history and locale had wrought in it during its long abeyance have been allowed some relevance to its renewal?

On the contrary, the idea seems to have been of a land somehow put into limbo until recoverable, immune, like 'the Seven Sleepers of Ephesus', from the passage of un-Jewish time. Then, as repossession came, it had to be in European guise, Jewish, that is, in the culture that diaspora itself had imprinted – the very diaspora that was read as incapable of proving compatible with things Judaic except on its terms of assimilation or dominance.

Thus Palestine was passionately necessitated and effectively discounted in its long history. Herzl referred to it as 'a plague-ridden, blighted corner of the Orient' to which they would bring 'the well-distilled customs of the Occident'.[30] It was as if a nostalgia for place could despise the fact of history, covet location and yet disown it. Vladimir Jabotinsky, one of the most forthright of Zionist 'separatists', strenuously insisted that the Jewish

State was, and must be, emphatically 'European and not eastern'. At the other end of the Zionist spectrum, the outstanding diplomat Abba Eban, with his South African nurture, was convinced that Israel must be studiedly 'European'. In *An Autobiography*, he stressed 'the basic Zionist concept of a Jewish state saturated with Jewish identity and associations', and continued:

> Israel is no more and no less than the Jewish people's resolve to be itself, to live renewed within its own frame of values . . . [31]

These would be essentially those of European Jewry. Elsewhere he saw Israel's 'right destiny' as not Middle Eastern but Mediterranean. He invited Arab nationalism to forget the tiny piece of its vast extent which Israel had occupied, and went on:

> The Israeli policy is one of cultural autonomy. There is no attempt to make the Arabs into Jews or Zionists.[32]

Acknowledging Israel's 'separation' in the Middle East, he argued that it was due not only to Arab hostility but also to the nature and ethos of Jewish nationalism – an act of Israel's deliberate will. What the Jewish people achieves through the State of Israel, wrote Emmanuel Levinas, is 'withdrawal into itself'.[33]

It is clear that the Herzlian idea of Zion as the solution of the Jewish problem by 'abstraction' from the midst of 'Gentiles' still obtains, yet with the paradox that in Israeli terms it is at the same time an 'insertion'. 'Neighbourhood' is inescapable in this world, given bodies in places as being what all humans are. Thus land *per se* is no solution. The Zionist task of 'taking Jewry out of the ghetto' required also 'taking the ghetto out of Jewry'. Could statehood, in Zionist terms, do the second? The decisively chosen land – Palestine, as distinct from Argentina or Uganda – only intensified the dilemma. If return to *that* land was seen as the urgent alternative to a relinquishment by Jewry everywhere of their ethnic, historical and religious identity through assimilation, they could hardly re-tenant it in assimilative ways.

Writing in the 1940s, the eminent British Zionist Harry Sacher made this separatism brutally clear in the form of a de-Arabizing of 'Palestine' *in toto*:

> Of such an Arab world, Palestine can never form a part . . . Palestine cannot be an Arab country . . . The moral is plain: Palestine can never be part of a free, independent Arab world . . . In the realm of real politics,

if there is to be a free and independent Arab world it must exclude Palestine . . . hard inexorable fact.[34]

What 'Zionism restored to its original biblical significance' was 'Jewish particularism'.[35]

Other aspects of 'the fate of location' will concern us in a later context. The will of many Zionist thinkers for a 'European' character to Israel might seem to be queried by the abandonment of Yiddish and the fascinating revival of Hebrew, led in splendid energy by pioneers like Ben Yehuda and Bialik. Nor was it a Hebrew, as Jabotinsky demanded, in Latinized letters. The newly vibrant language, however, became the instrument of sharply Western culture. In the pens of writers like the novelist Moshe Shamir, it could also serve the worst passions of separatism. His novel *Tahat Hashemesh* names the hero's girl-friend Balfouria, to whom he says:

'I know this piece of land of mine: I know it better than does any unwashed Arab whose ancestors were here hundreds of years ago, because my ancestors were here three thousand years ago. Men like me don't ask many questions. The world belongs to men like me in an absolute sense. They take, and that's that.'[36]

Balfouria, we assume, was suitably impressed.

VI

Israeli Hebrew writing has many gentler, happier authors than Moshe Shamir, but to note him serves here to introduce other dimensions of the land in the story. The European bias we have sketched with minds like that of Abba Eban belongs with the origins, from the far west to the far east of Europe, of the several *aliyahs* or migrations into Palestine. These, however, after 1949 and the securing of the state, at least by 'armistice', were followed by large numbers of Arabicized Jews of the Middle Eastern dispersion. Moreover, European Jews themselves came as settlers, breaking ground – often with their bare hands – as 'lovers of Zion' *qua* farms and settlements in which mercantile, academic or professional Jews took up a totally new habit of life in their new habitat. Becoming tillers of the soil and 'soilers of their hands', they developed the virile *sabra* image – the word adopted from the prickly pear or cactus bush.

Thus the land meant the sheer physicality of things Hebraic tempering but in no way subduing the technical, scientific counterparts of land possession, typified by Weizmann's Rehoveth Institute. In some measure the *sabra*-izing of the Europeans brought them closer to the incoming Arabicized new Israelis from the eastern areas round the state. But never placidly so. The tensions between the different 'origins' of common citizens have long been a strain within society and a complex factor in politics. Those tensions were accentuated by the disparities between Ashkenazi and Sephardi in the traditions of Judaism.

Israel was determined to be in no way a 'Levantine' entity, yet ethnographically 'Levantine' elements were a significant element in the mosaic of its people. The actual, gradual, stubborn, arduous land occupancy which Herzl had discounted, pending the diplomatic sanctions on which he relied, proved the very saving grace once political 'chartering' was secured. But the land factor, *qua* draining, watering, planning, cultivating and fructifying, proceeded in very Western shape and did not avail to create any local community between Jews, whether European or oriental, on the one hand, and Palestinians on the other. On the contrary, the *sabra*-making quality of the land, as Jews knew it, tended to the despising and repelling of the Palestinian dimension. This was accentuated by the increasingly technological shape of Jewish land cultivation, whereby, in due course, Arabs constituted no more than a labour market for the fields they had once owned and differently tilled. The clash was not only between rivals for tenancy but between sophisticates and primitives, with corresponding emotions of disdain and resentment. Some even argued that Palestinians, as well as being displaced from their lands, should be discouraged from farming altogether lest emotions of affection for the land should anchor them more doggedly to it. Thus Chaim Weizmann in 1907:

> The Arab retains his primitive attachment to the land. The soil instinct is strong in him and, being continuously employed on it, there is a danger that he might feel himself indispensable to it with a moral right to it.[37]

Such sentiments left absolutely no hope that the land, and the two-people use of it, might have exerted a unifying, reconciling impact on both parties. Zionism had to think in resolutely exclusifying terms – odd as the perception was, given the long reality in subsequent Israel of Palestinian labour in its economy.

Despite the Israeli resistance to the very notion of ever becoming 'Levantine', and the sharply distinctive *sabra* types, some Arabicized Jews in Israel have dreamed of an authentic Judeo-Palestinian culture. A recent survey by Ammiel Alcalay discusses novelists and poets in this context but cites, with sad concurrence, a critic's verdict who

would prefer a more Mediterranean Israel, though she knows that such
an Israel is, in literary as well as political terms, still very much within
the realm of Utopian fantasy . . . Israeli literature moves willy-nilly on
paths determined by European literature.[38]

The paradox seems irreducible whereby a state and society, determinedly
located in a land tenaciously demanded by their identity, possess it, nevertheless, in studied segregation from its physical implications as place and
time define them. The very form of Zionist land intention meant a land
contention not only in its being competitively loved but also in its being
conceptually privatized. Despite the same rains from the same westward
waters, the same occasional snows, the regional climate and the enduring
hills beneath the same heaven, Palestine–Israel lives in a waning/waxing
dichotomy of human tenure and love, a land about a people and a people
about a land. Zionism sees it as a single land about a singular people – the
prize and the price of location, the boon and the fate.

The Palestinian minority within the Israel of pre-1967 borders, with
their representatives in the Knesset, and the great demographic circumstance of Palestinian population in unresolved status on the West Bank,
though part of the land theme, will concern us in a later setting. They do
not qualify the fate of location we have intended to study in its land aspects.
Indeed, they underline and embitter it. 'The land had rest' was a familiar
conclusion of the biblical annalists in ancient times. The words have only
a wistful contemporary ring.

Notes

1 Recalling Thomas Hardy's 'Wessex novels' and Najib Mahfuz's masterly evocation of his
native Cairo in his now widely translated Arabic novels. On Robert Frost, see *Complete Poems*
(New York, 1964), p. 467.

2 See Toynbee's monumental *The Study of History*, vols 1–10 (Oxford, 1934, 1939 and
1954).

3 The proviso is necessary inasmuch as Herzl was at one point ready to visualize a Jewish
State on *any* viable location. See below.

4 'Metahistory' is a useful term covering idealized or symbolic versions of events as bearing
mystical significance beyond the reach of 'factual' analysis. See, for example, Hayden White,
Metahistory: The Historical Imagination in 19th Century Europe (Baltimore, 1973). Cf. 'The idea
of the nation – a thought of God', p. 172.

5 Joshua 5:14 and 15. It begins to have other connotations also in the Psalms and Isaiah.

6 Pagan mythologies are full of this theme of land bestowal and protection via celestial
patron powers. The nexus is a natural one, given the vital role of sowing and harvesting in
people survival. The famous passage (on swords and ploughshares) in Micah 4:1–5 says as
much. See also the list in 2 Kings 17:29–33 of national gods and sundry peoples.

7 See below. The doctrine of 'diaspora mission' had to be denounced in favour of 'Zion
nation'.

8 It is, of course, 'a foolish saying'. Walter Brueggemann, *The Land* (Philadelphia, 1977), p. 18.

9 David Ben Gurion, speaking in 1925 at the 25th Zionist Congress; cited from *The New York Times* (8 January 1961), p. 53.

10 Even though two and a half tribes were given dispensation to remain on the east side. The narrative is stylized and ritualized and the actualities uncertain.

11 This despite the perception of 'the wilderness' in Hosea as the place of purity to which Israel must be recalled. It was precisely 'landed' experience of compromise and guilt that made Hosea yearn for the nomadic simplicity.

12 Some scholars have surmised that perhaps the stories of conquest in the Book of Joshua in fact represent a series of peasant revolts against the tyranny of Canaanite city states. Such conjecture does not alter how the narrative understood itself as land acquisition *in toto* by divine design.

13 See Uriel Tal in Laurence Hoffmann (ed.), *The Land of Israel: Jewish Perspectives* (Notre Dame, 1986), p. 321.

14 Talmud: Tractate Ketuboth, 110 b; quoted in Dow Marmur, *The Star of Return* (New York, 1991), p. 130.

15 See Abraham Heschel, *Israel: An Echo of Eternity* (New York, 1968).

16 Abraham Kook, quoted in Eliezer Schweid, *The Land of Israel* (New Jersey, 1985), pp. 171–2.

17 Zvi Yehudah Kook on 'The sanctity of the Holy People in the Holy Land' in Y. Tirosh (ed.), *Religious Zionism: An Anthology* (Jerusalem, 1978), p. 141.

18 Amos Oz, *In the Land of Israel*, trans. Maurice Golberg (Jerusalem, 1984), p. 12.

19 *Metahistory*, p. 129. The theme is uncannily close to the words of Jesus, according to Matthew 5:45, bidding us 'be perfect [i.e., 'inclusive in our compassion'] as our heavenly Father is perfect, making His sun to rise on the evil and on the good'. One might recall Walt Whitman's line in his poem, 'To a Common Prostitute': 'Not till the sun excludes you do I exclude you.'

20 Gush Emunim, 'the block of the faithful', was founded in 1974. Its Rabbi Meir Yehiel declares: 'We have not settled here to look for peace and quiet: we have come here despite the sound and fury in order to fulfil the Lord's command, consequently no obstacle shall obstruct or hinder us.' See Amnon Rubinstein, *The Zionist Dream Re-Visited* (New York, 1989), p. 105.

21 Ibid., p. 113, quoting Joel Florsheim.

22 W. D. Davies, *The Territorial Dimension of Judaism* (Berkeley, 1982).

23 Ibid., p. 30, quoting from the Psalms of Solomon.

24 Ibid., p. 45: Jerusalem Talmud: Kilayyim vii.5, ed. Krotoshin, 31 a, line 32. For Lieberman, see *Proceedings of the Rabbinical Assembly of America*, vol. 12 (1949).

25 Theodor Herzl, *Der Judenstaat*, trans. in Arthur Hertzberg, *The Zionist Idea* (New York, 1973), pp. 204–26.

26 Moses Hess, *Rome and Jerusalem: A Study in Jewish Nationalism*, trans. M. J. Bloom (New York, 1958). J. L. Talmon sees Hess as affirming: 'There are ultimately no universal religions: there are only national cults': see *Israel Among the Nations* (London, 1970), p. 99. For all his idea of proceeding as 'innocuous' Herzl still declared: 'The Maccabees will rise again.'

27 Golda Meir was among many who noted this irony, deploring that, circumstantially at least, Jewish colonization had come to a contentious place.

28 Theodor Herzl, *Complete Diaries*, ed. and trans. M. Lowenthal (London, 1960), vol. 1, p. 41. Chaim Weizmann said much the same in his turn: 'If I want to take a decision, I stand in front of a mirror and hold a conference with myself and that is how the organisation [i.e. the Zionist Executive] is run.' See B. Litvinoff (ed.), *The Essential Chaim Weizmann* (New York, 1983), p. 211.

29 Chaim Weizmann, *Trial and Error* (London, 1949), pp. 74–5.

30 *Complete Diaries*, vol. 1, p. 343.

31 Abba Eban, *An Autobiography* (London, 1977), pp. 493f. (speaking in Geneva, December 1973).

32 Ibid., p. 286.

33 Emmanuel Levinas, *Difficult Freedom: Essays in Judaism*, trans. Sean Hand (London, 1990), p. 288.

34 Harry Sacher, *Zionist Portraits and Other Essays* (London, 1959), p. 179.

35 David Hartmann, *Joy and Responsibility: Israel, Modernity and the Renewal of Judaism* (Jerusalem, 1978), p. 280.

36 Moshe Shamir, *Beneath the Sun*, in *Modern Hebrew Literature*, vol. 3.3 (Autumn 1977), p. 16.

37 *Jewish Chronicle* (London; 25 October 1907). Weizmann was speaking in Manchester. The words reveal an astonishing attitude. 'Primitive'? Jewish settlers 'employing'? The 'danger' of an age-long population *acquiring* 'a moral right'? Can anyone be rightly subject to what is designed to make him 'feel dispensable'? The obtuseness seems incredible.

38 Ammiel Alcalay, *After Jews and Arabs: Remaking Levantine Culture* (Minneapolis, 1993), p. 253.

3

The cost of inconsequence

I

When the Romans decided to name old Philistia and the southern land of the eastern Mediterranean shore 'Palestina', they had historical precedent but were also signalling their quittance of the turbulent Jews of 'Judea'. The map had better register the actuality of politics and war. The Romans were unashamedly and unambiguously imperial in so doing.

It was perhaps a natural reactive instinct for modern political Zionists to reverse the process and cease to admit the Palestinian name. This happened in the far different strategy of a progressive acquisition but – ironically – only after happily using it themselves. The sorry element of the ambiguous in the story will concern us, politically, in the next chapter. The immediate significance here has to do with the way in which the entire Zionist enterprise was capable of either ignoring or dismissing the crucial Palestinian dimension of its whole intention. Palestine, the Palestinians and Palestinianism could be treated as inconsequential. What Jewish realists knew to be of central relevance could be left as a marginal irrelevance. It is the subjective experience of this 'un-thought-on-ness' that we must document and assess as an aspect of *Palestina Agonistes*.

It is a familiar detail of this entire history that 'Palestinians' were not mentioned in the famous Balfour Declaration.[1] There was intended evasiveness in talk of 'the existing non-Jewish population' – a curious expression for people already belonging to a territory that was, and could then be, named as 'Palestine'. The country needed its recognizable name but the inhabitants could be imagined not to carry it. If we read the worst, then the process of nullification had already begun. 'Civil and religious rights' were not to suffer 'detriment' – a negative formula – but those for whom the safeguard was meant to be reassuring, if not fully protective, could be left anonymous.

Herzl's *Der Judenstaat* made no mention of the Palestinians, his diaries only rarely. In his novel *Altneuland* ('New–Old Land') he pictured them eager to share in Jewish society for its benefits. He was essentially the diplomatic contriver, concerned with the Sublime Porte, banking potential and a legal charter for the 'right' to settle. But the 'legal' did not incorporate the people locally at stake. The Israeli historian Jacob Talmon commented truly in observing that

> The Balfour Declaration, the Palestine Mandate and the U.N.O. decision in 1947 were all Herzlian realisations in content and in spirit.[2]

That is, they were documents of 'great power' warranting, ignoring any local consent. The *quid pro quo* in Herzl was legality for lobbying, monetary aid for constitutional order. In his lawyer realism he may well have assumed that nothing else, local, psychic, ethical, was relevant to the matter in hand.

Yet a Palestine was nameable – not least in Zionist usage, at least until the Second World War. The Jewish Agency after 1921 pleaded the terms of 'the Palestine Mandate'. It is interesting how the memoirs of Harry Sacher, Chaim Weizmann and Golda Meir referred unblushingly in early days to 'the Palestine people', meaning, always, Jewish settlers. Sacher has three chapters of reminiscence headed 'Palestine Memoirs' – all of them concerning Jewish figures. He explains how the Zionist Commission helped 'the Palestine Jews' prepare for the implementation of Balfour.[3] Golda Meir wrote:

> The first Palestinians I ever encountered were . . . I listened spellbound to the Palestinians.[4]

They were Ben Zvi, in due course Israel's second President, David Ben Gurion, its first Prime Minister, and Ya'akov Zerubavel, a writer. When the second-named did refer to 'the Palestinian Arabs', he saw them as 'placidly vegetating in their poverty under the Turks . . . in a forgotten corner of the Turkish Empire that nobody wanted'.[5]

This usage of 'Palestinian' ceased after the 1930s, though it was not until May 1948 that the decision was taken to speak of territory and state as 'Israel'. That decision, however, simply regulated the inconsequentiality of 'Palestine', memorably expressed in the oft-quoted words of Golda Meir in *The Sunday Times* of London on 15 June 1969:

It was not as though there were a Palestinian people in Palestine considering itself as a Palestinian people and we came and threw them out and took their country away from them. They did not exist.

Similarly, Menahem Begin later declared in *Yediot Aharanot*:

If this is Palestine and not the land of Israel then you are conquerors and not tillers of the land. You are invaders. If this is Palestine then it belongs to a people who lived here before you.[6]

Those were anguished words. It is sometimes the casual remarks that say as much. Thus Raphael Patai in *The Arab Mind* observes:

After settling in New York, I was a frequent visitor to Palestine – now independent Israel.[7]

A laconic comment on a tormented history. Could it, then, all have been, as Herzl suggested in the first volume of his *Diaries*, a case of 'trying to spirit the penniless population across the border discreetly and circumspectly'?[8]

II

'To spirit', 'penniless', 'discreetly' and 'circumspectly' were all tragically misconstrued notions. Yet it is right to see the emergence of Palestinianism as the creation of the Zionism that denied it any recognition. This paradox may in part explain why so many Zionists saw only a vacancy for their enterprise. There was doubtless much wishful thinking in that situation and it was, by some criteria, readily excusable. Yet the very impulse that generated nationalism in Jewish terms ought to have anticipated the countering reality it was itself evoking in the other party. The *sacro egoismo* of Judaism had no reason to assume a unilateral occasion. For Zion to will a Palestinian irrelevance was to misread its own Judaic significance. It is this tangled irony we have to explore.

It is often alleged in Zionist thinking that 'Palestine' as a definable entity only exists because Israel does. It is, on this view, essentially a copy having no validity other than these imitative terms. It is like an act of coveting aroused because others possess. This perception in turn allows a sort of Jewish absolution. It affords an alibi of exoneration. One might almost phrase an aphorism that '"Palestine" is of no consequence, being only a consequence of ours'.

There is truth in the sequence; there is none in the alibi. Undoubtedly, the reality of Israel, and the processes by which it was achieved, served to denominate in desperate terms the Palestinian identity. For it had incurred adversarially what the reality and the processes entailed. Even if only defining the relevant piece of territory, Zionism gave it a definition intrinsic to its occupants. Once Revisionists like Jabotinsky had been halted and the Mandate, *de facto* if not *de jure*, applied to land west of the Jordan, a 'Palestine' was confirmed as the space in question. That single fact inevitably availed to give it what might be called a territorial consciousness.

That, however, was by no means the sum of the matter. On the contrary, throughout the final decades of the Ottoman Empire, Palestinian Arabs had been playing their part in the counsels of fellow Arabs within it. These, to be sure, were in anxious debate and contention, moving with the oscillations of imperial policy. The cruel regime of Sultan 'Abd al-Hamid II kindled brave Arab resistance – both aspects recurring again during the First World War. In between, with the Young Turks and others in divided mind, there were hopes of genuine provincial autonomy within a dignified Arab 'Ottomanism'.[9] The overall power being Islamic, revolt against it was not religiously congenial to the Arab mind (despite inter-Arab–Turk tension). Many Palestinian notables, Turkish-speaking, were ready for a continuing Arabism in an Ottoman frame, provided the incipient nationalist form of their Arabism had genuine and secure expression.

When this proved illusory and the case for 'the Arab Revolt' became paramount – despite a continuing Ottomanism which the Turks themselves torpedoed in the war situation – Palestinians took due part with their Syrian and Iraqi partners in the costly business of Arab nationalism. Federalism yielded to the demand for the 'nation' principle. The victory of Allied arms in 1918 and the total defeat of the Central Powers *seemed* to Arabs like the threshold of authentic national fulfilment.

It is strange that so many of Zionist mind in Jewry failed to take the measure of this Arab counterpart. Brought up on the ideas of Moses Hess, Leo Pinsker and Max Nordau, of Judaism as 'a nation', and as a nation demanding 'a state', fired with the visions of Mazzini and Garibaldi and directing these irresistibly to the Palestine destiny, Zionism contrived to be oblivious of the same logic and the same emotions in the Arab setting. With exceptions rare enough to be remarkable, it seemed capable of ignoring, dismissing, or simply failing to register the local Palestinian counterpart.

Was not Arab policy negotiating, comparably to the Zionists, with 'world powers' – such negotiation being the necessary order of things? A 'home' – national or otherwise – they did not need. For they were already resident. What they certainly sought, and believed they had been promised, was a 'state of their own', once the Ottoman relinquishment of their territory had been contrived by the same power-equation on which Weizmann and his colleagues also relied. Were Arabs not calculating comparably on the outcome of the 1914–18 War, having opted, like the Zionists, for the British alternative, without – again like the Zionists – entirely burying the German option should that, in the end, emerge victorious? Pragmatists are by instinct opportunists.

Perhaps this Zionist capacity to discount things Palestinian was merely wishful. Or, since it was clearly necessary to persuade the massive Jewish resistance to Jewish nationalism, from a Jewry that wanted to be in loyal diaspora,[10] that *aliyah* was feasible, there was no point in drawing attention to the Palestinian dimension except as a waiting vacancy. Or, if serious cognizance was taken of it, it could nevertheless be presented as manageable, one way or another. As early as 1901 when Herzl negotiated with the Ottoman power about a charter to colonize, he included the right to deport Palestinians. Or again, as a cynic said, some problems are best handled by intelligent neglect. In that event, and in some cases, they may come home to roost. When Herzl visited Palestine in 1898 he produced a report which made no mention of Palestinians, who then numbered around half a million.

Neglect might be rationalized into ideology by other Zionist thinkers. Thus Ber Borochov saw a Zionist state as the form in which Jewry would play its unique role in an international class-struggle. Inclusive socialist revolution would transcend the Arab/Jew issue by bringing both, under Zionist auspices, into Marxist liberation. Palestinians would have every reason to participate. Zionism, to his mind, was not authentic as a crude nationalism responding in kind to anti-Semitism. True nationalism was to be realized only through progressive minds leading it into the common emancipation of the masses in which ethnic motives would be drowned in socialist ones. Seen nationally, he argued,

> the Jewish problem migrates with the Jews . . . Emigration alone does not solve the Jewish problem. It leaves the Jew helpless in a strange country . . . It accelerates the rise of national competition in the countries into which the Jews have recently emigrated.

Borochov's prescience in this analysis, however, related only to populated industrialized countries. Immigration had to mean outright colonization. This argued a territory where colonization was feasible. This meant 'a country having no attraction for immigrants from other nations and not highly industrial . . . but rather semi-agricultural'. Palestine was that country, 'a land of spontaneously concentrated Jewish immigration'.[11] This proletarian Zionism would be 'a step toward socialism' in which the recipient territory would enjoy the proletarian ideology.

Borochov's thesis had much relevance at the turn of the twentieth century and his ideas had influence in the labour element so prominent in the years prior to and after the formation of the State of Israel. Among his associates in the Ukraine was Isaac Ben Zvi, destined to be President of Israel. It is clear that socialist ideology meant colonization and colonization relative 'emptiness', with 'an existing population' virtually irrelevant for its own sake and on its own terms. Borochov's point about 'the rise of national competition' referred to cities like New York or Philadelphia, where Jewish concentrations provoked ethnic tension and so vitiated economic ambitions. For Borochov,

> Anti-Semitism flourishes because of the national competition between the Jewish and the non-Jewish petty bourgeoisie and between the Jewish and the non-Jewish proletarized and unemployed masses. Anti-Semitism menaces both the poor helpless Jews and the all-powerful Rothschilds.[12]

By its very emptiness, its availability for colonization, Palestine would resolve that tension, its consent being inconsequential. Its attraction was its undeveloped vacancy. The appeal to economic calculus reached, in effect, the same conclusion as virile racial nationalism. Borochov, *vis-à-vis* Palestinian concerns, was one with Nordau and Jabotinsky, no rise of national competition being there foreseen.

It did not need Marxist reasoning alone to argue the benefits of Palestine perceived in solutions to 'the Jewish problem'. The theme of its emptiness could exist on romantic concepts of the Arab as 'the nomad', a population not even 'semi-agricultural'. Nomads can always move on. Their mobility is the settler's occasion. Outside the Negev, nomadism had not obtained in Palestine for centuries. 'A land of milk and honey', 'out of whose stones you may dig brass', was scarcely nomads' land even for the biblical narrative. Was it not 'the wilderness' which the tribes had left behind? Was it not 'the vines and fig trees' of others whom the incomers were to possess? Fit the paeans of the Deuteronomist about the land into the notion of a *nomadia* and the ludicrous is reached (Deut 8:7–14). According to the Joshua saga, it was hardly a drove of nomads the invasion had to incite to flight. There had to be trumpets around the walls of Jericho and the immolation of populous cities.

It is true that when many observers, with Zionist intent, came to Palestine they saw destitution and privation and an unsophisticated agriculture. What they were also witnessing, without perception, was decades of Turkish oppression, a peasantry victimized by absentee landlords and a degree of lethargy not without a kinship to the ghetto. None the less, the villages were there, the family structures sacrosanct and the memories tenacious.

Being right in one's own eyes, one can ignore contrary evidence, the will to innocence, or at least for exoneration, being so strong. Insofar as 'Israel would represent', in Ben Gurion's words, 'the land of the championship of God', a distinction would be usefully made between Palestinians being a physical presence and their having any moral and historical right. In a theological, as distinct from a literal sense, they were 'non-inhabitants'. This was a sentiment that Jabotinsky could make even more explicit.

III

The sundry ambiguities attending the political history which call for review in the next chapter contributed powerfully to the disqualification of the Palestinian dimension. Taken on the wrong foot on many occasions, as we must see, their reactions supplied endless alibis for the Zionist mind. Why should it be reproached for in fact succeeding? It could be alleged that only Palestinian intransigence had occasioned the idea, and then the fact, of partition and that after 1948 and 1967 Palestinians had for the most part displaced themselves: [13] Palestinian acts of omission and commission were responsible for the establishment of Israel. Throughout, those Zionist figures who agonized over conscience or conceived of federalism could be vilified or decried as eccentrics or near imbeciles. Thus Harry Sacher dismissed Judah Magnes as

> believing himself to be a saint and as such entitled to differ from others on fundamental matters . . . He believed he was the man to achieve harmony and co-operation between Jews and Arabs and . . . that soft words could break down stubborn facts. Politically he lived in a world of fantasy, which he confounded with a world of lofty morality.[14]

This of a leader capable of founding the Hebrew University and of weeping gently in fervour at the ceremony of its inauguration.[15]

The same Harry Sacher has very dismissive words for those in the British Mandatory Administration who inclined – as many genuinely did – to the Palestinian 'side' of the tragic equation. Their motives, often honest and authentic, could be trivialized as those of deluded and romantic 'Arabists'. Marie Syrkin, referring to Palestinian property 'abandoned', likened it to Egyptian villages lost in the High Dam project, or new motorways

41

requiring the shifting of populations for the public good. Ignoring the different factors of 1948 and 1967, she added: 'Only in the case of Arabs has village patriotism been raised to a sacred cause.'[16] The belittlement aside, did the final phrase betray a perception for which only one 'cause' might be 'sacred', while, in point of fact, Palestinianism of the PLO majority has never played the sanctity card?[17]

In various other ways it was tempting for Zionist activists to read Palestinian consciousness as artificial and inauthentic precisely because it lacked the qualities belonging to the Judaic version of the same emotions. Or it emanated from British encouragement – a theory that fitted well into the Jewish Agency's concern to swing the Mandatory Power entirely behind a Zionist interpretation of the Mandate itself. Alleged British connivance lay behind the Arab troubles, which ought not, therefore, to be related credibly to the Jewish presence. Ben Gurion insisted that to align any 'nationalism' of Palestinian Arabs with 'the Jewish ideal of Israel' made no sense at all.[18] Given Judaic destiny and Judaic force of will, all else was of no consequence. Nor was it calculated to give pause, except as an obstacle for prowess to overcome.

In more suave and erudite minds than Ben Gurion's there was a different kind of alibi concerning Palestinian 'rights'. It had to do with a necessary futurism. Futurism had always been a concomitant of the Messianic idea in Judaism, as Gershom Scholem demonstrated in his classic study of that theme.[19] Zionism being 'the Jewish re-insertion into the creative stream of human history',[20] the cause, the state, the ideal, must all be given time. Adverse verdicts ought to be muted until the full day of righteousness had dawned. Israel, before and after 1948, was *in via*, on the way. Patience was imperative. Was she not embattled, struggling for survival, in straits between defiance and despair? No new nation could be expected to attain social justice and coexistence in such times. The ideal, however, was inviolate and would one day come true.

There was much that was legitimate in this plea, as we must note elsewhere. Yet, all the time, the *way to* was taking the *way from* in respect of the innocent legitimacy, the ideal perceived in its own frame of reference. Means tend to become ends in themselves when the end approves them. But to be *in via* is not of itself to be *ex culpa*. The very term 'peace process' may be a naïve or malign illusion, a contradiction in sense. What delays may spell what denies.

That there were also powerful alibis from the far and the immediate past, enabling Zionism to hold Palestinian implications of no vital consequence to its overriding purpose, will come more properly into Chapters 5 and 6.

One other feature in the present context is the instinct to avoid anything that might as it were Palestinianize Israel itself. It was noted in Chapter 2 how the fact of common location was not allowed to serve the expectation of a common culture.

The Jewish settlers were escaping from the ghettos of cities or the habits of commerce in diaspora, becoming by strenuous and deliberate effort tillers of the land and followers of the plough. This was integral to *Hibbet Zion*, 'the love of Zion'. The early pre-political, innocuous settlers, whom Herzl's logic had so deplored, had shown the way. The rugged quality of *aliyah*, into and on to the land required and attained, might have suggested an active kinship with a Palestinian peasantry engaged for centuries on the same soil and in the same struggle with nature. For Palestinian life was emphatically rural and plebeian, villages being many, cities very few. Some aspects of the Jewish *sabras* might have been kin to the local patterns on the same terrain.

To be sure, their methods were different. They were increasingly served by sophisticated farm technology and disciplines as kibbutzniks that adjacent villages could not command and to which they were not attuned. It needed more than adjacence, washed by the same rains and sharing the same water-table, to fuse these two agricultures, and in due course the physical factors made them sharply competitive. But the finally decisive factor was a will to a sort of apartheid, a conscious separatism springing from the Zionist consciousness pursuing a private destiny. If the land of itself did not marry the parties, how could the human neighbourhood? Men could gaze across from the new watch-towers to the clustering village roofs, from the new irrigation pumps of the one to the old wells of the other as by a tacit mutual exclusion. Or, when economic factors demanded, they might work out a strictly practical *modus vivendi* of wage paying and wage earning that only deepened the psychological apartheid. When war supervened, the dire human consequences of dispossession and land loss could be reckoned inconsequential, wars entailing such things.

This avoidance of Palestinianization – if the phrase is allowed, the fact being manifest – was, of course, implicit in the entire Zionist logic. Zionism meant stringent self-expression, based on total self-reliance, secured by entire self-sufficiency, land and state being the prerequisites. There was no desire for an eastern 'host-nation'. Local compatibility would turn, if at all, on Zionist dialectic, events facilitating. That story belongs with Chapter 4. There was no final doubt about the fact that Zionism hoped and intended to create. All elements in the equation were to be grist to that mill. Yet, humanly, would it be possible to hold to such an adamant conception of all that was afoot in a populated country with a humanly caring cargo of human traditions and human heritage?

There were many, many Jews who thought not in their hearts. Yet heads also counted. That Palestinianism should be discounted, held at arm's length, has been a posture borne out by one notable feature, namely the Hebraization of literature and society by the emergence of modern Hebrew. From within Zionist consciousness there was legitimate enthusiasm and creativity in this development. It was a cherished dimension of what has been called 'the elimination of the diaspora'. However, it worked effectively against the freedom and morale of the large *Arab* and Arabic dimension of the diaspora itself. State-building and the avowed aspiration to incorporate all Jews of whatever vintage might have been expected to afford greater tolerance and liberty for what they brought with them. Moreover, the new state contained within its borders a minority of Palestinians who became technically its citizens.

Both these Arabicized elements within Israel, the incomers as Jews deriving from cities from Iraq as far as Morocco and the locals, were sadly disadvantaged by the official status of Hebrew. Lively playwrights, novelists and poets in the Arabic vein found their talents either discouraged in the politics of culture or deterred by the necessity of attaining expression in a completely new language medium. Numerous Arabic terms and usages have penetrated into Israeli Hebrew, as inevitably happens when an old language renews itself for current relevance. There has been nothing like the same Arabic infusion in Israeli literature. The elimination of the diaspora affects even anthologies and the literary market.

The Sephardi dimensions of Israeli Judaism, which might have been expected to weigh against disfavour towards Arabicized elements in Jewish Israeli society, have in general not been allowed to do so. Europeanism, as noted in Chapter 2 relating to that context, competes against a more inclusive Semitism within the state. There are worthy Arabic Departments in Israeli universities but the Arabic ethos at large is not greatly aided thereby. The Sephardi Council of Jerusalem stated:

> By doggedly dismissing the idea of a Palestinian personality or entity the present 'hawkish' leaders of Israel have naturally stifled any signs of the existence or growth of such a personality.[21]

Many ordinary Palestinians, in relations with the state and its officialdom in endless matters of permits and procedures, have been at a loss either to comprehend or to survive through the imposition of a mandatory language in which they cannot operate.

Literate writers, of course, do not incur these practical troubles, yet instinctively they are at home creatively in the speech of their native culture. Incoming Arabicized Jews have suffered in this way because the 'ingathering' – so nobly cosmopolitan in its physically absorptive ambition – has proved partial in its hospitality to cultural Jewish diversity. The diaspora has been undone in more ways than the geographical. That this should have been the case in respect of 'Arabic-speaking Jews' only underlines the odds against Arabic-speakers who are not Jews at all.

What witnesses to this conclusion without undoing it may be noted in the emergence of Israeli-Jewish groups which accent their 'oriental' sympathies. The heterogeneous character of the old city of Jerusalem in earlier days served to stimulate 'the Hebrew Canaanites', represented by novelists like Binyamin Tammuz and Aharon Amir, who sought to identify with the local ethos.[22] They witness to the protest against a falsely unilateral consciousness in Israeli letters which chimes with direct de-Palestinianizing motifs in Israel's perception of its destiny. They resist what amounts culturally to a state of internal exile, while from the Palestinian side a literature of resistance is engendered by the very absence of equal conditions.[23] In some measure Israel generates the antipathies that wait on marginalized emotions. One Israeli writer, Samir Naqqash, rejects Hebrew and continues to write in Arabic.[24] At least in cultural terms the undoing of diaspora has been in a highly partial form, as a consequence of the prevailing Zionist conception of a spiritual separatism explicit in the way historical Zionism has both conceived its nature and contrived its eventuation. Israel was always insistent in seeing Palestinianism as a pan-Arab or an arch-Arab entity, refusing it as a contributor within despite the positive affinities it could have coveted, and partially found, within the diaspora's own yield of an articulate Arabism of Jewish vintage. Responding to a bitter poem by the Palestinian Mahmud Darwish, Yossi Shiloah, a noted Israeli writer, kindled sympathetically to him even at the beginnings of the Intifadah.

> I am in search of my roots, my identity, and I cannot find it within Israeli culture: if I do, then it is only negatively. I went to Palestinian Arabic literature in search of my culture and, being Oriental, found that I feel much closer to certain Palestinian poets than to Israeli writers . . . No initiative has been taken in Israel, neither in the theatre nor in the educational system, to bring the cultural and spiritual dimension of the Palestinian people to light. I reject the common idea that the two peoples are 'condemned' to live together. This is a coercive, negative concept . . . about life in common.[25]

45

It would almost seem that in repairing the diaspora, Zionism had not understood how wide it was, or was repudiating it as everywhere a hostile experience. The politics of Zionism clearly made inescapably for confrontation. Need its culture and spirit have followed suit in the gathering-in of 'oriental' Jewish communities whom the politics of its creation put in danger? The further paradox is that political exigencies have conspired to make the state a 'Gentile' entity in respect of the ways of *realpolitik*, security and finesse in strategy. Zionism could not have achieved what it has attained in our sort of world without behaving in terms akin to those of any nationalism and every nation. Could it be that in the very impossibility of remaining in *realpolitik* distinctively Jewish – still less Judaic in a prophetic sense – it was the more minded to disavow what it saw as an uncongenially oriental Jewishness in its own cultural make-up? What might have been a bridge into Palestinianism served to induce a further distance from it.

IV

It will be clear from later chapters why political Zionism disallowed the cultural and spiritual consensus, or at least compatibility, it might have reached with the Palestine element in the whole equation, especially given an Arabic-speaking Jewry in the context. Despite the gulf the politics of statehood created, the human setting might have generated – at long range – its own fusions of culture and ethos, but for a quality implicit in the very texture of Jewry. It is a mystery very difficult to probe, still more difficult to surmount from without or dispel from within. What we have been seeing here as marginal and inconsequential to the Zionist mind about Palestinian reality belongs with the age-long Judaic category of 'the Gentiles'. Jewry has long been burdened with a radical suspicion of the rest of humanity and all too often the rest of humanity has given tragic warrant to the suspicion. That dual situation has blighted and darkened history. That it is *dual* none can deny. Anti-Semitism defines a negation: the 'Semitism' it opposes is, and ever was, an affirmation, a concept of sharp differentiation consciously esteemed and requiring to be conceded by those excluded from it. That requirement kindles its own repudiation.

Trying, however patiently, to unravel this complexity can all too often be suspected as conniving with it. Such is the tangle of the situation. One can be thought 'anti-Semitic' precisely in the effort to understand the 'Semitism' from which it is identified if not derived. 'Semitism', insofar as the term can be current except in and with the 'anti', embraces much more than Jewry. It must mean all that springs from Shem of the sons of Noah in post-diluvian humanity. Conspicuous among these are Arabs themselves. There are three great religions properly called 'Semitic', in respect of whom 'anti-Semitic' might more precisely describe Buddhists and non-theistic Hindus. These are certainly 'non-Semitic' and, in controversial mood, also 'anti-Semitic'.

Anti-Semitism, however, means effectively 'anti-Jewish', a disputing of Jewish exceptionality, a disavowing of Judaic self-perception and, more darkly, a hostile obsession against it. Obsessions ought always to be suspect. But is Judaic self-interpretation one of them, the more obsessive for being rooted in a theological frame of 'covenant' and 'election'? Can it be only coincidence that the world's most insistently 'elect' and 'separate' people are the world's most consistently persecuted people? Or, if not coincidence in the casual sense, certainly so in the causal sense? Just as the ghetto was necessitated by what despised it as well as by what needed it, so anti-Semitism responds to what invites it, decries what defies it. How far, it might tragically be asked, does Jewry *need* anti-Semitism in order to be sure of itself as Judaic? Rabbi Abraham Heschel used to ask if 'the Gentiles' really wanted 'a world without Jews', for that is what persecution and assimilation might seem to intend.[26] Then, perversely, might not anti-Semitism be the way to prevent that ever happening?

Chapter 5 below must undertake the biblical origins in 'the holy' of Jewish self-consciousness and the urgent problems about 'chosen-ness' of people and 'promise' about land. There is no doubt that all arose in a context of tribal identities and tribal worships and was perpetuated within a resplendent monotheism. Even when Judaic monolatry developed into monotheism there was still retained an exclusive duty of Yahweh to the Hebrew nation and a unique status of that nation under Yahweh. Even for the Deuteronomist, and certainly for the narrator in Joshua, the claim to separatism did not admit of peaceful co-existence with other cults and peoples. But the 'religious' differentials remained rooted and validated in the ethnic. Resistance to the Philistine *baalim*, 'lords many', retained its tribal overtones even when the undertones were those of monotheists.

These deep-lying issues are crystallized in the notion of 'the Gentiles', a denominator of all mankind except the Jewish segment, an ecumenism by exemption.[27] Tragically, when Judaism decided – by no means unanimously – to take nationalist form in political Zionism, the resident people of Palestine, already a 'Gentile' category, became the acute physical symbol of a 'Gentile' contradiction to Jewish self-understanding as 'elect'. Their resistance to settlement, occupation and displacement could be read as 'anti-Semitic', even as a guilty conniving with Hitler.

This has been the bitterest experience of their history. Their being inconsequential to the proper proceedings of Zionist intentions, reinforced as these were by the enormities of the Shoah, was in complete line with a traditional Jewish concept of 'the Gentiles' among whom these Palestinian 'Semites' were to be numbered, and numbered more sharply for their inconvenient existence and locale. The Halakhah classifies non-observant Jews as having been taken captive by 'the Gentiles'. Maimonides used the word to disavow Jews who go their own way, aloof from 'the congregation of Israel', 'as if they were Gentiles, having no portion in the world to come'. The very word 'Gentile' thus lends itself to disavowal and betrays the instinct that uses it as strangely biased. T. S. Eliot once described D. H. Lawrence as 'an ignorant man in the sense that he was unaware of how much he did not know'.[28] Similarly we may be biased the more by our non-register of its degree. The enormities of anti-Semitic bias go unspeakably beyond the word. But what are we, what are Palestinians, to think of the bias that makes us all 'Gentiles' in separation from the divine benisons of Israel?

These chapters are revolving around distinguishable but still convergent aspects of the Palestinian experience of political Zionism. Others will follow. That it is painfully caught in the tangle of Judaic self-perception is not in doubt, nor the fact that Palestinianism has been fated by history to bear the contemporary brunt of that issue. For the State of Israel is yet another venture in Jewish self-segregation, perceived as required of it, indeed forced upon it, by Gentile antipathy. On the one hand, Jewish nation-making is a political form of assimilation to 'Gentile' norms of 'nation' and 'state' and 'power', yet paradoxically pursued as asserting Judaic exceptionality. Ideologically it denies the old ghetto condition but in a conceptual sense resembles it, with the supreme difference that it is virile, armed, defensible and self-reliant.

It is a difference which Palestinianism registers as being at one and the same time the victim of the virility and the setting of the normalcy. On neither count could it think to escape dire and bitter cost-bearing as long as Zionism fulfilled its purposes. Diaspora could not be politically repudiated or undone without particular 'Gentiles' incurring the penalty. The old *goyim* image of the 'non-Jew' was configured with the Palestinian Arab.

Notes

1 This feature of the document, apart from its ultimate consequences, has always exasperated Palestinian feeling. If unintended as nugatory of a whole identity, the long sequel told heavily against that charitable view.

2 J. L. Talmon, *Israel Among the Nations* (London, 1970), p. 125.

3 Harry Sacher, *Zionist Portraits and Other Essays* (London, 1959), pp. 316–25.

4 Golda Meir, *My Life* (London, 1975), p. 39.

5 David Ben Gurion, *Recollections*, ed. T. R. Bransten (London, 1970), pp. 24f.

6 See Arie Bobor, *The Other Israel: The Radical Case Against Zionism* (New York, 1972), p. 77.

7 Raphael Patai, *The Arab Mind* (New York, 1973), p. 5.

8 Theodor Herzl, *Complete Diaries* (London, 1960), vol. 1, p. 88.

9 The issues are well reviewed and documented in Hasan Saab, *The Arab Federalists of the Ottoman Empire* (Amsterdam, 1955); Hazem Nuseibeh, *The Ideas of Arab Nationalism* (Ithaca, NY, 1956); and C. E. Dawn, *From Ottomanism to Arabism: Essays on the Origins of Arab Nationalism* (Ann Arbor, n.d.).

10 It is often forgotten how massive was the Jewish reluctance to accept the idea of return to 'Zion', and how forlorn a cause Zionism at first seemed. It jeopardized diaspora Jewry, exposing them to suspicion about the integrity of their local loyalty; it seemed to contradict all that was most spiritual in religious Judaism; and it implied, for the strictly Orthodox, that 'Messiah's work' could be done for him.

11 Cited from Arthur Hertzberg, *The Zionist Idea* (New York, 1973), pp. 361, 366.

12 Ibid., p. 361.

13 Yehoshafat Harkabi, *Arab Attitudes Towards Israel* (Maryland, 1972), p. 365.

14 *Zionist Portraits*, p. 319.

15 Judah Magnes (1877–1948) was a patrician who, after an early Herzl discipleship, developed a lonely advocacy of immigration and Judaic culture for which statehood was not indispensable, given a federal agreement with Palestinians for which he sought against increasing odds. To the likes of Jabotinsky and Ben Gurion he was a traitor outside the camp, an appeaser of the unappeasable.

16 Marie Syrkin, *People and Politics in the Middle East* (London, 1971), p. 316.

17 For the reason that the Palestine National Charter sought to provide for Arab and Jew of prior-1947 residence as equal elements in a Palestinian statehood.

18 *Recollections*, p. 116.

19 Gershom Scholem, *The Messianic Idea in Israel and Other Essays* (New York, 1971), p. 35.

20 *Recollections*, p. 131.

21 *Towards Jewish/Palestinian Reconciliation* (World Union of Jewish Students, n.d.), p. 70.

22 See James S. Diamond, *Homeland or Holy Land? The Canaanite Critique of Israel* (Bloomington, 1986). 'The Hebrew Canaanites' aimed at a more local, integratist perception of the Zionist task.

23 One strong example of such 'resistance literature' was the work of Ghassan Kanafani. See his survey in *Al-Adab al-Muqawamah fi Falastin al-Muhtallah* (Beirut, 1975). See also Khalid S. Sulaiman, *Palestine and Modern Arab Poetry* (London, 1984).

24 Apart from his own writings (more received in Cairo than in Tel Aviv) Samir Naqqash is discussed in G. N. Giladi, *Discord in Zion: Conflict Between Ashkenazi and Sephardi Jews in Israel* (London, 1990).

25 Cited from Ammiel Alcalay, *After Jews and Arabs: Remaking Levantine Culture* (Minneapolis, 1993), pp. 231–2.

26 In a lecture at Union Theological Seminary, New York, Rabbi Heschel asked this question: 'Would it really be *ad majorem Dei gloriam* to have a world without Jews?': *UTS Journal*, vol. xxi, no. 2 (January 1966), p. 129. See further my *Troubled by Truth* (Edinburgh, 1992), pp. 107–26.

27 *Goyim* ('Gentiles' is a word of Latin origin) simply means all others, not us. Every identity is aware of distinction from the rest. Only the Judaic tradition requires a single

word to denominate all other humans in a category turning on a special theology about themselves. Can there be theological discrimination between one people and all others? Judaic faith has never really faced the implications in 'Gentilizing' fellow humans.

28 T. S. Eliot, Foreword to M. Jarrett-Kerr, *D. H. Lawrence and Human Existence* (London, 1961), p. 10.

4

The prey of ambivalence

I

Isaac has always seemed the kindliest of the old patriarchs of biblical story. There are few more charming scenes than that of his serenade in the evening as the camel-train drew near bearing the bride of his dreams from a far country, the daughter – as yet unknown – of his distant kin. In his old age this gentle trustfulness was the more deceived. His twin son Jacob would take advantage of his blindness to pass himself off as Esau and steal the first-born's blessing. The bride–mother he had welcomed to his bosom was party to the deceit. In the deathbed moment he had had his own misgivings: 'The voice is the voice of Jacob but the hands are the hands of Esau.' It was the hands he had trusted, gloved in a huntsman's skins, when the voice was the surer, the undisguised, credential.

Trustingness, as Kant observed in contriving his categorical imperative, is necessary to the success of deceit. To allay suspicion is part of the policy in situations that deserve it, just as keeping it alert is the safeguard against being deceived. The two strategies, unless there is trust, are likely to abet each other. Poor Isaac let the hands win against the voice.

In the history of conflict over Palestine–Israel the ambivalence of hand and voice has sometimes been the other way round, what has been done being more telling than what has been said. There has been deep ambiguity in both spheres, ambiguity which has kindled misgivings, caused these to deepen into entire distrust and so tangled positive purposes in crippling enmity. To study Palestine as 'the prey of ambivalence' is to measure the pain of location and the cost of inconsequence in their political incidence.

Ambivalence has attended the story from the outset. It is the corollary of opportunism and opportunism always lives uneasily with scruple. Zionism had enormous odds to face in first establishing its credibility within Jewry, then its legitimacy for at least one 'world-power', then its goal within the British Mandate, its status with the United Nations and its lobby role in Washington and US policy-making. In all these arenas of its century-long sequences, it needed to be both dogmatic as to its claims and somehow legitimated concerning them. It needed at the same time to demand and to plead, to navigate in ways at once precarious and determined. Opportunism was its only option but, by definition, the opportunist is not his own master however inwardly overmastering his purposes may be. It is at once the glory and the indictment of political Zionism that it became so doggedly manipulative of circumstance and occasion at the price of subtlety and contrivance.

What was gratefully partitionable in the debates of the 1930s and the decision of 1947, and was briefly negotiable in the aftermath of 1967, had become indivisible and inalienable for the policy-makers of the 1980s. 'Why do you want to partition our country?' could be Menahem Begin's question forty years after the Biltmore decision of 1942 that fervently agreed that it was both prudent and permissible to accept the idea of partition then developing. To be sure, ideologues at that meeting had protested that Palestine, as 'holy land', was not available for partition. The pragmatists overruled them with a sounder logic of clinching what might be currently feasible on the way to the hidden future. Their sagacity was amply vindicated when Palestinians, cherishing a whole territory they saw as their own, rejected any notion of its division.

The imperceptions of Palestinian reaction to political Zionism will concern Chapter 8 as 'the ifs of hindsight'. That they have played critically into the hands of an 'Israel on the way and in being' is evident enough. They are the counterpart of a hidden agenda which was all the more effective for its hiddenness. The aim here is to trace a Zionism always in debate with itself about its programme and its ends but almost always contriving to contain them within a subtle adaption to events whereby ends came into definition in the act of being realized. In this history personalities suited to the successive junctures of leadership were readily to hand, even if, as with Chaim Weizmann, they were ceremoniously relegated to the margins when their political utility had passed. Zionism somehow succeeded in being opportunist as the very condition of its success. It was not that Palestinianism was taken unawares, except perhaps at the early stage. Rather, it was matched with a resilience more subtle and more adaptive than its own.

II

The invitation of Ben Gurion to Chaim Weizmann to allow himself to be nominated in 1948 as first President of the new state described Dr Weizmann's presidency as 'a moral necessity for the State of Israel'.[1] His long leadership through half a century had certainly been a political and practical 'necessity' in the attainment of statehood. Just prior to his acceptance of the office Weizmann had written about

> the programme of the Jewish State. An enormous amount will have to be left to trial and error and we shall have to learn the hard way . . . The goal is the building of a high civilization based on the austere standards of Jewish ethics. From these standards we must not swerve, as some elements have done during the short period of the National Home by bending the knee to strange gods. The Prophets have always chastised the Jewish people with the utmost severity for this tendency.[2]

'Trial and error' became the title of his memoirs. They are the stock in trade of all politics. Prophets may be right to fulminate, though pragmatists prevail. There is no honest exploration of the 'error' in Israel's 'trials' that is unilateral or exclusive of all that is necessarily reciprocal in human conflicts and ambitions. Our thesis here is that much of the trauma of the Palestinians stems from their own obduracy and 'evil counsel'. That is a large part of their being *agonistes*. *Mea culpa* is always the heaviest of *culpas*.

Yet 'other parties' have their part in this vicarious human field. The intricate ambivalence belonging to all the Zionist story, while playing into the hands of Palestinian deficiencies, also served to exploit and provoke them. The constant factor of discretionary interpretation, of disguise – plausible enough to avail yet thin enough to be suspect – controlled the situation long before and long after Balfour. The likes of Jabotinsky might be forthright and frank but reassurance was always at hand to mitigate and mollify. A Jewish writer's analysis runs:

> Weizmann and the Labour Movement saw the demand for a Jewish State as a general final goal which should be publicly expressed or suppressed according to the exigencies of the tactical demands of the political struggle for Zionism. Meanwhile, they insisted, the Movement should not waste time on declaratory politics but create in Palestine [*sic*] the socio-economic infra-structure which would make such a demand into a viable possibility at the right moment.[3]

It is not only religion, as John Donne thought, that profits from 'least light'.

It has become notorious now how far this guise of things was hallowed by the Balfour Declaration itself late in 1917. 'Home' was the word: 'state' was the intent. 'In' was the preposition: 'of' was the hidden sense. HM Government 'viewed with favour the establishment of a national home for the Jewish people in Palestine'. It was not to be such as in any way to prejudice 'the civil and religious rights of the existing non-Jewish communities in Palestine', but did the word 'communities' suggest that these would never be a 'state', the 'rights' then belonging only to individuals as such? Or it could be argued that they would never be 'a nation' in state form, since in that event no *caveat* about 'rights' would be necessary, states having them inherently. Even so the proviso sounded reassuring.

What status anyway was the Declaration assumed to have? It was couched as a personal letter to Lord Rothschild and spoke of itself as 'a declaration of sympathy with Jewish Zionist aspirations'. When vested in the League of Nations Mandate and that Mandate interpreted by the Jewish Agency, 'sympathy with aspirations' had become 'obligations about rights'.

Long negotiations lay behind the text. Zionist readers not only read 'between the lines' but proceeded on what they read with mingled guile and frankness. Max Nordau, who coined the 'national home' language, wrote that the term (in German, *Heimstätte*) would 'deceive by its mildness' and did not mean to exclude a passionate claim to statehood in the land.

> I did my best to persuade the claimants of the Jewish state that we might find a circumlocution that would express all that we meant but would say it in a way that would not provoke the Turkish rulers of the coveted land. I suggested *Heimstätte* as a synonym for 'state' . . . We all understood what it meant. To us it signified *Judenstaat* then and it signifies the same now . . . Now there is no need to dissimulate our real aim.[4]

Later, in 1936, Lloyd George, the Prime Minister involved, told the Peel Commission that the idea of the Declaration was

> that a Jewish State was not to be set up immediately by the Peace Treaty without reference to the wishes of the majority of the inhabitants. On the other hand, it was contemplated that when the time arrived for according representation to Palestine [*sic*] – if the Jews had meanwhile responded to the opportunity afforded them by the idea of a national home and had become a definite majority of the inhabitants – Palestine would thus become a Jewish Commonwealth.[5]

It is hardly surprising that Palestinians should read Jewish immigration as a foster-child of the Declaration and be in periodic – and violent – alarm about it, while softened by protestations of its inherent 'innocence'. It seems appropriate that until 1920 the Balfour Declaration was kept in a file marked 'Secret'. Other organs of British policy found it unwelcome, if not villainous.[6]

Balfour readily acknowledged how devious – if not iniquitous – its provisions and evasions were. When the Declaration became part of the Mandate, he conceded how distant its implementation would be from the Covenant of the League itself, from the Wilsonian idealism to be pondered in Chapter 10. 'The policy', he wrote,

> would be even more flagrant in the case of the independent nation [sic] of Palestine [sic] than in that of the independent nation of Syria. For in Palestine, we do not propose even to go through the form of consulting the wishes of the present inhabitants of the country . . . The four great Powers are committed to Zionism, and Zionism – be it right or wrong, good or bad – is rooted in age-long tradition, in present needs and future hopes of far profounder importance than the desires and prejudices of the seven hundred thousand Arabs who now inhabit that ancient land.[7]

Perhaps Jacob Talmon meant more than he said in opining that 'the group of men' behind the Declaration 'did not know what they were doing'. Yet he was ready to complain at the Mandate time about 'a whittling away of its provisions', when 'provisions' in it there were none.[8] It has to be remembered that at the time of its issue the area referred to was Ottoman territory yet to be acquired at great human cost by the British forces in battle from Egypt to Damascus. That Ottoman sovereignty is sometimes used to assert that, prior to 1919, Palestinians had no 'status', which ignores the independence movements from the 1880s and is, in itself, a strangely un-Zionist case-making.

The ambiguity of Balfour and the Mandate persisted into the long unease and final despair of the British in Palestine. By Jewish Agency lights, their function was to facilitate unimpeded and urgent immigration. In Arab terms they were required to honour other pledges and observe the majority rights to which the Mandate paid tribute as conditioning all else. Their dilemma could not have been more forcibly underlined than by the totally unambiguous Vladimir Jabotinsky:

> It is impossible to dream of a voluntary agreement between us and the Arabs of Eretz Israel . . . Every nation [sic] civilised or primitive, sees its land as its national home, where it wants to stay as the sole landlord for ever . . . Every nation fights the settlers as long as there is a glimmer of

hope of getting rid of the danger of foreign settlement. Thus they behave, and thus will the Eretz Israel Arabs behave, as long as there is a glimmer of hope in their hearts that they can prevent the changing of Palestine into Eretz Israel.[9]

Ironically, in his very terminology ('Arabs of Eretz Israel') Jabotinsky had already done the changing.

Meanwhile, the Mandatory was supposed to preside over the irreconcilable – a task compounded by the fact that the inevitable resistance to Zionism would be teased, cajoled, bewildered and held in suspense by intentions which waited prudently on events and reactions while being at core implacable. As Chapter 8 must record, Palestinian ineptness, not lacking in suspicion, failed to master the dynamics in the situation.

It might be said that the dynamics were at once at issue in the appointment of Herbert Samuel, a prominent British Jew, as the first High Commissioner; he at once picked for his Chief Secretary 'the one military man with a deep-rooted implacable faith in the Zionist cause'.[10] Did his appointment mean that the British would apply a pro-Zionist bias? Hardly, for Samuel sought to be even-handed and in due course his successors would be accused by Jews of a strongly pro-Arab bias.[11] Samuel, however, had himself earlier submitted to the War Cabinet a plan for the establishment of a Jewish state. He might therefore symbolize in the present context the hazardous pro/con query (whose pro and whose con in the stakes?) which hung on the entire Mandatory administration, with the other built-in items of ambivalence: policing, the holy places, diplomacy and land law. The nuances of politics are always volatile, most of all when contention rules the very ends in view. Any bias of sympathies had to be controlled until both bias and sympathy were overwhelmed, by the 1930s, in the sheer and hapless business of holding the ring for incompatibles.

III

The sorry theme of ambivalence returns when the War's end and the Mandate's demise into relinquishment conveyed its persistent quality to new realms of power and counsel in the post-war United Nations. It might seem that there was nothing equivocal about lines drawn on the map in 1947 delineating two 'national territories' and so acknowledging the 'rights' of two independent national autonomies. Had not 'partition' – so long and so far studied and mulled over – been decisively adopted? The parties might finally be mutually at ease.

Here, nevertheless, lurked deep ambivalence. The politics of the vote concern us elsewhere, but even the major parties harboured sharp misgivings which had surfaced before the die was cast and stayed even afterwards in the interval prior to the evacuation of the Mandatory power. There was an idea of reverting to some kind of 'trusteeship' mechanism, only quashed by desperate representations on the part of Weizmann.[12]

Truman trumped those notions with his recognition of the new state, but what of the internationalization of Jerusalem which the decision enjoined? What of the 'joint customs union' between the states? What of the mutual 'peace' supposedly regnant between them? The very decisiveness of the founding UN Resolution was an exercise in evasion, a virtual perpetuation of the bedevilments that had made impasse for the Mandate, a solution simply decreeing the unsolved. Not more than 8 per cent of Arab land had been purchased by Jewish funds, yet 52 per cent was granted. Arguably the fragments needed to be garnered into something defensible, but at whose expense? And what of the miscarryings in the womb of the future? By the elements in the equation, 'partition' could only aggravate them, giving now the sanction of statehood in territorial demarcation to entities for whom statehood was the quintessential point at issue.[13] Here was ambivalence masquerading as finality, answering by ignoring the question. It was a question only conflict could intensify and only arms resolve. In the resolving the arms only 'hardened all within'. Meanwhile, as J. L. Talmon noted, the UN vote, from the Zionist point of view, had been 'a masterly exploitation of propitious circumstances in a fluid historical situation'.[14]

The tragic option for hostilities which Arabs then took will be studied elsewhere in these pages. Before hostilities supervened, Weizmann and others had sought to be conciliatory. He wrote:

> The Arabs [i.e., within the new Jewish State] must be given the feeling that the decision of the United Nations is final, and that the Jews will not trespass on any territory outside the boundaries assigned to them.

He agreed that 'such a fear [existed] in the heart of many Arabs . . . and must be eliminated in every way'. 'The world', he opined, 'will judge the Jewish State by what it will do with the Arabs.'[15] Within three years the official Israeli Year Book noted that 'the State had been established in only a portion of the land of Israel', while the Sephardi Chief Rabbi declared that there was a religious obligation not to return the newly occupied territories. It was the difference between 52 and 80 per cent of former Palestine.

A new sort of ambivalence supervened. The difference sprang from trial of arms, regulated by truces – but by truces only. In that sense it became an acquisition by force which, in voting partition, the UNO (as the only available 'legality') had explicitly ruled out. But the successful force had triumphed in the teeth of unsuccessful war-making. In measure, then, the situation was de-legalized and warranted the familiar comment: 'Are we to be blamed for winning?' Do the victorious, having been challenged to arms, ever revert to all the risks of a *status quo ante*? In all the traumas, why should they? The case seemed absolute.

The territorial difference, of course, was vital to the viability of the new state. Moreover, it served well the vital objective of as thorough a Jewishness as possible, seeing that warfare had occasioned a wide evacuation of 'natives', enabling a strong majority Jewish presence. However, the assumption or doctrine that 'winners' retain their winnings removed, in territorial part, the juridical validity. In so doing, it spelled a steady abeyance of international order. For what war gains, counter-war can regain; *force majeure* enjoys only the immunity it can perpetuate and as such reaps no gentle peace. On the contrary, it necessitates perpetual vigilance.

This inherently indeterminate situation was reproduced with more dire effects after the sharply definitive results – as they appeared – of the June War of 1967. Israeli victory had been swift, total and dramatic. Palestinians read the disaster as utterly catastrophic and groped for clues to a shattered future. There was deep irony in Israeli Ambassador Abba Eban telling the United Nations on 8 October 1968 that there was 'nothing normal or legitimate or established to which to return'.[16] Did the middle adjective concede that Israel still had to search for a legitimacy other than military victory? Or did he imply that all prior UNO decisions had been overtaken and cancelled? He was to write elsewhere that 'Israel is no Esperantist nation writing its history on a clean slate'.[17] What then of the unclean slate in 1967?

While Palestinians, in dazed confusion, reached for a response via the lately developing *fatah*, 'resistance' – to which the calamity gave new impetus – Israeli thinking wrestled with the dilemma of success. About Jerusalem and its environs there could be no question but annexation of an 'inalienable capital'. But annexation of that last 20 per cent of Palestine (the West Bank) with its heavy concentration of non-Jews would be unthinkable.[18] Let it then be 'administered' and let others name it 'occupied' or 'seized'.

The ambivalence, standing in much more than terminology, persisted until the advent in 1977 of a Likud government brought a vigorous Jewish settlement policy into the equation without resolving it juridically. Abba

Eban promoted the idea of 'land for peace', i.e., the surrender of territory which, in care for homogeneity, it would be well to forgo if doing so could be enshrined in a peace treaty. Noting what he called 'a deep-seated discomfort in Israel about the idea of ruling a foreign [sic] people', he believed that

> in the policy and doctrine of Israel this was regarded as a temporary paradox that would somehow be resolved in the context of peace.[19]

The 'paradox' and the 'somehow' would survive at least three decades. The idea of relinquishment receded and, for some in Israeli counsels, the 'somehow' about the nature, length and term of 'discomforting occupation' could dispense with 'the context of peace'.

In any event, at that critical juncture of complete humiliation the defeated were in no state to initiate negotiation or to come forward to try out the frail proposals about land for peace. The PLO was only in its infancy, still far from the politic 'admission' of Israel that it could reach, through yet unforeseeable vicissitudes, by 1988 and 1996.[20] Palestinian thinking was searching its soul over Al-Nakbah, 'The Calamity', and musing on how that which could have been secured by acceptance of partition in 1948 had been lost for ever – at least in 1948 dimensions.[21] 'Abd al-Nasir's Egypt, the main catalyst of the débâcle of 1967, would be too prostrate until 1973 to contemplate negotiation. Indeed, it would seem that Anwar Sadat's peace initiative of 1977 first required the measure of recovery his Yom Kippur War attained in the psyche, if not for long on the ground around the Suez Canal. There was no ambivalence about 1967 – only categorical victory and total defeat.

IV

The Camp David negotiating marathon between Sadat, Begin and President Carter, following on Sadat's response to Begin's invitation to the Egyptian leader to visit Jerusalem and address the Knesset, was a ripe arena for a resumption of ambivalence. There was the heroic determination of the American President to go on until formulae were reached. There was the deep fixation of Begin's mind. He had come from the bitter Jabotinsky tradition of believing in armed struggle against any Palestinian pretensions to statehood during the Mandate. He had long been excluded from political power prior to 1977 and held tenacious views about the inalienability of 'the holy land' and the utter uselessness of international guarantees for Israel.

Sadat, it might be said, had the least complicated hand in bargain making. A peace securing his southern border was obviously attractive to Begin, while Sadat had urgent need to recover Sinai. There were the makings of a bargain there. But Sadat could not be seen to be betraying the Palestinians for whom Egypt had already suffered so much. Any agreement must in some sense incorporate 'the legitimate needs of the Palestinians' and reaffirm Resolution 242 about return of 'territories'.

In the event, these were achieved. Begin agreed – in words – to a solution of the Palestine issue 'in all its aspects'. He meant, however, as he later insisted, in 'Eretz Israel'. The Sinai Jewish settlements he had to forgo had never been in 'promised land'. He could ensure, despite the antagonism he suffered from his own party in the Knesset, that the 'linkage' with the Palestinian solution which Carter and Sadat sought could be fudged, disowned or otherwise nullified.

So, in fact, it proved. The Prime Minister whose 1977 election manifesto had pledged to 'take action to exterminate this organization' (i.e., the PLO characterized as an agent of Soviet Communism and 'a murder organization') had only defaulted on that pledge in order to fulfil it in more subtle terms. He had earlier neatly side-stepped the question about 'annexing' the West Bank (which he invariably called Judea and Samaria) by saying 'It is foreign land one annexes, not one's own country'. However long President Carter's patience had prolonged the meeting, he could never have overcome a fixation so firm. This one of his partners was not open to negotiation in any terms of significant give-and-take, except to forgo the settlements in Sinai whose retention, by his own rubric, was not imperative. His partners were only the more deceived. One paid for it dearly in 1981.

So, in different terms, did Menahem Begin himself. Seeing the Six-Day War of 1967 as a repulsion of foreign aggressors and so arguing the irrelevance of Resolution 242 about its 'return' in any sacred inch, and fobbing off the 'West Bank' with a derisory proposal, he turned to pursuing the Palestinian foe into its Lebanese havens. The upshot we will study further in the chapter to follow. Was he inveigled into the attack by Ariel Sharon or was it that the complete defeat of the PLO in Lebanon would demoralize West Bank Palestinians and make possible an imposed annexation coupled with depopulation by force or dismay?

Either way, the ambivalence persisted. The PLO was indeed eliminated from Lebanon but in no way from contention, while the invasion generated an anti-Zionist fervour in Lebanon which would plague Israeli arms and conscience as far as 1997, necessitating the occupation of a large border zone with all its attendant provocations. Begin had been long obsessed – as we must see – with the idea of Palestinians as Nazis. In 1983, in the wake of a curious withdrawal from the zests of office, Begin resigned and Yitzhak Shamir, a man in the same Jabotinsky mould but a dour contrast to Begin, succeeded him. In retrospect that self-elimination of Menahem Begin from the political scene might be said to symbolize a turning-point, undetected at the time, in the process, to be studied in Chapter 8, whereby Palestinianism attained, in its conceded stature, its long-sought, long-denied reward, the beginning of the end of its political wilderness-years. What was implacable began to founder in the mysterious passing of the figure who had epitomized the armed struggle of Zion against the Mandate and all else, who personified the adamant quality of mind and will without which Israel could not have come to be, but with the unyielding persistence of which it could in no way find its peace.

The significance, however, was not immediately apparent. In his own prosaic style Shamir continued the hard policy of rejectionism, dismissing the 1988 Palestinian acceptance of an Israel at peace with it on territory yet to be agreed and in state form, as criminal and bogus. As he saw it, the only 'peace' the PLO could offer was that of a burial in the sea. Resisting the suggestion of an international conference, he had to accept in 1984 a shared governance with the Labour alliance, a 'National Unity Government' in which the premiership alternated, with Shimon Peres taking first turn and Shamir the second.

Ambivalence about peace thus took concrete political form, the arrangement measuring the deep cleavage within the nation as a whole. By 1987 Shamir was scuttling Peres' more forthcoming ideas and the two men were concealing policies from each other. Shamir saw all peace ideas as a menace, not an urgent necessity.[22] Stalemate continued until the election of 1992 and the premiership of Rabin with Peres as his Foreign Minister. With American policy via James Baker more in active peace posture, events moved towards the Oslo Accords. The ever-recalcitrant Shamir was out of the way.[23]

V

The most noted Jewish writer on 'the Messianic idea' concludes that it should be seen as 'perpetual futurism',[24] a quality of Jewish fidelity in hope of God which, however, withholds identifying hope-fulfilment at any point in time or place. His perception stems from long deferment and disappointment in Jewish history concerning Messiah.

It might be said that the Oslo Accords 'futurized' the data of peace in an agreement to be prospective, via a calendar of future steps, each turning on the prior attainment of the other, and setting the most difficult and contentious as the last. In no way meaning to be 'messianic', there is much wisdom in the notion of progressive movement. For mutual confidence is at once far to seek and vital to find. Both procedural and substantive ambivalence hang over the meaning and the implementation of what was agreed at Oslo. The context was far from reassuring, given that the antecedents had been so compounded. Remoteness in Norway, initially with academics only, may have been a happy tactic, given that the 'official' meetings in Washington had proved so inconclusive, tortured by indecision and prevarication as they were. Shimon Peres called Oslo 'the back channel' and its sequences were only precariously contrived.

Yet there was a certain nobility about the resourcefulness and tenacity with which lines of agreement were drawn amid nervous emotions. There was also charm in the strategy whereby the Americans, who had had no part, were deftly taken on board when finality was near.[25] The reality was that the Palestinians had so few assets, except the undesirability (to the then Israeli Government) of their permanent embarrassment to Israeli peace of mind and peace of state. Realists could say that the bargains were broadly fair, given that the most contentious issues were deferred to stated timings in the five-year period, i.e., Jewish settlements, Palestinian refugees and the status of Jerusalem.

However, 'empowerment' was to be immediate in the Gaza–Jericho hand-over, subject to Israeli security on which consultation was promised without agreement being needed. Jericho would not include the vital bridges over the Jordan. Despite the Jewish settlements within it, the forgoing by Israel of the Gaza Strip might be thought a 'good riddance'. Philistine territory had no special religious significance – Samson apart.

Deferment of vexed issues meant also deferment of fixed positions, notably the status of East Jerusalem. Even the right of Palestinians there to participate in the elections of their National Council had to be safeguarded by odd devices lest their doing so should imply that the city was, by implication, Palestinian. Temporary residence elsewhere would be necessary or, maybe, their suffrage could be exercised in Muslim or Christian 'holy places'.[26] It remained unclear how Palestinian jurisdiction in ceded centres would relate to areas not ceded, to the Jewish settlements on them, and to transit within them. The 'statehood' to be 'explored' at the end of the interim 'empowerment' remained obscure. Yet it was made clear by the Israeli team that insistence on present clarification of all these points would kill the negotiations. There is no such word as 'whitemail', but had there been it was clear who was practising it on whom. The Palestinian team was anxious throughout as to whether some subtleties were not being worked to ensnare them. Only the long sequel would show. Nevertheless, the Oslo Accords and their piecemeal exercise in mutual trust represented a brave achievement against strong odds. All knew well that sometime during the interim period there would be a fresh election in Israel.

VI

When the election took place in May 1996 there came the cruellest ambivalence of all. Were Israeli governments bound by the undertakings of their predecessors? Or, more deeply at issue still, did the sharp division in the mind and soul of the Israeli nation itself dependably admit of a conclusive policy? For the very narrowness of the electoral verdict made crystal clear that here stood a people unable or unready to reach common ground concerning their most vital decision, namely their co-existence with the Palestinians.

It might have been possible, in the aftermath of the murder of Prime Minister Yitzhak Rabin in November 1995, to have ended the long prevarication inherent in the fundamental purpose of Zionism. For that assassination set the issue down in the most traumatic terms. This was a deed writing in blood the intrinsic crisis itself – a deed deriving from the religious radicals, preceded by much verbal violence from within Likud against its victim and that victim the esteemed hero of the wars of Israel's survival and the taking in 1967 of old Jerusalem itself. It was Israel's first experience of interior outrage against its own established authority and against a resolute yet still tentative initiative towards a feasible *modus vivendi* with the Palestinians and, thus, an ultimate solution of a hitherto endless imbroglio.

An election in that aftermath, called to challenge the nation in its self-image to resolve its will for integrity with peace, could have given Shimon Peres the sort of decisive majority Israel's electoral patterns had rarely yielded since Ben Gurion. No election was called before the implications of the murder had been somewhat mitigated, with shock partially overcome and extremism busy with exoneration, so that the basic 'normalcy' of controversy could reassert itself.

It was ironical that the new system of direct popular election of the Prime Minister should have coincided with the pre-election trauma. For it was designed to surmount the complexities to which the old pattern was prone. In the event, the verdict was the narrowest imaginable, yet the cruellest. It might be argued that the Netanyahu government has no clear mandate for reversal of the inherited agreements, given a near half of the nation voting for their continuation. Yet that kind of solicitude is no match for the ideologies that give no quarter. These would also note that had the narrow verdict gone the other way without the kind of margin an election nearer to the assassination would have given, Shimon Peres might have owed it to the votes of Arab Israelis whom later, it would seem, he bombed into abstention by 'The Grapes of Wrath' on Lebanon.

A majority, then, is a majority, the closeness only underlining a nation's inner quarrel with itself concerning the self it means and needs to be. On that quarrel hinges the question whether Oslo can survive. The Likud-led coalition under Netanyahu made electoral vows and slogans hardly conducive to good hope. To talk with the PLO and the new Palestinian 'authority' without pre-conditions sounds forthcoming, except that the Oslo Accords should be understood to constitute pre-conditions in themselves. They include the deferred, but in no way obsolete, issue about the final status of Jerusalem; the cessation of West Bank settlement by Israelis; and the vexed matter of Palestinian 'repatriation'.

Much that had been achieved, albeit with postponements of original timings, after September 1993, was heartening and substantial, but was it truly irreversible? Beginning with Jericho and Gaza and then Jenin, major Palestinian urban centres, with adjacent villages, had been transferred to Palestinian control, putting some 75 per cent of Palestinians under their own authority. Elections to that authority were successfully held in January 1996, though tensions persisted over duly democratic control of its policies and decisions.

Yet, in the event of serious Intifadah-style unrest, Israeli force was readily able to reinstate control, such unrest being the more likely the more ambiguous the rest of the Oslo programme became. In parallel progression, a contrivance and aggravation of ambiguity would make the possibility of violence more certain and, with it, the Israeli case for the priority of the demand for security over all other criteria. This, in turn, would be a formula for at best perpetual stalemate or at worst tragic explosion.

Sadly, in the post-election period of 1996 this proved to be the pattern. The scenario is not hard to describe. The Labour leadership after the assassination had discerned but not seized the occasion to clinch, in electoral terms, the sudden moment of self-awareness that the horror of an Israeli political murder had aroused. The nation had been forced to look into its soul and see an unmasking of its depths. There might then have been a 60 per cent mandate for genuine peace purposes to seal the vision of Yitzhak Rabin and Shimon Peres. The moment, being in truth momentous, was not taken.

Slowly belligerence was allowed to reassert itself. There came those 'grapes of wrath' on Lebanon. Hamas bombings callously revitalized Israeli fears and contributed perversely to the Likud argument in the May elections. A wafer-thin majority was Likud's reward. Prevarication about Oslo and the further steps it had enjoined was easy to adopt, meanwhile reserving all the bitter options. Likud philosophy reached right back to Jabotinsky, via Menahem Begin and Yitzhak Shamir, for whom 'land for peace' had never been a policy. Netanyahu's task, therefore, was to employ suspense to prepare surreptitiously a *de facto* abandonment of Oslo while protesting some continuing 'peace process' on the new Israeli government's terms.

Prior to the election, Likud had engaged in policy assassination of Rabin and Peres by the venom of their accusation of treachery to a true Zionism Jabotinsky-style. So doing, they had been in no way ambivalent in final terms, while using it for a hiatus in the immediate sense. A situation, meanwhile, could be contrived in which the policing 'good faith' – and efficiency – of the Palestinian armed authority could be called in question, thus admitting of making a case, namely, that until it had been proved worthy, in prolonged terms, of 'delivering' an Oslo-agreed 'security' to Israelis, the rest of Oslo could legitimately be 'on hold'. Meanwhile, the 'settlements' had more time to implant their irreversibility on the landscape.

The immediate lighting of this fuse was the opening of the tunnel from the great 'Wailing Wall' Plaza to the Via Dolorosa, in September 1996. The order, it seems, came personally from Netanyahu without informing or consulting the army leadership likely to be involved in the aftermath, and despite the prudence of the previous government in refraining from an act they knew to be inflammatory.

On one count, the readying for public use of an intriguing piece of archaeological initiative and interest would scarcely deserve to be greeted with an uprising of violent anger. But the facts were less simple. The opening could be seen as a further step in the steady Judaization of Jerusalem which had been proceeding apace for decades. The tunnel alongside the Haram al-Sharif skirts an area long sacred to Muslim tradition. It brings the unique shrine of Israeli nationhood – the Plaza afront the Wall – into direct, if subterranean, link with hallowed Muslim and Christian territory. It fans the ardour of Jewish zealots and the apprehensions of Muslim devotees concerning the Temple Mount above it, in Islamic legal hands but coveted for repossession by Israeli Levitical religion. It also marches with the diminution of the centuries-old tradition of a Jerusalem shared by faiths each of which had their own territorial securities inside the walls. It was read as being in line with the demolition of an allegedly 'illegal' Palestinian hostel and the ever precarious access of foreign governmental and other representatives to Orient House, the Palestinian HQ in East Jerusalem.

Coupled with the pledged but still ambivalent evacuation of Hebron by Israeli forces, the opening of the tunnel provoked the anticipated uprising of Palestinian and Muslim anger, made the sharper by perceptions of heightening frustration overall. At once the issue arose precisely as contrivance had expected. Would the armed Palestine forces of law and order in the enclaves give full proof of their pledge to give Israelis security by controlling their own unruly and disorderly people? By and large they did.

In the immediate passions some 200 out of 40,000 Palestinian militias and/or police did fire on or resist the Israeli army, 30 of these in Ramallah. It was a tiny proportion. The Palestinian authorities were able to rein in these elements and after two days there was the strange spectacle of Palestinian forces restraining their own and defending Israeli personnel. But the pretence of Palestinian defaulting on something fundamental to Oslo was now available as warrant for delaying, or arguably renegotiating, its 'peace process', this latter being still honourably 'in being'.

The whole situation was full of sharp paradox. The Palestinian entity, proverbially expressed, was 'in a cleft stick', called upon, in a way, to do Israeli policing by proxy in a cause subtly ambiguous. The task of giving no occasion to Israeli reproach that could or would cancel hopes of further acquisition of Oslo's provision, entailed sustaining a situation totally adverse to one's sympathies and sense of justice. It was indeed a subtly contrived ambivalence.

Moreover, their irreducible human numbers apart, Palestinians have no countering assets. European financial aid is liable to be deterred by uncertainties; the urgent facility of an airport in Gaza remains shelved; access between the Gaza Strip and the West Bank Palestinian enclaves remains withheld; the enclaves are increasingly economically isolated from each other by the network of inter-settlement roads around them; the access of Palestinian workers into Israel can be turned on and off at will; release of prisoners tarries and the fateful issue of Jerusalem is open only to staying closed.

All is a far cry from the surge of peace emotion in the wake – as then perceived – of the martyrdom for peace of Rabin at the will of most pernicious evil. Jewish casualties in February and September 1996 renewed the ever-sensitive case against compassion from the loss of Jewish lives, though in September the proportion was 14 to 56. The image of implacable Palestinians is rekindled and Hamas stands ready to enforce it further.

The gradualism of Oslo was deliberately designed to serialize solutions in the hope that emerging cycles of trust would undergird them from the readiest to the hardest. For suspicions have been chronic throughout in the very nub of the issues. In the event, a contrary process seems in train whereby 'hope deferred makes the heart sick' and every surmise of bad faith ensures occasion for it.

Meanwhile the protagonists of peace among Israelis find themselves disheartened by the sheer dismay of the contrasts between September 1993 and the same month in 1996, and all the irony of that narrowest of majorities. What course avails to them? How might they bring around again a Rabin–Peres momentum with election so far away? Is there hope in the sanity and goodwill of American Jewry that might ignite a perception of fundamental Jewish values in the guidance of Zionism, and perhaps incline US policy to a more genuinely mediatorial role in the issues and away from the potent agency of the American Israeli Public Affairs Committee, supreme in the arts of the Washington lobby?

Short of a more equable 'honest brokerage' of super-power prestige it is difficult to see how at best impasse and at worst violent upheaval can be avoided. Jerusalem apart, Hebron holds in symbol the entire stakes, Hebron the quintessence of Abraham, father of covenant and the sacred seed. But Abraham is also essentially Islamic, the great iconoclast, the founder-*Hanif*, a monotheist who was – in the Qur'an's phrase – 'neither Jew nor Christian', relating to God, as indeed all Semitic monotheists believe, before Sinai and the Mosaic Law. Could he not, therefore, symbolize, and even generate, a compatibility among his heirs?

The city–shrine, to be sure, has bitter memories of mutual massacres, early and bitter by Arabs on Jews in the enterprise of Zionism; late and dire by Jews on Arabs in the pride of zealot Zion. The mutual memories are desperate. Yet, currently, a mere 400 armed and belligerent Jewish settlers, purposely implanted for their ideology, jeopardize the normal existence of no less than 100,000 Arab inhabitants. Sanity might suggest their peaceable withdrawal but that would signal, or rather seem to signal, surrender and forfeiture of sacred right and story. For lack of it, however, the mass of citizens are subject to virtual house arrest and defenceless against vigilantes armed and fanatical, until solution supervenes. The resting place of patriarchs and consorts is haunted with the unease of Zion.

In prolonged and chronic sequence ambivalence grows the more unpredictable. Were the parleyings of the autumn of 1996 in Washington and Gaza a scenario of total renegotiation from which it would have been wise for Palestinian minds to have been absent in order to repudiate that implication? Was participation a necessary gesture, in hope that implementation of Oslo was sincerely meant? That nice diplomatic question cannot continue to be a riddle on the ground. Tension breaks unless it is resolved. Not even the subtlest ambivalence can for ever negotiate with nemesis.

Books and authors on the Middle East are likely to be outpaced by events in the time of publishing. That risk is run here. Hebron could be thought resolved in the spring of 1997 thanks to revisions in the Oslo formulae. It would seem that great-power pressure was involved in rare effectiveness but great tensions remain which could violently explode as the dividing wall and the street provisions and the hatreds lurking are tested in the time unfolding.

Stable success there could help the vexing tasks ahead. Release of prisoners, secured access from Jericho to Gaza and between Palestinian towns and rural enclaves (as and when the latter are handed back) and the consolidation and multiplication of Jewish settlements – all these await agreement or sustain contention as the case may be. Meanwhile confiscations persist and with them measures to inhibit Palestinian fulfilment and viability in economic and social terms. There is no doubt who holds the whiphand. The rapid programme of the road network linking Jewish elements on the West Bank suggests, at best, a very distrustful 'land-for-peace' equation and, at worst, a territorial expression of a fragmented apartheid. The Palestinian dream of 'statehood' would thus appear to remain one in perpetuity. It is hard to see how Palestinian policy can surmount the emerging shape of a sharply attenuated political and physical existence.

For it has only two discernible negotiating assets. The one is demography – the sheer numbers of Palestinians that Israel cannot ignore, suppress, eliminate or minimize without staining the Zionist vision and surrendering its Judaism. The other is the significant degree to which the security of Israel's population from the violence of continuing – or latent – Palestinian extremism turns on the co-operation of Arafat's security police (with arms Israel has provided). Any decision to terminate that co-operation would jeopardize all else Palestinian, so that it becomes a dubious asset and could look, instead, like a wise Israeli device to have 'good' Palestinians do policing and 'securing' for them. Insofar as that is so, Israel contrives to keep its negotiating 'partner' compliant while broadly determining developments in its own time and on its own terms. It would seem that – short of disastrous eruption – there is little the other can do than 'go along' caught between hope and frustration.

Over all looms the question of Jerusalem. Decision is projected into some 'final' calendar but its intractability persists – an inalienable capital of the Jewish State or an achievable symbol of sheer human community possessed in the possessing of three great faiths. It is over Jerusalem that the utmost Israeli/Jewish adamancy obtains. Yet – by something like divine irony – and short of utter catastrophe dislodging it, the sacred Islamic Haram on Temple Mount abides. Only the most rabid Zionist passion could think to include a recovered Temple in its equation or exclude the Haram from the 'final' accommodation. It will be a further historic irony if, in the end, Palestinian stake in the Holy City remains irreducibly religious to console a political forfeiture. Only guesswork could currently discern whether Jerusalem will attain 'her peace' as the long constraints of history demand or dream to be 'at unity in herself' in solely Jewish terms. Either way, 'demand' and 'dream' are the verbs in option.

Notes

1 Chaim Weizmann, *Trial and Error* (London, 1949), p. 587.

2 Ibid., p. 571.

3 Schlomo Avineri, *The Making of Modern Zionism: The Intellectual Origins of the Jewish State* (New York, 1981), p. 182.

4 Cited from Christopher Sykes, *Two Studies in Virtue* (London, 1953), p. 160.

5 See Harry Sacher, *Zionist Portraits and Other Essays* (London, 1959), p. 169.

6 Ibid., p. 316.

7 See Leonard Stein, *The Balfour Declaration* (London, 1961), pp. 649–50.

8 J. L. Talmon, *Israel Among the Nations* (London, 1970), p. 145. He added: 'No one gave a precise thought to the ways in which the Declaration would be implemented' – meaning in the approving British Cabinet.

9 Quoted from Eric Silver, *Begin: A Biography* (London, 1984), p. 12, translating from the Russian of Jabotinsky's *On the Iron Wall*.

10 *Zionist Portraits*, p. 321.

11 The essayist Harry Sacher (see note 5), a prominent British Jew, and other Zionists have written with some disdain of 'Arabists' in the Foreign and Commonwealth Office with 'grudge' and 'bias' in their preferences. At times it takes bias to detect bias.

12 See *Trial and Error*, pp. 577f. Weizmann made feverish representations to argue prompt reversal in March 1948 of what was a strange reversal of US policy. This was, he said, 'utterly unrealistic. Palestine Jewry had outgrown the state of tutelage. Everything that had made the Mandate unworkable would be present in the trusteeship.' In April, in a private letter, he told President Truman: 'The choice of our people is between statehood and extermination.' Happily, the notion was dropped and Truman compensated for the aberration (whose?) by his immediate recognition of the new state.

13 See in Chapter 8 the logic in the Arab rejection of the 'solution' of partition. Jewish statehood – given Zionist doctrine of an indivisible Eretz Israel – spelled an international recognition of an entity ideologically expansionist. Palestinian statehood, seemingly fair had the parties' antecedents been the same, only sanctioned a half-expression, subtracting the other half irrevocably.

14 *Israel Among the Nations*, p. 132.

15 *Trial and Error*, pp. 566 and 569.

16 He called for recognition of what 'common interest demanded', and argued, from

physics, that 'fusion at high temperatures' might also happen politically. How interests could feasibly be 'common' in the given context was itself the problem.

17 Abba Eban, *Heritage: Civilisation and the Jews* (London, 1984), p. 333.

18 For annexation would swamp democratic processes with non-Jewish numbers and jeopardize the Jewish homogeneity the State was dedicated to ensuring.

19 *Heritage*, p. 332.

20 The 'recognition' accorded to Israel as a state in the decision of the Palestine National Council of 1988 did not amount to a deletion from its Charter of the clause calling for the 'de-construction' of Israel. That move was taken only in April 1996, significantly in the very midst of the sixteen-day Israeli attack on Lebanon in which many thousands were made refugees and a hundred civilians killed at Cana. The 1988 affirmation of co-existence in separate statehoods anticipated and awaited Israeli response. None credibly came until the Oslo Accords, many points in which had to be tested for good faith in events deliberately dated ahead. The more formal 1996 decision was meant to take account of those imponderables partially but still dubiously fulfilled. It was a mutual process of building – and deserving – confidence.

21 The disaster of 1967 stirred a mood of introspection and self-accusation in Arab minds. Writers like Constantin Zurayq, Fawaz Turki, Albert Hourani, George Hourani and Fa'iz Sayigh analysed the reasons behind the humiliation. See, e.g., Albert Hourani, 'The moment of truth', *Encounter* (November 1967); and Constantin Zurayq, *Ma'na al-Nakbat* ('The Meaning of the Débâcle') (Beirut, 1948) and *Ma'na al-Nakbat al-Mujaddadah* ('The Meaning of the Débâcle Renewed') (Beirut, 1968).

22 See Shamir's autobiography, *Summing Up: An Autobiography* (London, 1994); also Moshe Arens, *Broken Covenant: American Foreign Policy and the Crisis Between the U.S. and Israel* (New York, 1995). Arens, who was close to Shamir, traces his stubborn loyalty to old Irgun concepts of 'the enemy' and how Shamir's 'Peace Plan' of 1989 (pressured by Baker) excluded statehood, banned the PLO from any participation and offered elections on the West Bank to chosen representatives. It was abortive from the start.

23 Shamir's tenure had been a sort of postscript to the moribund old order and the Jabotinsky mind, taking a long time in its decease parallel to the slow arrival of a Palestinian legitimacy in Zionist eyes.

24 Gershom Scholem, *The Messianic Idea in Israel and Other Essays* (New York, 1971).

25 Shimon Peres' account is in his *Battling for Peace: Memoirs* (London, 1995), pp. 325–37. He explains how the Israeli Cabinet was no party to the talks prior to the announcement of the Declaration. He also pays warm tribute to Abu Ala'a, the main Palestinian figure.

26 An intriguing question follows: Can one be a 'citizen' of 'holy places'? If so, might not the extra-territoriality of these (implied in their use for voting) be absorbed, by physical location, into some shared political 'territory'?

5

The anomaly of the holy

I

'The Holy Land' is a term in ready use and most users will be in no doubt, geographically, where they locate it. They mean old Canaan, Philistia, old and new Judea, Zion, Israel, Palestine, the land bordered by the Mediterranean, Lebanon, the Jordan and the wilds of Sinai. Geography locates it but where is it otherwise? By what right is it exclusified with that definite article? 'A holy land' might be a humbler, wiser description. For unless all lands are potentially holy, could any be so? There has to be more warrant than mere geography if the absolute term is to be a synonym for any stretch of territory.

'There *is* more', voices will insist, meaning the words to signify some unshared dimension that justifies the precise singular they claim. There is history, there is acquisition, there is covenant, there is election, there is an inalienable given-ness about a people and a place. About all these there is something final, incorrigible, irreversible, perpetual. 'The promised land' can never be unpromised. Unpromising history will not undo it: its status is perennial. What happens there cannot undo the primary history of a once-for-all bestowal.

Yet there is neither geography nor history without demography. The area bestowed was not then, nor since, a vacancy, an untenanted wilderness. It was anticipated in terms of the 'milk and honey' with which allegedly it 'flowed'. These presuppose tillage, verdure, cultivation and inhabitants. The 'holy' would not supervene on virgin soil but would enter into pagan labourings, the husbandry of folk already present. Was not warning of their presence a crucial factor in the antecedents of the 'holy' entry? How then does 'holiness' comport with dispossession or with the debts owed to prior occupants? For vines do not yield grapes for newcomers overnight.[1]

Perhaps, then, 'holiness' might have to do with interrelations from old to new, from past to present, unless it is identified with mere imperialism. There are few places on the earth where 'aborigines' – if still identifiable – remain securely dominant. Are not the original Dravidians long centuries corralled into the tip of India? Where are the ancient Britons in the 'English' population? Lands may, or may not, be called by their 'proper' denizens. Canaan, Judea, Samaria, Palestine has been variously named and the time to which the covenant concept returns was one of tribal migrations and endless shifts of claimants. Is 'holiness' in origin then merely the incidence of Yahweh's patronage, even as Chemosh bestowed Moab on his Moabites?[2]

Geography, history, demography – what of climatology? Is there a different rain falling upon Israel than falls on the slopes of Hermon to the north or Gilead to the east?[3] Do the Mediterranean clouds differentiate the winds that carry them shoreward with their cargo of vaporous benison upon all the reaches of their cycle? How, in these terms, may 'holiness' particularize? Or if it might, does its incidence in the only place not necessitate the ecology of an entire region far beyond its borders? Can it somehow be edged into surrounding nothingness like a penumbra?

The questions are not trivial. They raise the vital issue as to how any human habitation can be held uniquely sanctified, seeing that human coexistence competes through them all and natural resources, however diverse, in common sustain them. Is it perhaps that the usage 'the Holy Land' has bemused us too long, been insufficiently interrogated for what it could, or could not, mean?

We defer the 'But surely . . . ' that some readers are urgent to interject to stay these unfamiliar thoughts. For it is evident that whatever 'holiness' might signify as assigned to 'the promised land', it has to do with a universal trinity of people, place and posterity that belongs to all human experience. We are all, indifferently, 'native' to a land, native with a tongue and native to a tribe. We all revere ancestry, cherish memory, plough or otherwise subsist on pieces of earth, and belong with ethnic identity. Habitat, haunt, history and kin characterize us all. Our total diversities are rooted in these common factors. The ethnic, the economic, the environmental are the vital features of all humankind.

There was, therefore, nothing exceptional in the Hebrew consciousness concerning a who and a where and a whence about themselves. All identities have tenancy, time and tribe in their earth experience. We cannot, then, locate the singularity of *the* holy land in dimensions so manifestly shared. Exile, so crucial in Hebraic consciousness, only reinforces the point. For the exile, the refugee, knows displacement as threat to viability itself and a rude disruption of ethnic assurance also. 'How shall we know it's us without our past?'[4] is the haunting question of the wanderer from the familiar place. We cannot well sing our folksongs 'in a strange land'. Calling the lands by their own names, their names by their own lands, is the manifest instinct of all peoples. Judah and Jewry are thus one with France and the French, Finland and the Finns. 'Israel' as a name makes people and place identical.

The point here is no idle one. To think their 'who' one with their 'where', as one element in the notion of 'covenant' (distinctive features apart, to which we must come), is no perquisite of Jews or Israel. It must follow that there is, and can be, no exclusive copyright on the ambition for 'a holy land'. The elements being common, the ambition can be shared. All lands through their peoples may be hallowed. This is the sense in which the usage '*the* holy land' is cruelly ambiguous, insofar as it implies an ecology that elsewhere is not divinely potential of righteousness and glory. By Christian sights, there is a kingdom into which all the nations may 'bring their glory and honour' and all cultures do God service. All nature under man is capable of holiness; or, in biblical terms, any meaning feasible in this context to notions of Abrahamic or Davidic covenants belongs only with the Noahid covenant.[5]

Indeed, it is clear that many nations have fully aspired to this kind of emulation of the Hebraic sense of election to responsible glory. Did not Abraham Lincoln see Americans as 'the almost chosen people'?[6] Scenarios of destiny link many lands with many peoples. How possessed by thoughts of 'holy Russia' was Fyodor Dostoevsky! Peoples will not consent to dub themselves 'uncircumcised'. 'Gentile' is a denominator that needs to find itself undeserved.[7]

Emulation of Hebraic self-perception, however, has its perils and these must be part of our misgivings. For, in some measure, things Hebraic are implemented to the scorn of others and the consequences have been dire for those who, like the Canaanites, found themselves on the receiving end of 'chosen' privilege.[8] It is this experience which, under Zionism, has made twentieth-century Palestinians a paradigm of the several other people-obstacles to land right exercised in the name of destiny. Did not Prime Minister Golda Meir remind British, American and other reprovers of Zionism that such very critics had their own colonizing story and, therefore, were in no way warranted to call Zionists to book?[9] Indeed, she contrived to turn the tables completely by insisting that Israelis were no 'colonizers' of aliens' shores but the long-dispossessed recovering their 'mother country'. Yet, if Zionists are not at all analogous to Virginians on the Potomac, Pilgrim Fathers in Massachusetts, or Afrikaners in the Transvaal, the actualities for Palestinians have meant comparable resentments, tensions and displacement.

This is an aspect of 'the holy land' that is difficult to recognize. There may be a strange irony in that the author of the lines on Liberty Rock, Emma Lazarus (1849–87), also wrote 'The Banner of the Jew', in which she celebrated the Maccabees crying 'Wake, Israel, wake! O for Jerusalem's trumpet now.'[10] There was indeed about modern Zion a rousing call: 'Give me . . . your huddled masses yearning to be free . . . send these, tempest-tossed, to me', but the hearers were to be Jewish and there would be refugee camps necessitated. The builders of the State of Israel had title such as the British never possessed on the White Highlands of Kenya but that truth in no way diminishes the clear analogy between Jomo Kenyatta's Mau-Mau and Yassir Arafat's PLO, the recipients' trauma being comparable in terms of a vexing deprivation of ancestral territory.[11]

There was no sense of any redemption of holiness in European coloni-zation in Africa. Motives were merely imperial and economic. Zionists had long historical vistas of tenancy and celestial right. Diaspora jeopardy, not imperial pretension, was their impetus. Yet, in the event, their impact and effect were experienced by 'the existing population' as a colonizing venture. What was held by Zionists as divine mandate was known by Palestinians as human intrusion. The tangled factors which are traced in other chapters, for all their complexity and 'might-have-beens', do not qualify this basic situation. The underlying injustice, tentative at first and final in its incidence, needs to be part of the reckoning in any measure of 'the land as holy', or of 'the holy' via the land.

II

Conceding that vital distinction between colonialism and Zionism only makes the issue of 'the holy' the more searching. Imperialists are not exonerated by nonchalance about ethics,[12] seeing that only the idealists among them sought sincerely civilizing, liberating ends. Still less, then, can Zionists be absolved from their consequences by claim of divine mandate and historical recovery of a land made sacrosanct. For the rubric must surely be: 'The more holy assumed, the more ethically liable'.

It is this inter-relevance of 'the holy' and the moral – the burden of this chapter – which underlies all else that may be written about *Palestina Agonistes*. For there have been occasions and attitudes in which it seemed that no inter-relevance belonged. The urgencies and the toils of Zionism in the given context of Arab antagonism called for a resolute set of mind that could brook no scruples save those of a discrete opportunism. Zionism need in no way be reproached in conscience for what it had enterprised in sanctity. The alibi about action could always be invoked in the imperative legitimated by heaven and the sufferings of diaspora. Palestinianism, one might say, could expect, on its part, no more than a silence from heaven.[13]

All returns, then, to those divine 'promises' in the Books of Genesis and Exodus and elsewhere which so dominate and determine Judaic (and much Christian) thinking about 'the holy land'. How should they be understood? The view to be taken here is that they are, overwhelmingly, facts of belief but that the degree to which they are facts of history is deeply problematic. The distinction between the two orders of 'fact' may not matter for many. Can history finally control religion, or historians theologians? What is deeply believed becomes – in its own right if not its own truth – a veritable fact of the situation. The experts in archaeology and the other disciplines of research and the experts in Midrash are divided.

There are those who purport to vindicate the clear historicity of Abraham and his odyssey around the Fertile Crescent. Others detect a narrative designed to associate the Exodus and the Sinaitic covenant with earlier migrations of ancestors. Others again perceive in the narratives of the entry an idealization of a much more obscure story in which Hebrew tribes were already inside Canaan and had no part in the Sinai scenario.

Most radical of all is the notion that the whole epic was the work of a literary genius who might be called the J-Yahwist, writing late in the tenth century BC in the aura of Solomonic power. He/she for the first time gave shape to a heroic Yahweh and 'his people' in a drama from Abraham to Joshua that ever since has dominated the Judeo-Christian tradition. Culminating in David, it fixed the theme of a land-possession made for ever inviolate by virtue of a saga of nomadic wandering, settled flock-rearing, Egyptian bondage and miraculous liberation into a destiny of divine patronage and complete ethnic exceptionality. 'Such', writes a recent reviewer of Jewish historiography, 'is the Biblical story, whose verification defies . . . historical and archaeological science.' He concludes: 'It is a romantic fantasy . . . a contrived archaism' which 'gave plausibility to a people of distinctive quality who by their superhuman fortitude and literate intelligence came to be where and what they were'. The myth of divinely ordered beginnings was in fact 'the impact of a transcendent deity upon a small obscure people of shepherds and farmers'.[14]

Another Jewish man of letters is even more explicit and credits the myth of divine covenant, by bold conjecture, to Bathsheba, mother of Solomon, and, after her, to elaborating editors and redactors of her pristine genius. All stems from this female 'J' and 'her Yahweh':

> a literary character, an all too human figure, incommensurate with us and impossible to avoid . . . the hidden story of how a solitary warrior-god, apparently one among many godlings, established himself as the supreme figure . . .

and came to command Jewish, Christian and Muslim worship down long centuries.[15]

There have been leaders of contemporary Israel, like David Ben Gurion, prepared to welcome this explanation of Jews not as a 'chosen' but as a 'choosing' people who, so to speak, created their own legend. A cluster of tribes from or among the Canaanites in fact devised their own story. All biblical loyalists and many scholars will round on this version of 'covenant' between Yahweh and Israel, reasserting the honoured traditions as veracious, however at odds among themselves over chronologies and sequences of place and century. For present purposes, in respect of Palestinian experience, the crucial fact is the actuality of the belief, the tenacity with which it is held and the procedures it sanctions and demands. Whether what is 'historical' is ever reliably recoverable or remains intellectually debatable, 'the holy land' and 'the promised land' remain for ever in the equation of current politics and ethics.

Those who find only a historization of myth in the alleged status of the land will never thereby elide either myth or history from the annals of this century. For, either way, actuality is the *de facto* truth of the empirical situation. No Palestinian misery is going to be redeemed by finding Abraham's encounter mythical when the feet of a nomad were promised the régime of a state; no refugee camp is going to be comforted by disavowing a pregnant volcano in Sinai. The perceived Jewishness of the land being a psychic kind of certitude, Palestinianism may well interrogate history and find no respite in doing so. 'Holiness' being essentially a 'religious' order of reality, its obligations to the ethical realm become the more vital. It is not merely territory in fact, but territory by right, that is at stake. If Zionists do not consent to see themselves as invaders, then by the same token Palestinians are not to be seen as usurpers. However pragmatic twentieth-century Zionism has been, it was never acquiring mere acres: it was restoring forfeited meanings. Palestinians who would have been only fugitives in the first case, surely had to be acknowledged as participants in the second, unless 'holiness' is self-deceiving, self-deceived and, in that event, no longer 'holy'.

There is one interesting feature here that requires general comment. It has to do with the extent of the land 'promised'. Exodus 23:31 delimits it between 'the Red Sea, the sea of the Philistines and from the wilderness to the Euphrates'. Numbers 34:3–12 sees the southern border bounded by 'the wilderness of Zin marching with Edom' eastward from the end of the Dead Sea. Westward is the Mediterranean shore. Northward the frontier moves from Mount Hor to Lebo-Hamath, to Zedad, Zephron and Hazar-enan. Eastward the land is defined from those points southward to the Jordan. However, Genesis 15:18, Deuteronomy 1:7 and 11:24, like Exodus 23, take the eastern frontier to the Euphrates. By that larger measure – the Euphrates not the Jordan – there has been a massive relinquishment by the mainline Zionists of covenanted territory, against the grain of Revisionists like Max Nordau and Vladimir Jabotinsky who urged that lands beyond the Jordan river were as inalienable as Palestine. The case against them was no doubt a matter of demography. Pragmatic reasoning suggested that Israelis could never compete with Arab masses all the way to Baghdad and Basrah. It has long been prudently concluded that demography dictates the viable limits of Israeli expansion and that the river Jordan is the place. Strategy doubtless concurs.

But there is an abiding – and growing – demographic Arab factor *west* of that river. It is growing within the pre-1967 borders of Israel proper.[16] It is irreducible, either by expulsion or attrition, in the West Bank and as long as it is legitimately restive it jeopardizes the moral character of the Jewish state in respect of human rights and political sanity. Indeed, it would be fair to say that sheer demography is the only discernible asset Palestinians have in the whole equation.[17]

It was, of course, easier to forgo dominance and concede neighbourhood to the east of the river, but at least there is a territorial precedent in Zionism for a will to accommodation that could facilitate rather than forfeit its ideals.

III

Whatever believers and pundits may or may not conclude about things Abrahamic, Mosaic and Davidic in the biblical history, there remain the vexed questions around the exile, the prophecies and promises of return. Here the reading of Scriptures comes more readily within the range of critical scholarship and intellectual discourse. We can be more alert about

Jeremiah than Melchizedek. The question presses: Is contemporary Zionism in proven, or provable, line with the hopes and visions of Deutero-Isaiah, Ezekiel and their peers?

Asking these days what texts 'mean' is a taxing enterprise. Do texts 'say' or do readers 'find'? In the latter case, then which readership? These subtleties of hermeneutics are bewildering and may leave the simple-minded far adrift. The Scriptures of the prophets are in no way immune from the notions of the philosophers of language. Jacques Derrida, conspicuous among these this century, is no Talmudist but his ideas of 'deconstruction' have been traced by some to Talmudic associations of exegesis in which authorial intentions are yielded up to reader autonomy.[18]

It must be clear that what reader autonomy in Zionist practice is likely to do with holy writ is to find itself necessitated and foretold. It is, however, a sound – and urgent – principle always to ask what could be meant by texts for, and in the context of, their first hearers. This criterion of exegesis must govern whatever latent or prescient meanings might be deducible after the lapse of long centuries. Pained and puzzled Jews hanging their harps on the willows in Babylon were not credibly heartened by hidden significances cryptically contrived for legibility twenty-five centuries after their decease. Both they and their mentors were in immediate crisis of perplexity and dismay.

There can be no reasonable doubt that the several promises of return from exile reflect the tenacity with which the land of promise was loved and existentially cherished. Exile had to be seen as a contradiction of an entire self-perception in Jewry and, therefore, as assuredly only an interim condition. To be sure, Jeremiah exhorted the exiles to adapt creatively to an environment unlikely to be promptly terminated, but he also tellingly purchased an inheritance in Judea in love for his native Anathoth. To have conceded that exilic circumstance would be endlessly perpetuated would have been to abandon the entire self-belief Jewry owed to the will and loyalty of Yahweh. Their expectation of redemption was simply the measure of their very identity, a tribute to the whole theme of their physical and spiritual being.

Symbolic time measures, like 'seventy years', were never a precise calculus or calendar but an apt binding into one of hope and patience, of time awaited and, by the same token, time not yet. Exiles would find solace only in terms of their own conviction. Pledges of 'return' were pleas of faith. They meant that no alien residence could cancel the crucial bond of land-nexus – itself the evidence of their God-association. Thus the pagan powers, for all their political domination and their military clout, were no more than pawns in the behest of the God of the Jews. When, thanks to Persian counsels of tolerance, Cyrus allowed the return, he could be seen as Yahweh's 'Messiah' (Isaiah 45:1). Thus all circumstances and therefore all eventualities, con or pro, could be read as divine appointment. It seems eminently sane and honest to read promises through exile in these clear terms.

That still leaves open the question whether they can or should be invoked as either foreseeing or sustaining twentieth-century politics. On one count, perhaps, they could be taken contemporaneously now as they were then, enshrining an unchanging land-love sealed by a divine bond. Diaspora would then be read as 'exile', in neglect of how far, in parts, it was proving, in fact, to be congenial and would be needed as the very resource of return. Insofar as prophecy may be read as people-fulfilled in Ben Gurion terms of self-determination, Zionism may arguably find its mandate in the sermons of Jeremiah.

A little reflection quickly realizes how, on other counts, this case becomes incongruous. In biblical exile only the Lord could 'hasten His word to fulfil it'. It becomes ironical in that Zionist 'scripturality' (if we may so speak) precludes prophetic fulfilment in purporting to implement it. This thought was the dilemma of those Jews who demurred about Zionism in faith that only the Messiah could bring promises to pass.

This thought takes us at once to the predominant secularity of twentieth-century Zionism. Do its political and military concomitants allow it to invoke promises so contrastedly received through the tears of Jeremiah and the pious parables of Ezekiel? Here one may answer that exegetes will find what they desire and that all is grist to the ardent mill. No critic may deny that Zionists may see themselves bringing promises to pass and finding heartening sanction in their logic. But that *they* were what the prophets 'meant' will always be in question, not merely because of all the lapsing times but the incongruities between whence and whither.

However, even if self-fulfilling, it may reasonably be claimed that Zionism in this twentieth century 'fulfils' the biblical promises in the sense that it expresses their age-long sense of inalienable habitat, from which exile is inauthentic and therefore necessarily terminable. Jewishness can never be, as it were, 'departicularized' either ethnically or land-wise. Identity is always *sui generis qua* people and land-tied *qua* geography, however widely dispersion scatters it. Judaism counts divine people-relation without land a Christian aberration, the Church being esteemed overly 'spiritual' in supposing that 'people of God' could have no necessary physical address. For Jews it is as if Yahweh himself has 'an address on earth'. For him and his people there is a steady cohabiting, as Zechariah 8:2 has it: 'Thus says the

Lord: "I am returned to Zion and will dwell in the midst of Jerusalem and Jerusalem shall be called 'a city of truth'".' Diaspora was thus a sort of divine displacement, the Shechinah going into exile, and 'return' is a co-journey of Yahweh and his people.

It follows that promise concerning land and land recovery is the map expression of the divine status of Jewish identity. It would therefore have been unthinkable for modern Zionists not to have appealed to those faithful Baruchs who wrote down from the lips of prophetic souls the heavenly pledges of renewed cohabitation. Was it not a Talmudic principle that meanings of texts were never exhausted in their first parameters? Even Moses, sitting meekly in a *yeshiva* seminar, conceded to the pundits that he had not understood himself aright.

IV

If, then, we legitimate the application of ancient exilic promises to current politics, we only make the more pointed Zechariah's pledge about 'a city of truth'. If exile had stemmed from the guilt of profanation, return was not assumed to re-enact it. On the contrary, it would have to be 'in righteousness and truth'. The holy soil was to be, and known to be, 'the place of the Name'. If exile had to be seen as a temporary episode of divine ubiquity for his people's sake, the re-enlandisement on every prescript of things Judaic must be a radical renewal of divine locality. As long as it claimed to be biblical, even if for pragmatic and secular reasons, Zionism would have to judge itself by 'holiness'. Palestinians would be the test-case of how well it did so. 'Holy Yahweh, holy people, holy place' would be the rubric, retrieving and reinstating the perennial triangle sung by psalm and prophet. and told in the 'star of David' on Israel's flag. If failure to return was, as many thought, itself a deed of profanation, returning would have to mean re-domiciling with God.[19]

It follows that returning Zionists would be caught in an ancient quandary about the bearing of the 'holy' on the 'ethical', and of both on the political. For it has been noted in other chapters how necessary to the whole Zionist vision was statehood. The state was inevitably seen as the vital condition of having the land, even as the land was the critical arena for the state, each for the sake of the other, seeing that Zionists were not looking to Palestinians to provide them with yet another 'host nation'. The triangle of people, land and God would involve the other triangle of holy, moral and political.

In all human history the ethics of politics have stayed problematical. The art of the possible is more likely to be the preoccupation of states than the art of the holy. Israel was not to be reproached, differently from any other body politic, for having armed forces, Beth Shins, cunning diplomats and cynical fixers. Her circumstances have been tangled and her urgencies cruel. Political entities necessarily practise compromise and incur guilt. The justice they can render in their affairs domestic and their relations foreign will only and always be a bare modicum of righteousness and compassion, not least when survival is crucially at stake.

It is not, therefore, primarily the political within the triangle which is here the concern, but rather the mutual bearing of the other two. How ethical is the holy required to be? On some counts the very question would seem inane and the answer: 'totally'. How else could we, should we, think of the 'sacred' as other than the 'righteous'? Presumably, there is about 'holiness' a dimension of awe, wonder, mystery and the sublime. These somehow transcend mere 'right and wrong'. They belong with the numinous that is at the heart of right religion. It may surely be assumed that, in their presence, the moralist is more fully embraced and secured as such.

Sadly, it is not the case. 'The Name', the very ground of holiness, is 'taken in vain', unholily invoked, recruited to override its due demands and thus effectively reverse them. From this feature of some readings and actions of Zionism the Palestinians have experienced their deepest spiritual travail. It is not simply that old Philistia was the ancient enemy, the nuisance factor in Samsonic or Davidic epic story. It is rather that sacred repossession of the land can hold the sanction of a divine mandate that entails a tragic dispossession, an authentic homecoming that in Yahweh's name can validate another's exodus and find it 'holy'.

The incidence would be easier to take, to undergo, to suffer, were it perceived and pursued in entirely secular terms of superior power or merely adroit exercise of it. Those terms, indeed, have never been absent from the equation but the pain is sharper – though the losses may be equal – if and when events are underwritten as being heaven-meant and God-enjoined. For then the holy seems at total odds with the ethical. At odds with the ethical is a situation which need raise no eyebrows among politicians; should it be the same in the eye of sanctuaries? Or is the land 'holy', one might ask, willy-nilly?

The query may be blunt but it is not un-Jewish. For at the heart of prophetic religion in Israel there was always the demand for unsullied righteousness. In respect of theologies like that of Gush Emunim, one might say that Palestine for half a century has been the arena of something like the age-long tension at the Bible's core between the priest and the prophet. It has proved the land's strange destiny as competitively prized. One might almost say further that the best Palestinian hope of justice and compassion at the hands of Zionists must lie in a recovery of the superb Jewish prophethood of an Amos or a Jeremiah, to accuse the self-justifying instinct that bestows on Zion 'holy' warrant to take guilt for righteousness. When David, as king and so 'the Lord's anointed with oil', conspired guiltily for Bathsheba's body against her Hittite husband, it would seem that no conscience troubled him until a seer called Nathan brought home what was criminal in his very crown.[20] It needed a prophet to intervene. Is it significant that when something like conscience intervened in David's noble deed of sparing Saul when at his mercy in the cave, it was because he, Saul, unlike the Hittite, was 'the Lord's anointed' and as such inviolate?[21]

Events in the saga of David are remote from current history and no precise parallel is meant. The point, rather, is that in Judaic tradition (unless we think of mavericks like Spinoza) the place of conscience is taken by Torah righteousness and comes therefore under the purview of religion; thus, under religion, it may have other than ethical constraints. The phenomenon runs through all faiths but has acute incidence in Jewry by virtue of how religion, there, uniquely authenticates ethnic particularity and, *qua* Zionism, arbitrarily reckons with territory.[22]

Since the puzzle of Abraham's recordedly divine summons to 'offer' Isaac, i.e., to put him to death, there have been endless debates about the priority of the apparently divine over the otherwise ethical. In the Judaic norm, conscience and the ethical imply a personal moral self-sufficiency, unless the voice of conscience is received as the voice of God. On certain counts, conscience might almost seem a supersession of Yahweh and a deification of the human. A Jew, then, must subdue conscience in obedience to God. What is understood as claimed by obedience to God is thereby beyond or above what should otherwise be moral scruple.[23]

This situation, so far entailed in the Zionist story, emerges as the bitter factor in *Palestina Agonistes*. Any pondering of it – certainly by Western thinking – is at once exposed to the charge that observers are thereby diverting attention from the far more onerous and odious violations of conscience at work in the Holocaust. They are engaging in a subtle variant of anti-Semitism.

That charge reverts upon itself. For any reproach of anti-Semitism requires a final appeal to conscience and cannot rely on the doctrines of chosenness which it decries. The burden of Palestinianism this century has been squarely to disavow anti-Semitism by the very zeal of its appeal to have Israelis hearken to conscience for the very truth's sake of Yahweh. In that appeal they have the greatest Hebrew prophets on their side.

For did those prophets not passionately call for 'righteousness to roll down like a mighty stream' and for a total end to 'vain oblations', asking 'Who has required this at your hand?' and saying that it was assuredly not Yahweh? They were even ready to deny that sacrificial rituals had ever been commanded in the wilderness, disowning, at least rhetorically, the whole priestly apparatus. Orthodox scholars, appalled at this radicalism, might argue that it was well-meant hyperbole to be taken with reserve. But at least the vehemence of its realism against the falsities of 'calling on the Name' was case enough against the immolation of ethics in rituals, the strangulation of conscience in sanctuaries.

That conscience might effectively reinstate itself inside, if no longer against, the pieties of religion is the ultimate hope of Middle East peace. Justice demands to be honest with its referents. The point belongs with the happy, oft-quoted, care of Exodus 23:9 about 'knowing the heart of the stranger' and the command in the Decalogue and elsewhere against oppressing him. It was apt and benign to recall Jewish 'strangerhood' in wandering nomadism and in bonds in Egypt. Yet how does the warning apply when 'the strangers' are the aborigines, the people already in the land and indeed outnumbering the incoming practitioners of compassion? Does one first make strange in order to befriend, create an alien to practise kindness, with 'grapes of wrath' leaving gleanings of pity? Might Palestinians be justified in borrowing the prayer of Lithuanian Rabbi Izak Goller, referring to his fellow Jews?

> O God, help me
> For I have fallen into the hands of the righteous
> And the sons of the pious have encompassed me.
> Their gentle hands are choking my life from me.[24]

Nowhere was the priority of the ethical more gently enforced than in the comment of Jesus, according to Matthew (5:23–24):

> If you bring your gift to the altar and there remember your brother has something against you, leave your gift there by the altar, go your way, first be reconciled to him, and then come and make your offering.

Why 'remember there' unless the very access to the sanctuary nudged the memory and so alerted the conscience? That should be the way altars work, given that the scruple aroused is promptly and truly discharged in action.

Then worship may suitably resume. How far may this be from the tumult of Israeli–Palestinian politics?

V

If tragically, and all too often, the 'holy' in Zionism has unwittingly or deliberately offended the ethical, how might 'the sense of the holy' reinforce and sustain it? It certainly, if potentially, holds dimensions calculated massively to fortify and illuminate all things ethical, if only sanctuaries are sacramentally understood. 'Sacramental' in this context would be a Christian usage, meaning the sanction of 'association'. 'Holy places' are then foci of meanings that are quickened by the sight (site) or feel of them but are not idolatrously fused with them. Land or place are not, then, as in Judaic dogma, inherently 'holy', but can be regarded so by virtue of what has happened in them. The holy aura they then possess is governed by the import of the drama they served to stage or locate. Such, broadly, is the associationism that underlies Christian pilgrimage and its accompanying sense of the sacrament of geography. If the land is held holy it is by dint of divine dramas, not divine donation. The significance of a drama may be carried without essential loss across endless territories, none having exclusive prerogative even if one has the sole honour of incidence. Events, in that sense, will not engender a kind of idolatry to which places are vulnerable.

It is noteworthy, in this context, that Zionism has rarely, if ever, celebrated explicit sites, as Christians do Galilee, Nazareth, Gethsemane. The whole land is for the sake of the holy city, that city holy by virtue of the Temple (or its non-possession in 'vacant' place). In turn, the Temple hallowed the city and the city the land. Unified worship, after a prolonged struggle, disqualified local sites and shrines. Thus it would seem that there is no special associationism about Anathoth, birthplace of Jeremiah and now almost overtaken by the urban spread of northern Jerusalem, nor about Carmel for Elijah, or Jericho for Joshua's trumpeting inaugural.

Perhaps it is significant that the one exception in Zionist associationism is the Mount of Masada, ancient symbol of the heroic self-suiciding Zealots, where recruits to 'Defence Forces' take their oaths still. Those Zealots had perforce fallen back from Jerusalem under Roman power and had decided to hold out their resistance in the seemingly impregnable fortress which, reassuringly for their faith, still lay within the border of the inviolate land. When that final *locus standi* proved a fatal trap, they resolved to die by their own hands rather than live in patient self-vindicating piety under the

Roman yoke that they, and others, had done so much to provoke. Masada thus has more celebrity in Zion than the scrub around Tekoa because of Amos or the Gilgal of the first king in Israel. Hebron, it is true, has special sanctity, thanks to patriarchal tombs and competing Muslim shrines. Jerusalem, epitomizing the whole land, remains 'the inalienable capital' and the supreme emblem of recovered Zion. The continuing associationism is sharply politicized. How far, then, is 'holiness' embarrassed in its deepest relevance? It was different with the old devout rabbis of Safad, 'the city set on a hill', but they antedated the will to power and statehood that political Zionists after Herzl found indispensable to their ends.

The sacramental idea of a sanctity, to be cherished but not dogmatized, attaching to 'place-holiness' was exemplified in the purely agricultural Zionism of the 1870s which the politicians found toothless and ingenuous. They could hardly be blamed for arguing the vital necessity of statehood with power as the only form in which Jewish self-salvation could be ventured. The doctrines of covenant and election were certainly available for that reading, despite centuries of diaspora perspective to the contrary. But the sacramental yearning of the Passover plea 'Next year in Jerusalem' has its innocence tarnished by the activism in fact fulfilling it. We are back with the moral in the toils of the political and so of the holy in ambivalent, if not precarious, relation with the moral.

Even so, the sense of 'the holy' as perceived by the great prophets still has deep potential relevance to the future of the land. If it is truly interiorized it can still avail to guide and sustain the search for coexistence in the land, depending on how, in both Jew and Palestinian, it perceives itself. The latter has a more earthy, even secular, land-love. If Israelis read this as merely a pseudo-Zionism, a copy fraud, they understand neither its deeply human quality nor their own different theology.

Either way, the holy, as the sacramental, means that which is 'set apart'. The 'apartness' might have been, in origin and later, a sheer apartheid, a segregation making for taboo and even superstition. The very 'ark of God' might then take bizarre revenge on the fumbles or stumbles of the unwary.[25] There had to be total isolation from the mundane and the ordinary, a kind of manic antiseptic and mysterious power to be only feared and revered, whether attaching to places, roles or times.

Or, in a spiritual sanity of mind, the holy may become the inherent worth and worthiness of the human dignity, of place and time as inclusive wonder, entrustment and awe. Land, as soil and sustenance, home and haunt, vista and inheritance, may thus be read as vocation – vocation to be held apart from ethnic cleansing, political strife and spiritual competition as the ground of an experience of which we say: 'Truly the Lord is in this place: this is none other than the house of Yahweh.' So understood, the holy may then massively reinforce and educate the ethical and impart even to politics a reverent reticence about the lusts of power and the techniques of rule.

Such a reckoning with the holy, if duly interiorized so that it ceased to be unilateral either with Yahweh or the land, would be the truest measure of 'This year in Jerusalem', the surest fulfilment of the meaning of election and covenant. 'Chosenness' does not need to be made ethnically or spiritually exclusive in order to be inwardly distinctive as a conviction of the heart. If, as secular Jews like to think, Israelis are 'the choosing people', let them 'choose' in these terms, thereby remaining more splendidly themselves while happily undoing the 'unchosenness' of all other peoples, and of the Palestinians as being physically the nearest.

It may all seem far to seek but the hope of it, even if unconscious, is what *the* holy land, as the usage still goes, desperately awaits. These are times in which theophanies are not supposed to happen. Yet they may whenever humans are ready to realize and say with the poet ''Tis a place of wonder, meet 'tis, the ground is holy'.[26]

Is it only the music that makes William Blake's *Jerusalem* so loved a song? For the words are lyrically elusive, elusively lyrical. It is almost folly to ask naïvely what he 'means':

And was Jerusalem builded here
Among those dark Satanic mills? . . .
Bring me my arrows of desire . . .
I will not cease from mental fight,
Nor shall my sword sleep in my hand,
Till we have built Jerusalem
In England's green and pleasant land.[27]

The shift from 'I' to 'we' seems to be recruiting *agonistes* like himself. Be the 'mills' and the 'arrows' what they may, Blake seems to mean a holiness which is at once local and ubiquitous, the place of a name which may be everywhere the name of the place. There is a 'pleasant land' more immediately Jerusalem's than England for 'building' by unceasing 'mental fight'. Meanwhile the anomaly of the holy remains as grimly captured in the parting words of Samuel to Saul: 'Do as occasion serve thee for God is with thee.'[28]

Notes

1 Hence the frequent note in the Hebrew prophets of inhabitants 'sitting (unafraid) under vine and fig tree', these being symbols of idyllic security. Does the same inference lie behind the warning in Revelation 6:6: 'See that ye hurt not the oil and the wine', the olive and the grape being so slow to recover after devastation? The Palestine of 1918 knew this desperately, the Turkish army having felled so many trees to fire their war effort – leading some incoming Jewish settlers in the 1920s to think the land was unloved.

2 Judges 11:24 has Israelites telling the Moabites to 'possess' what their god, Chemosh, had given them, while Israelites enjoyed what Yahweh had assigned to them.

3 Rabbi Abraham Heschel, in *Israel: An Echo of Eternity* (New York, 1968), lyricized about the very climate and soil of Israel.

4 The plaintive question of Grandma Joad in John Steinbeck's *The Grapes of Wrath* when, trekking west after being uprooted from their homestead, they have to jettison precious mementoes of themselves.

5 The Noahid being the 'covenant' of 'seedtime and harvest' in Genesis 8:22 which would avail for all and sundry, everywhen and everywhere.

6 Lincoln's phrase comes in an address in 1861 to the Senate of the State of New Jersey. The theme of 'election' to land possession and thereby to special status and stature in the world runs through the whole of American literature and matches the 'continental' sense of things engendered by the ever-open frontier and the 'Westward ho' of the Atlantic that led to it.

7 As happens for readers of the New Testament; see e.g., Galatians 3:16–29 and Ephesians 2:15–19. Has not Judaic thinking always been ambivalent about who 'Gentiles' are and why they should be?

8 It is useful in this context to note the reaction of 'Indians' in northern America and elsewhere to Hebrew Scripture. See, for example, R. A. Warrior having to 'side' with the Canaanites in reading the Book of Joshua. Cf. R. S. Sugirtharajah (ed.), *Voices from the Margin* (London, 1991), pp. 287f.

9 Though Golda Meir was prudent enough not to air the point in her highly successful pleas to President Nixon for aid to her country.

10 Emma Lazarus, *Songs of a Semite* (New York, 1882). See also H. E. Jacobs, *The World of Emma Lazarus* (New York, 1949).

11 It is intriguing how Gikuyu religion held its land tenure by a divine bestowal to their mythical ancestors, so that deprivation was in no way merely economic but a sort of sacrilege. Jews were not alone in their perception of a 'holy' land possession. In its will to be secular, the PLO invoked not divine sanction but national and moral justice, no doubt reinforced for Muslim minds by the due sovereignty of Allah.

12 'Nonchalance' implies no neglect of the deep spiritual objectives exercising many 'servants' on the ground in the dreams of 'empire'. For some 'the white man's burden' was seen as a divine 'vocation' but that did not make it, in the corridors of state, other than a power scramble.

13 Recalling the enigmatic words of Revelation 8:1, when the 'silence' lasted half an hour. There were many times for the psalmists when they wondered why heaven had nothing to say (cf. Psalm 74:22).

14 Norman Cantor, *The Sacred Chain: A History of the Jews* (London, 1994), pp. 11, 68, 175.

15 Harold Bloom, *The Western Canon: The Books and School of the Ages* (New York, 1994), p. 6. There is an opinionated bombast about this author, who seems to enjoy the pontificating oracle status he assumes.

16 'Proper' here cares for vexed questions of international law. Strictly, the juridical 'right' of the State of Israel springs – if at all – from the partitioning Resolution of the United Nations in November 1947. That was never implemented in its legal terms. The *status quo*

on the map, pending any 'peace agreement' with the Palestinians, hinges on battles and truces. The initiating Balfour Declaration of 1917 was no more than that and carried no legal force. Even so, 'proper' is a serviceable word for Israel as of 1949.

17 Apart, of course, from the great potential for the much beset Israeli economy of any future 'free market' across the whole Near East which final peace could bring about.

18 See *The Sacred Chain*, p. 422.

19 The 'star of David' is a double triangle that can be taken as representing the physical triangle of place, people and past, enshrined by Yahweh in election, covenant and power, i.e., place donated, people chosen and possession mandated.

20 The story is told in 2 Samuel 11 and 12.

21 See 1 Samuel 24:1–15.

22 'Arbitrarily' is meant strictly here in the sense that an *arbitrium*, an exercise of (divine) will, has suspended criteria that might otherwise obtain. It is precisely this which has been the burden of Palestinians throughout their experience of the incidence of Zionism.

23 Michael Wyschogrod argues that there is no classical Hebrew term for 'conscience', and that Judaism 'lacks a doctrine' concerning it, contrasted, say, with Stoicism. He traces this to the primacy of revelation. Exodus 23:3 about *not* 'favouring the poor man in his cause' he takes as symptomatic of the rigorism of Torah claim, i.e., no privately derived 'bias'. He asks whether 'Isaac' is the conscience we must be prepared to offer. Even so, Torah-owning Jews have, like others, to undertake individual decisions. See A. Finkel and L. Fuzzell (eds), *Standing Before God: Essays on Prayer in Scriptures* (New York, 1981), pp. 313–28.

24 Quoted from Lionel Blue and Jonathan Magonet, *Kindred Spirits: A Year of Readings* (London, 1995), p. 33.

25 As in the incident in 2 Samuel 6:1–7 when Uzzah steadied the Ark of the Covenant as it rocked in the cart of his father Abinadab *en route* from Baale to some other abode. He died on the spot because of 'the anger of Yahweh'. Alternatively, later the Ark brought unusual good luck to a certain Obed-Edom who was ready to risk housing it.

26 T. S. Eliot (ed.), *Selected Poems of Ezra Pound* (London, 1928), p. 69.

27 William Blake, *Complete Works*, ed. Geoffrey Keynes (Oxford, 1966), p. 481.

28 1 Samuel 10:7, words of the ageing prophet to the man he chose to inaugurate Israeli kingship after first demurring about the popular clamour for monarchy like the rest of nations. Was Samuel unwittingly an inaugurator of Zionism?

6
The victim of the victimized

I

From the bus window on the way, in the area of Mahane Yehuda market, by the light of a street lamp, he saw a black placard with the words: 'Arabs out!' He translated them into German switching Arabs with Jews, and was overwhelmed by fury.[1]

The Israeli novelist Amos Oz, writing in 1991, allows the novel's hero to make the unthinkable association of Nazi anti-Semitism with the Palestinian experience in Israel, of Jewish tragedy in Europe with the incidence of Israeli power-holding in the Jewish state. When non-Jews have ventured to imply or allege some discernible parallel between the Shoah undergone and any Zionist oppression inflicted, world Jewry has responded in incredulous repudiation of outrageous calumny. And rightly so, for the Holocaust must be acknowledged *sui generis*, an unparalleled barbarity intending the total, brutal, pitiless elimination of an entire people, their culture and their meaning, a calculated bid for 'a Germany without Jews'.

Even so, when Israelis themselves perceive some reason to suspect that theirs has been a triumphalism not entirely unconnected with their age-long victim status in a world of 'Gentiles',[2] those same 'Gentiles' have reason to attend. The guilt of Europeans must always disqualify them from reproachful assessments of Israel that argue a vengefulness vented on Arabs. Guilt here is never a feasible custodian of conscience there. It is too liable to be scheming its own exoneration. It suffices to have all parties search their own hearts.

For many Israelis the Holocaust affords a totally inclusive alibi for whatever successful statehood requires in the effort to outlive its ravages. But not all; there are those who have identified that temptation for what it is and refuse its arguable warrant to ignore human rights in the pursuit of Jewish ones. This, for some, includes the perception that the victimized have deep in their experience a logic of retaliation, if not against the original party, then in any encounter entailed in survival. Such encounter, however external to the primary victim-experience, must carry enmity and bitterness to be released into some new equation. Palestine and Palestinian lay squarely in the path of that logic.

Human history is full of such entails of pasts into presents, of wrongs undergone requiring avenging wrongs. It could hardly have been otherwise, given the sheer enormity of the Shoah. Its victims made every survivor a debtor to their memory by every measure of things unforgettable and unforgivable.[3] The State of Israel itself, though conceived long before its direst urgency became apparent, emerged as the central positive discharge of what the Shoah laid upon the Jewish soul. It could not escape the negative emotions such fulfilment bore within itself, given the awkward Palestinian obstacle that was innocent of the anger's origins.

Fima, the central figure of Amos Oz's novel, is no heroic specimen. His 'fury' over the realization of a comparability between some Israelis and all Nazis only leaves him bewildered and frustrated, desiring somehow to be at peace within himself in the privacy of an ineffectual conscience. Readers can readily sympathize with his surrender to mediocrity under unmanageable burdens. Other actors, in real life, as we must see here and in Chapter 10, have been more robust. The need now is, first, to understand and document the case against some dimensions of Israel's history since the 1950s as those of the erstwhile victim victimizing, and then to explore the deeper factors in the Jewish perception of the *goyim*, the non-Jewish humans.

II

It has often been remarked that young Jews of post-Shoah times, schooled in the resilience of Israel, have invariably asked when told of its defenceless sufferers: 'But where was our Army?'[4] They found it hard to realize that none existed. From this tragic victimization, deprived of all dignity and herded into powerless immolation, came the compelling determination never to allow such total jeopardy again. Hence the fever of proud, defiant, self-reliant will to adequacy within themselves that has characterized Israeli Jews since the state began. To be sure, political, military and monetary allies, sponsors and sustainers have been imperative, so that viability is no solitary achievement. But the will, if need be, to suffice for themselves of themselves is palpable. Despite its catastrophic end, the defiance of Masada lives in the memory. The final bastion is the will alone, ready to stand alone. For, as Menahem Begin observed, 'There is no guarantee that can guarantee an international guarantee'.[5]

This adamant self-sufficing, congenial and decisive in Israeli thinking, could hardly fail to generate something correspondingly impatient about the Palestinian impediments in the whole equation. Demography, not to say also ethics, creates both inconvenience and embarrassment for the inherent self-reference in the Jewish soul. Oh for a world without Palestinians! They are the awkward presence in the will for their absence. How this sense of things in the psyche rides with Israeli democracy and conscience – with which it co-exists – we must note in due place.

The memory of the Shoah being for all Israelis the spur to entire adequacy to, for and in themselves, it was natural that for some it suggested anti-Palestinian emotions descending from annoyance to intolerance and so to enmity and finally to victimization. The oppressive and utter irrationality of what Jews had undergone under the Third Reich made a rational compassion irrelevant for such minds. How could post-Shoah survival concede a claim on forbearance, pity and justice when these had been so desperately denied? What sort of state might have emerged to be 'Israel' had there been no Holocaust, history will never know. The state that did emerge in its aftermath has carried in its psyche the trauma of that overwhelming antecedent, with Palestine in vicarious connection.

That tragic mutuality was, of course, played out in the politics and conflicts that history records. Victims have no occasion to become victim-izers unless they are first victors. Palestinian resistance set the struggle sharply enough in physical, territorial and combative terms. It was in that otherwise 'ordinary' confrontation that the feature we are concerned to isolate in the present context comes to light and into play. Israeli arms developed a ruthlessness required, it might be said, by the desperate exigencies of the situation, but also revealing a subtle exultation akin to biblical tradition. A 'backs-to-the-wall' quality blends with a 'destiny awaits'. The adversary is more than a foe: he is a denier of the right of way. A destiny is at issue and not merely a battle.

This quality was especially evident in the Begin-led forces in the push to the outskirts of Jerusalem in the spring fighting of 1948, with its grim symbol of the massacre of some 254 villagers of Dair Yasin. The tragic event, symptomatic of the brutality on all sides but itself a salient in the enormity, at once became – and has remained – a subject of controversy concerning the facts themselves, a circumstance which in itself is witness to the Jewish desire to mitigate, or at worst suppress, the significance of a dark atrocity.

The forces of the Stern Gang and the Irgun Zvi Leumi (the former cherishing the legend of Abraham Stern (alias Yair), the latter under the direct command of Begin) were alongside but insistently distinct from the Haganah, the military arm of the Jewish Agency. Dair Yasin lay in the path of these uninhibited fighters urgent to relieve the pressure on the Jerusalem front. Stern had been fanatical in his perceptions of Zionism, hating Jews who opposed him hardly less vehemently than the British administration by which he was briefly imprisoned, only to be killed early in 1942 in a police raid. His violence lived on in his armed followers, their passion in arms fortifying the bigotry of their intelligence. Stern saw 'Gentiles' at large, whether Nazi, British or Arab, as all pernicious obstacles to the success of Zion. Had he lived he could have proved the supreme victimizer – had the mind of new Israel been minded to allow him.

Menahem Begin, though comparably fierce in will, was a more complex character whose story must be pondered in the light of his strange withdrawnness in the traumatic aftermath of the invasion of the Lebanon in the mid-1980s. He always strenuously repudiated the description 'terrorist', though his career up to 1948 and his role in the sinking of the *Altalena*[6] amply warranted it. It must be noted that after the establishment of the state, he showed patient respect for constitutionality and bided his time before savouring power when the Likud attained it in the 1970s. In war, however, he was implacable and occasioned frequent tensions with the Haganah and Ben Gurion.

Ben Gurion offered immediate apologies to King Abdallah of Jordan when news of Dair Yasin spread – to the chagrin of Begin. There was no doubt of the acute embarrassment when the Red Cross official counted 254 corpses of Arab men, women and children. Had the villagers in fact harboured armed Arabs, had they been 'invited' by Begin's forces to leave, had they or had they not refused to connive with either side? The propaganda that overtakes atrocity never makes amends but only compounds or smothers the reality. Mutual retaliatory outrages rapidly followed in the passion Dair Yasin had signalled. The village became a password for a vindictiveness fuelling the perception of the enmity it fired.

Dair Yasin had another tragic consequence. It quickened the panic which induced a massive exodus in flight of the Palestinian peasantry. That story, too, is enmeshed in controversy. If news of Dair Yasin was not the only factor, the departure in fear in large numbers of what Balfour loftily called 'the native population' certainly suited the Zionist aim of a homogeneous Jewish society, in the event of peace. The will to make space was not feasible without a will to make victims in displacement. Villagers caught in the fray had been no party to the Arab decision to confront Jewish objectives militarily rather than contain them by a shrewd acceptance of partition.[7] That being beyond their emotional reach and their political intelligence, warfare only proved their tragedy in not being first their option. The massacred of Dair Yasin were thus doubly victims but the deed was done by the Irgun. Begin survived to become at length Prime Minister.

The wilful making of victims reached from the graves of villagers into the highest level of peacemaking. As we have seen, the Israel coming to be in 1947–49 owed what juridical validity it had to the vote of the United Nations. It was the UNO's own mediator, Count Bernadotte, who was brutally assassinated by members of Stern's fighting group in September 1948. He aimed to turn armistice into agreed conciliation by adjusting the lines to something like the partition of November 1947, with mutual statehoods mutually recognized and with a dual status for Jerusalem. The plan would have foreclosed the options of frontier revision. The Sternists and Irgun would have none of it; neither, but more subtly, would the Haganah. For it would have enshrined the rubric of 'no territorial acquisition by battle', since it required the areas acquired beyond the partition line to be forfeited – areas conceded as Israeli in the 1949 armistice by Bernadotte's successor as mediator. The murder was easily deplored by an Israel content enough to reap its sequel. Extremists are often useful for the exoneration had in deploring their action as well as for the retention of what their action yields. Victims may be made, and had, by subtlety as well as violence.

III

A vast documentation has congealed around the Palestine–Israel history during its long century of declarations, resolutions, editorials and briefings, as well as diaries, novels, poems and memoirs. None are more striking than the soldierly reflections published in the wake of the Six-Day War of 1967 under the title *The Seventh Day*.[8] When the battle cleared, young men and women, for the most part from kibbutzim,[9] many of them born in the land and born around the moment of the founding of the state, ruminated on their experiences and their reactions to the impact of war. Their conversations were edited by older hands inspired by the frankness, depth and pathos of the themes discussed. The result was a rare testimony to the dark, yet noble, paradoxes of military conflict.

The participants were all conscripts, but willing ones. They saw their country as under mortal threat, a David ringed with brutal foes, faced with possible annihilation, and themselves called to arms from their farms and schools to do or die. Few, if any, had experience of wielding a bayonet or firing a gun in the immediacy of killing to survive, of surviving to kill. They registered their trauma in different ways, living through the emotions of hate, futility, desperation, pride and triumph. Their diverse attitudes to 'the Arabs' ran through a whole gamut of feigned indifference in an exchange of cruelty or puzzled confusion about the common humanness at such bitter odds with itself. Some, in the security of victory, queried the notion of sovereignty and nationality – the primary stakes in the combat.

Inevitably, the instincts these inspired, the belligerence these demanded, took them back to the Europe of their elders, to the Shoah out of which their identity had come, to the sufferings they were, so to say, reversing by the military will to frustrate what, conceptually, was calculated to repeat that 'Jew-hatred' – the old idiom in a new locale. Given all the antecedents, the Nazi memory and the early summer build-up of 1967, it was impossible *not* to be fighting a battle, which proved triumphant, in the emotions of a memory that stayed ignominiously catastrophic. The association was reciprocal and vicarious, a past brooding in a present, a present fraught with a past.

No less inevitably, a perceptive reading of the triumph inspired a reversing of the roles. The here-and-now victors having been the there-and-then victims, imagination could not always suppress the realization that a sort of restitution was happening.[10] Could this be, if likewise the defeated were not now on the receiving end – at Jewish hands – of adversity in reverse? There was, emphatically, no parallel in the respective situations and the non-Jewish party in the two situations was totally different. Even so, the surmise came that the Jewish warriors in 1967 were in the entirely unfamiliar role of having their way against others by successful power – in effect, of making victims.

It is to the lasting honour of *The Seventh Day* that the surmise arose, that it was registered and, being registered, transcended. In the pages of *The Seventh Day* it was not indulged as a matter on which a vulgar mind could gloat. On the contrary, there was a large will, if not to repudiate hate for the Arabs, at least not to cultivate it. It was in 1982, as we must see, that vindictive victim-making became deliberate and preternaturally brutal.

One soldier ponders his reaction after the event, namely the Egyptian débâcle in Sinai:

Doubts continued to plague me after the war. I saw those wretched people streaming along the road, poor miserable souls carrying their bundles . . . some of them already with sores on their feet which they'd bound up with rags . . . I began to think about the Jews wandering through Europe and other places. One immediately rejects this idea. God in heaven! how can one compare the two things! Deep inside you you still have the feeling that it isn't quite like the wanderings and sufferings of the Jews.

After describing the surrender of a sizeable number of Egyptian soldiers, the same Israeli witness, unknown even by his comrades as being a medico, tells of treating on the sand a wounded Egyptian who, being unable to stand, had been told to lie on the ground. Expecting perhaps to be slain as the 'foe' bent over him, the prisoner knew tending hands dressing his wound.

An Israeli officer kneeling on the ground attending to an Egyptian private who was filthy, full of pus: not simply an officer attending to a private, but an enemy officer taking care of his enemy. This was something completely beyond their understanding and, just as previously there had been dead silence among them, now they suddenly shouted: Ya'ish Israel ['Long live Israel'].[11]

It was a rare moment of that 'Do unto others as you would have done to you' which war reverses on both counts.

The nobility of the dazed yet perceptive introspection of *The Seventh Day* registered the uniquely Jewish tension in being 'victorious' or in 'policing' hapless defeated troops or, still worse, their broken, fleeing populations. These erstwhile civilians felt they had not been trained for this kind of task, identifying their own dead while herding the captive enemy. They could hardly disown the human tenacity of people who kept faith with their dreams, refused to surrender their love for their heritage and yearned for the dignity of peaceful seasons and quiet lives – all very Jewish emotions, though belonging to entire humanity.

The Seventh Day soul-searchers discovered the 'conquest' character of Israeli actuality, though every fibre of their being and pride repudiated that version of their tenure of the land. They could neither deny nor concede the throes of their own experience as having, willy-nilly, made 'victims' with no option to do otherwise. Victory had etched into their new security the acid of their inward self-reproach. They could only leave unanswered the issue of what their politicians and the corporate mind of their nation would do with the stuff of victory so disturbingly contrived.

> Why should we regret having won, almost as if winning was a catastrophe? The war achieved more than we hoped for – and it's good that it did. As far as the rest is concerned: what to hold, how to keep it, how to run things there – that's something that has to be decided on the basis of political and security considerations.

In sum, they felt themselves characterized by 'the tragedy of being victors' and the 'hidden link with the destruction of the Jews'.[12]

It was the conquest of Old Jerusalem and the unification of the city which most fervently affected the victors and enthused their retrospect. In this context, they were living with the aura of the Hebrew Scriptures in the ambivalence between all-conquering Joshua and the heroics of the Book of Judges on the one hand, and the peace vision of Micah and Psalm 87. Many felt they had undergone a profound redefinition, in which the ethos of the ghetto, with all its arguable cravenness and godly torpor, had been forsworn in the virility of a triumphant nation on the crest of new assurance, the one both contained and cancelled within the other.

> 'I had a feeling I would like to bring all my ancestors, throughout all the generations and say to them: "Look, I'm standing by the Western Wall",' said an airman, educated to atheism.[13]

Having manfully averted what they had read as the threat of annihilation, 'they identified themselves with the Jews of the Hitler era'[14] by dramatically reversing the shape of their own Jewishness and crossing a Rubicon of new identity. The Palestinians and Arabs, whose defeat was integral to that transformation, became, by the same token, the counterparts of what had been Jewish losing and humiliation. In being dramatically the victors, Jews could never forget, by the sheer evidence of victims not themselves, that they had long been victims elsewhere.

The legitimacy of defensive/offensive war contrasted totally with the rest of the equation in the summer of 1967. It remains the dignity of Israeli arms that Palestinian victim-experience, dire enough in all conscience, was broadly confined to the war's own incidence, the illusion of 'a purity of arms' having been abandoned, at least by the soldiers of *The Seventh Day*.[15] They had been 'making victims', to be sure, but not after the manner of Nazi Europe. The malicious 'victor victimizing' lay ahead in the summer of 1982.

IV

The kind of self-esteem in which Israel could rejoice in the Six-Day War, contemplating the fruits of their prowess and the breathtaking issue of their crisis, told of emotions which could find no place in the sordid invasions of Lebanon, briefly in 1978 and criminally in 1982. No *Seventh Day* literature with its magnanimity emerged from those events but only a confused awareness of inauthenticity festering in part in the core of the nation, with the other part trapped in a brazen bravado. With crowds of the latter kind chanting 'King Begin, King Begin' in Tel Aviv, Israelis came their closest to the lust of victim-making in scarcely concealed revenge for Jewish victimization in Hitler's Europe. Soldiers of the quality revealed in *The Seventh Day* served in the blood-letting in Beirut with bitter revulsion. For the first time, 1956 apart, Israel's Defence Forces had belied their name in a wholly offensive war, initiated under the slogan of 'Peace in Galilee'. It was the Irgun in state uniform.

There is some evidence that the Likud Cabinet in 1982 was inveigled into the advance on Beirut, the more diffident members being cajoled into acquiescence by the more rabid. Be that as it may, the whole tragic adventure has many of the marks of a long-pent-up visitation of enmity on the Palestinian adversary and, in the violent sense, a psychic reality of victimization and a betrayal of all the finer instincts of Judaism. It is impossible to account for it merely as an unhappy aberration. For it had no rational political grounds and violated the integrity of many in Israel whom military duty drew into its pursuit.

The ever-present consideration about water had always given significance in Israeli eyes to southern Lebanon with its Litani river. The actual biblical extent of 'the land of promise' had never explicitly excluded the Lebanon in some sense from its borders. According to Deuteronomy 3:25, Moses had pleaded with Yahweh to be allowed to go over and see it. Joshua 1:4 included it in divine promise. Its cedars had served to build and adorn the Temple of Solomon, while Hosea celebrated its fertility.

The romanticism of psalm and prophet, however, was no part of the grim decisions of the summer of 1982. Palestinians needed to be pursued, harassed and eliminated wherever they withdrew. It is important to realize the inherently disruptive quality attaching to the Zionist presence, not only within the confines over which partitioning had debated, but also throughout the entire region. The Arabic proverb *Al-Jar qabl al-Dar* ('choose your neighbour before you choose your house') has a bitter wisdom here. For the adjacence of Israel has disquieted all its neighbourhoods, northwards most of all. The fact of contiguity and the bond of Arab kinship inevitably meant that adjacent states would be involved in the incidence of Zionism in its given territory.

To be sure, those neighbours aggravated their situation by their own belligerence and ineptness. The politics entailed concern us in other chapters. Israeli logic embroiled the whole environment inexorably in tragedy and tribulation. 'Hot pursuit' has always been a dogma of militarism. Wherever the enemy withdraws, shelters or conspires, pursue him. This seeking-out of Palestinians across Jordan or into Lebanon had a double merit. It crippled the main adversary but also potentially destabilized the régimes in the sanctuaries he sought. The latter, especially in the north, might be highly profitable if there were waters to fish in and parties to be cultivated or confounded, depending on their attitudes to Israel.

With the final implementation of the agreement with Egypt, Israel had ensured the security of her southern border by the end of the 1970s. That facilitated what she might devise elsewhere – hence the long exclusion of Egypt from the Arab League despite what Sadat had thought he was achieving by linking his regaining of Sinai and the eastern Canal Zone and canal traffic with autonomy – Begin permitting – for the West Bank.

Secure to her south, what of the east? Jordan had resolved the problem, for the most part, by the dire events of 'Black September' 1970. The Palestinian dimension in the Kingdom of Jordan was numerous and strong but the emergence of PLO militancy after the 1967 war, in the depths of which Al-Fatah was born,[16] queried the nature of Jordanian sovereignty. The armed Palestinians claimed the right to operate, within their free ability, from Jordanian soil. This invited retaliatory raids on the part of Israel, imperilling Jordanian subjects and putting in question local Hashimite control within the state. The PLO, unready to submit to inhibiting conditions, brought the issue to a head in a savage inter-Arab conflict which ended in the expulsion of armed Palestinians who, with their bitter losses, saw fellow-Arabs doing Israel's work. The details belong to Chapter 7.

Passing almost traceless through Syria,[17] these events only contrived to export the identical problem into the fragility of Lebanon, a state in no capacity to emulate the forthrightness of King Husain in Jordan. The near-Byzantine labyrinth of Lebanese politics need not detain us here. Syrian governments, for historical and territorial reasons,[18] had long had a legitimate stake in Lebanese affairs. The Maronite identity of the country, as alleged by that dominant section of the Christian population, competed with the mainly Muslim perception of an Arab – and therefore predominantly Muslim – identity as a state belonging squarely with the hinterland of Arabism. Other elements – Shi'ah as well as Sunni Islam, Druzes and various Christian entities – shared a statehood susceptible to fragmentation and political schism, a condition which became more serious with the shifting patterns of population growth, economic factors and feudal rivalries between local loyalties and powerful clans.

After the French withdrawal and national autonomy in 1946, a degree of cohesion was achieved, thanks to a working agreement between Maronite and Sunni communities in a constitution that reflected the 'confessional' balances. Corroborated by strong commercial interests, this cohesion might have survived despite the turbulence of Arab politics all around and the tensions within. It was the insertion of the Palestinian factor after 1970[19] that fatally undermined the fragile viability of Lebanon, and the Palestinian presence, in military form, was directly derived from the actuality of Israel in the shape Zionist ideology gave to it.

It would be false to hold Israel accountable for all that befell Lebanon and its people. It had no originating responsibility for Lebanon's territorial defining after 1920, nor for the stresses endemic in its feudal, composite and religious make-up. It did bear critical responsibility for the collapse of Lebanon into civil war that ensued from the Palestinian presence. For that presence exacerbated beyond solution the issues between the 'Lebanons' of competing factions. The Maronites saw the PLO – as the Jordanian Crown had done – threatening Lebanon's mastery in its own house and pulling it where it did not wish to go, that is, towards pan-Arab sympathies and away from Western, and so US, alignments. Intense enmity developed between the Palestinians and the Maronites, with ghastly massacres dealt out by the one and avenged by the other. The one resented a deviant usurpation of their sovereignty, the other an Arab betrayal of the common Arab cause against Israel.

As a recent historian observed about another context:

> The whole difficulty of historical reconstruction and writing lies in this fundamental truth about history: it contains a multiple situation for ever on the move.[20]

A situation, in our context, bitter with animosity and compounded by controversy. There were times when Israel made clandestine overtures to Maronite elements, exploring any mood for a small Maronite entity as a client useful to Israel and an ally against the PLO. It had its treacherous appeal, though nothing materialized. Suspicion of it did little to endear Maronites to other Lebanese. Israel was able to elicit and adopt a break-away Lebanese group on her northern border, under Major Haddad, thus contriving a proxy force to control a buffer zone and relieve Israeli forces accordingly, merely at the cost of a flow of Israeli, i.e., US, weaponry. The violation of Lebanese sovereignty was a negligible consideration, humiliating as it was to that state and accentuating the passions for or against the PLO.

Borders invariably figure where security on one side is under threat from armoury on the other. 'Peace in Galilee' became the slogan in the early summer of 1982 in an Israeli declaration of intent to push back Palestinian fighters 25 miles north of the exclusion zone. In the previous eighteen months there had been little serious disturbance of that peace. Precautions are always arguably pre-emptive. In the event, the 25 miles lengthened into full-scale invasion which finally penetrated into and beyond Beirut itself.[21] The policy seemed to gather momentum as it unfolded, as if driven by a half-submerged impulse towards a Palestinian annihilation, a deliberate elimination of a people organized for their self-defence, the 'final solution' of the Palestine question. The immolation of another people, a much afflicted 'host-nation', inspired no hesitation in Israeli government counsels, though it troubled the conscience of many citizens inside and outside the Defence Forces. The casting aside of all that had been best in Zionism, the sheer waywardness and vehemence of the invasion, the dire tragedy brought on innocent people in its train – all combined to characterize the invasion and its barbarity as a deep-lying act of vengeance in the Israeli psyche, a hidden passion of requital for the wrongs against Jewry. It was as if the founding impulse of Zionism and its idealizing determination to be 'innocent' had been decisively repudiated in a flagrant will to be guilty, as if asking: Need there be exclusive 'Gentile' copyright on the notion of 'final solutions'? For Menahem Begin, Ariel Sharon and their colleagues in the Israeli Cabinet and army, 'it had been proper', in the words attributed to Eleazar on Masada, 'to have conjectured at the purpose of God much sooner'.

V

The physical costs of the invasion were horrendous for village populations *en route* and for the civilian people of Beirut. Its ferocity intensified the already impassioned emotions of the factions in Lebanon. It completely failed to achieve any viable alliance with any significant element in that confusion, serving only to shame the sort of treason it required, for which earlier diplomacy had angled.

It proved a bitter education of Israeli minds and politics in three crucial fields: the ineluctable reality of Arab demography, the deep schism in Israeli society and, thirdly, the abiding irreducible actuality of the Palestinian fact in Israeli existence.

When the notional 25-mile range of occupation was extended beyond Tyre, beyond Sidon, beyond Damour, into Beirut, there was no military reason why it should not have proceeded at will to Tripoli, to Aleppo. Certainly Damascus was within easy reach for Israeli *blitzkrieg*, had command so ordained. Sound minds in Jewry had always known that there were limits by sheer Arab numbers to what a *Judea politica* could feasibly comprise. That awareness had reconciled the realists to the abandonment of Zionist claims to 'Trans-Jordan', which revisionists like Vladimir Jabotinsky insisted should continue to be claimed and coveted. Given the vast extent of Arab territories and Arab numbers, and the ideology of a homogeneous Jewish peoplehood as the central aim of the state, it was foolhardy to try and exceed a reasonable accommodation of land and people. Areas beyond would be proper for Arab emigration to them from Eretz Israel.

Overstretched in the morass of Lebanon and resisting the lure of carrying the punitive lesson into further reaches of humanity, Israeli policy had to turn to the terms that might extract the maximum assets from withdrawal, tempting as were the vistas of Damascus and Aleppo physically attainable. The state had taught itself in the costliest form the lesson it knew already – its necessary capitulation to the statistical reality of the Middle Eastern scene. The limits of military power were painfully underlined. Ben Gurion, twenty years earlier, had known and acknowledged that it was, above all, Arab population that circumscribed the territorial limits of the Zionist state.

It may be argued that the invasion of Lebanon in 1982 had not initially – or ever – intended to ignore this and that its aim had never been to annex Lebanon but only to deny it to the Palestinians as a haven and camp ground. Impulse, however, as distinct from strategy, took it further. For in the emotions, the logic was lost to view. Lebanon could not be denied to the Palestinians without being denied to itself. The flouting of its national sovereignty, of a state's dignity and self-pride – themes on which Israel so strenuously relied for herself – meant a violent repudiation of the inner integrity by which Zionism could alone hold itself authentic.

It followed that the invasion left Israel at urgent odds with itself. The result was an unprecedented fissure in Israeli society. Gone was the sense of sacred warrant and vindicating success that had characterized the campaign of 1967. Israel had been quite conspicuously the aggressor; all previous wars (the conspiracy of 1956 apart) had been responsive to attack, actual or forestalled. This one was signally assertive. Tit-for-tat exchanges of fire and threat in the north bore no resemblance, as a *belli causa*, to the *in extremis* quality of survival in 1948 and 1967.

The serious disavowals of the war by citizens at home, the desperate unease of many in the army, seemed only to rouse the architects of the policy and their supporters to wilder self-adulation. Begin, who had been so long maligned and isolated in the political wilderness, could savour with the sweets of power the still sweeter wine of ambiguous acclaim. When, a year later, in deep personal bereavement, he withdrew from leadership, there seemed a strange nemesis in the wearied withdrawnness of his spirit.

Be that as it may, Israeli democracy itself was never more deeply under strain than in the aftermath of the invasion. Underlying tensions in mind and soul were accentuated and embittered. These persisted in the effort to restore the image and somehow reinstate the authenticity of Zion.

All might have been vindicated, if not forgiven, had the elimination of Palestinianism been achieved. The third lesson of 1982 was simply the folly of the notion. To be sure, the retreating negotiations attained the evacuation of the PLO forces from Lebanese soil. They withdrew with appropriately ironical flourish to Tunis or elsewhere. For Israel it was a Pyrrhic victory bought at the enormous human cost of non-Israelis. It left Palestinian non-combatants, families and the old, in desperate exposure to Lebanese factions whose blood-lust had been aroused by the war itself. The massacres of Sabra and Chatila followed under the safeguard of Israeli guns, implicated though not involved. It was not the sort of Palestinian elimination that could bring Israel any satisfaction, but only a sharpened futility and guilt.

1982 may not have glimpsed the Intifadah but it served to engender it. There were more Palestinians than those who had wanted Lebanese ground for their valour. Their partisans proved tenacious on the southern border. 'Peace in Galilee' was no more assured than it had ever been, the only solution for which would have been to negotiate away the sources of the enmity. The will to this, of course, could not be unilateral, but the war of 1982 had done nothing to concert a dual will and everything to deter the case for it. Palestinian reality was more than demographic: it was people-shaped, spiritual and, in those terms, irreducible. The ultimate logic of 1982 was that neighbourhood has to be received as such and made good in co-existence. But 1982, with Israel punitively in Lebanon, seemed to be avowing that the Shoah could not – could not yet – permit that evident conclusion.

VI

The invasion of Lebanon by Israel receded into history, became an episode in an ongoing saga in the on-going-ness of all it had failed to resolve. Much of its rejectionist set of mind persisted in the obstinate refusal of the Likud government to 'recognize' the PLO as the legitimate expression and mouthpiece of Palestinianism. Zionists had battled with a determination to 'represent' world Jewry. Israel needed Palestinian collaborators at home and could always hope that it could determine who and what 'valid' Palestinians should be. The stance continued until the Madrid conclave of 1990 and even then a right was asserted to determine whom Palestinian delegations might comprise. American policy, which might have unlocked this bind, perpetuated it, conniving with it by insisting that issues belonged only with 'the parties' to them but delaying for long any full credence concerning one of them.[22]

Meanwhile, in 1988 the PLO had played its decisive card in acknowledging 'Israel's right to exist' within to-be-agreed borders, but without then affecting the Israeli pretence that there was no acceptable party to talk to.[23] It remains ironical that when talking with the Palestinians became at length Israeli policy, it had been, in measure, constrained by the rise of Hamas and the fear that there might come to be no negotiable Palestinian party in sight – while the rise of Hamas owed much to the stalemate that denial of negotiation had long created.

The precarious outlook for the Oslo Accords has concerned us elsewhere. It remains in the present context to ponder the most difficult aspect of all, stemming from the Israeli response to the Palestinian dimension in a century-long encounter, namely, Jewish perception of 'the Gentiles', among whom historically Palestinians are the most awkwardly included. The issues are haunted by the ancient association with which we began in Chapter 1.

It can be plausibly explained that it was only a wilful non-acceptance of Zion and the Zionists by the context that entailed the sequences of conflict and enmity which ensued from their coming. There was a determined local will to make their bid non-admissible territorially and spiritually. Resistance, not containment, was the Arab choice. Chance and Israeli courage built upon it in all the devious ways that we review in other chapters. Zionists could then hardly be expected to reproach themselves for winning, still less 'ungain their gains'. It is the instinct of power always to consolidate and, if enmities are wanted, enmities can be unleashed.

Tragically, passions latent in Zionism and occasioned by the Lebanese border tensions found cruel resurgence in April 1996 – resurgence darkly proving that the chronic victim-psyche by which Israelis could be driven had been in no way exorcized by the fiasco of 1982 or the introspection that had then ensued.

The familiar south Lebanon tangle persisted. UN peacekeepers could only monitor its tragic elements. Hizballah fighters found urgent reasons to target Kiryat Shemona in the northern confines of Israel on the ground that Israel was occupying one-tenth of Lebanese land as a zone for punitive 'disciplining' of those same Hizballah fighters and their hapless Lebanese 'hosts'. But that Israeli occupation itself engendered the fighters' dogged will to end it. The tally leads back dismally to Israel as a bad and angry neighbour, and Israel is a bad and angry neighbour because she insists on being there in Zionist terms. Only some mutual compatibility can turn the logic round to peace but logics, being plural, argue a rejection of compatibility. The word may be close kin to 'compassion' but that, too, is mutually wanting.

Why, observers wonder, was the April 1996 onslaught named 'The Grapes of Wrath'? The earlier, slighter one in 1993 had been more gently termed 'Operation Accountability' – a commodity that might hope to be reciprocal. Why was the exchange so cruelly unequal, with US-made how-itzers, equipped with precise, pilotless target surveillance, so remorseless? Why was the Fijian and Irish UN presence so negligible? Why should the pursuit of Katyusha rocket-firers require relentless seaborne attacks on the sole artery in a state as mountainous as Lebanon? The questions multiply. Maybe 'wrath' *was* their explanation – a conjecture sustained by high-ranking elements in the Israeli forces warning (*sic*) their Prime Minister not to suspend the action 'just yet'. Israelis, to be sure, must never more be attacked with impunity – so Holocaust memory ordains. Yet there were no scores of thousands of un-homed Israeli villagers trekking down to Jerusalem, no basic infrastructure decimated in Judea or Samaria. Disproportion is often the hallmark of anger.[24] In this context it was hardly the partner of wisdom. For the whole 'Grapes of Wrath' served to endear Hizballah to the Lebanese population and, in their eyes, justify their presence in the tenth of their country Israel had effectively annexed. Counter-productivity rarely fails to reward the wrathful.

'The wrath' no doubt had electoral point and force advantage but were its ultimate sources in a will to victimize, seen as concomitant to the will to be secure? Were there – as some have conjectured – operators in the Defence Forces ready to usurp a free hand in the flush of conflict? The subordination of things military to things political had been suspect in 1982. And, in the meantime, was not Israel tragically becoming a more violent society, putting the political process itself under threat if it were to yield, or seem to yield, action uncongenial to force-invoking elements? That there is an issue in the aftermath going to the very soul of Zion is clear to her deepest lovers.

VII

Are these, then, current Zionist dimensions of the ancient Jew–'Gentile' distinction which Judaism has still to de-signify? The issue of the peaceable viability of Israel with the abiding Arab 'neighbourhood' is not solved by power-in-wrath, only by power-in-compassion, i.e., in 'feeling with'. We return to the theme in Chapters 11 and 12 as the supreme spiritual test of three religions. Meanwhile, mutual enmity remains 'crouching at the door'. Palestinians in time of despair might ask whether Jewry ever came again to Palestine in viably compatible terms, statehood being paramount. 'Hosting', either way, was not in view. *Ex hypothesi* an exclusivity sought an implicit 'vacancy' – a severely minimal other element apart.

Given human demography, this could not be had without local 'forfeiture' of its physical reach and despair of its cultural identity. 'The promised land' would have to be, in some way, 'the compromised land'. The 'compromise' would have to be renunciation of the victimization brought by the one party from alien lands and shores and by the other sustained in their native immediacies. Naked anger can serve only a bitter futility.

Palestinians, an observer from beyond the fray might say, have been reliving in sharply concentrated form the 'Gentile' identity of old Philistia, as shaped by Zion's destiny today. The encounter is therefore an agonizing version of the ancient question only Jews and Judaism can resolve, namely how Jewishness belongs with humankind without 'Gentilizing' all the width and wealth of nations. The 'victims' on both sides of the Israeli–Palestinian divide are not merely casualties of a regional conflict but captives of an age-long story.

In 'Holy Cross Day', perhaps the grimmest of his poems, Robert Browning excoriates the sadistic cruelty of the medieval Church in requiring Jews to listen to sermons on 14 September in reproach for the crucifixion. There is no mistaking the fervour of his revulsion from the ritual nor the tragic query with which he concludes.

Ay, the children of the chosen race
Shall carry and bring them to their place:
In the land of the Lord shall lead the same,

Bondsmen and handmaids. Who shall blame,
When the slaves enslave, the oppressed ones o'er
The oppressor triumph for evermore?[25]

The poet recognized the human instinct but could not then know how it would miscarry.

Notes

1 Amos Oz, *Ha-matsav Ha-shlishy*, p. 40, quoted from *Israel Affairs*, vol. 1, no. 2 (Spring 1993), p. 217. The Hebrew title means 'The Third Position'.

2 The inverted commas are used throughout to suggest a characterization which, though common enough, needs exploration – later.

3 No one has made this point more eloquently, and with sustained insistence through a novel a year over two decades, than Elie Wiesel. This verdict about 'victims' and 'survivors' comes in *Legends of Our Time* (New York, 1968), p. 233.

4 Though, strictly, the word 'army' is not used. What Israel has are 'Israeli *Defence* Forces'. The question of youth is not affected.

5 The comment belongs with numerous occasions when peacemaking evoked assurances in those terms. Israel's 'security' cannot, ideologically, be at risk to factors not under Israeli control.

6 The *Altalena* was a supply ship bringing an arms consignment for the Irgun forces which contravened 'ceasefire' agreements made by Haganah and Ben Gurion. Begin was determined to have the arms, Ben Gurion determined – by the immediate politics of the agreement and by antipathy to Begin and his stance – to ensure they were not unshipped. Begin, on board, escaped when shore batteries fired at the vessel, named after the pen-name of Jabotinsky, the adored of the Irgun.

7 The hindsight argument that Palestinians could have 'contained' Israel by accepting the none the less grievous partition, instead of doing battle and allowing Israel to 'succeed by success' beyond Palestinian recoverability, will be studied in Chapter 8.

8 *The Seventh Day: Soldiers Talk about the Six-Day War*, various translators (London, 1971).

9 The kibbutzim played a major part and sustained, proportionately, the heaviest weight of casualties.

10 *The Seventh Day*, *passim*.

11 Ibid., pp. 148–9.

12 Ibid., pp. 175, 189 and 224.

13 Ibid., p. 23.

14 Ibid.

15 'The purity of arms' was a phrase frequent in Israeli circles and one that, for many, had to be strenuously repudiated in the invasions of Lebanon, however ideologically valid for the interpretation of 1967.

16 It is significant that militant Palestinianism was a direct consequence of the 1967 war. Initially the world thought of displaced Palestinians as 'refugees', stubbornly waiting for 'repatriation'. The war transformed that image. Begun only tentatively in 1964, Al-Fatah developed markedly after 1967. The war shattered any realism about 'return'. What *patria* remained? Further, it demonstrated the hopelessness of waiting for 'Arab nations' to deliver rescue. Thirdly, its trauma kindled a passionate resolve. In some respects, the impulses were not unlike those of Zionism itself and of Jewry *in extremis*.

17 Syria allowed in relatively few Palestinians and those it had (*Al-Sa'iqah*) it kept on a tight rein.

18 The French, with their Mandate, for reasons of their own, created a *Grand Liban* by adding areas in the north of Tripoli and in the far south (mainly Alouite and Shi'ah) that the Syrians regarded as theirs, transforming the Beirut region and the Shouf into a much larger, more complex identity at Syria's expense. Under that Mandate many aspects of what became two nation-states had been one.

19 'Insertion' here in respect of armed units. From 1948 Lebanon had received a large influx of tented Palestinians who were to suffer desperately in the civil conflict.

20 Geoffrey Elton, *Political History: Principles and Practice* (London, 1970), p. 177.

21 It is well to note that Lebanon is a very lopsided country, Beirut, its capital, being almost a majority of its total population.

22 On the US part in the whole equation see Chapter 9.

23 To be sure, it was not until April 1996 that the Palestine National Council deleted the clause in the Palestine National Charter requiring the liquidation of Israel in its state form. Israel, however, had not permitted the election of such a National Council until the year after Oslo, to formalize such a decision. The 1988 resolution was 'rubbished' by Yitzhak Shamir, and limbo-izing of the PLO persisted until the Madrid Conference of 1990.

24 Statistics, as in 1948, 1982 and again in 1996, pass themselves into bitter controversy and assuage no grief in doing so, but serious Israeli casualties in April 1996 were minimal compared with the more than a hundred deaths at Cana and the near half-million fugitives pouring into Beirut, with shelling on Tyre and Sidon. There need hardly be an urgent international appeal to restore the infrastructure anywhere in Israel. Nor was there word of Lebanese gunboats cruising lethally along the coastline between Haifa and Tel Aviv, nor were US warships in evidence shadowing the Israeli ones. Fewer than a hundred Israelis have been killed by Palestinian guerrillas since 1982. Katyusha rockets, to be sure, are horrendous on impact but merit little comparison with M109A1 howitzers, with their forward 'spotters' and M-172 proximity fuses, nor with helicopter-gunships of devastating fire-power over wellnigh undefended targets. Fond suspicions of bias cannot deflect – and ought not to silence – the witness of dire experience.

25 Robert Browning, *Poetical Works* (Oxford, 1949), p. 354.

7

The pawn of friends

The neat Lebanese proverb noted earlier advises you to 'choose your neighbour before you choose your house', *Al-Jar qabl al-Dar*. With noise pollution and much else it is, if feasible, a wise counsel. Territorially, however, nation-states have little option but to live with whatever contiguity history and geography have ordained. Palestine has long been unhappy because of its neighbours, often overrun by great powers round the southern corner of the Mediterranean and across the eastern deserts or, on one epochal occasion, inundated in conquest from the south-east. Its coastal areas have seen the traffic of empires, the flow and counter-flow of invasion and retreat. Jerusalem ranks among the most frequently ravaged and ruined of tribal capitals, the habitually besieged city.

In this century their Arab neighbourhood has proved a major factor in the woes of the Palestinians. The designs and then the steady outworking of Zionist intentions were seen from the beginning as constituting a challenge to the whole Arab world. The nationalisms had been concurrent, in contrasted terms, during the declining years of the Ottoman power. While Herzl cultivated the Sultan as someone with whom he might strike a bargain over a grant of Jewish right to settle, patriots already 'native' in Jaffa, Nablus and Jerusalem were urgently weighing whether their future lay in negotiated autonomy or outright rebellion. The contrast in those different cliencies had to do with comparable aspirations over which, at that point, Ottoman factors were seen to preside.

Even then the two parties, Palestinian and Zionist, were on a collision course, concealed or confused in the ambivalence we have studied in Chapter 4 but nevertheless inexorable, given the notions of ultimate statehood as the goal to which their logic led. Zionism could not fail to be an enterprise involving Jews everywhere, so Palestinianism could only live and have its being in the whole Arab milieu which place, time and culture gave to it. Arabism would be responding to the thrust of Zionism with emotions of political unison as one assertive identity, yet necessarily operating physically on the terrain of Palestine. For good or ill Palestinianism would always be a dimension of Arabness, yet one which needed to affirm its own particularity. The need grew, in fact, in reaction to the experiences stemming from the wider participation. The Arab sponsorship at large, on which, in the trauma of early refugeedom, the Palestinians first relied, proved such a dubious reliance that they were compelled to develop a resolute quality of their own. So doing, however, they could never contrive to operate except under the constraints of territory, power and politics determined by their neighbours. These, in turn, used their constraining roles to indulge their own rivalries and pursue their own ends, with lip-service to the emotions of Arabism and hand-service to their own illusions of grandeur or follies of power.

It is this sorry story that this chapter must review as not the least painful aspect of Palestinian experience. The story is a tangled one, its sometimes sordid details too devious to trace in full. The aim here is to sense, rather than to document, the sad ways in which Palestine was cruelly in pawn to the devices of the wider Arabism that might have been its saviour. There are few enemies so crucial as pseudo-friends.

II

The survey need not be chronological. It can well begin with its most dramatic index in the débâcle of 1967. The events of that fateful summer might almost have been deliberately devised to present Israel with the perfect scenario, a setting in which to accomplish its dearest objectives and do so with the aura of total legitimacy and decisive finality. So far was this the case that one might imagine a subtle and sinister 'double-agent' in the very heart of Egyptian policy, creating Israel's golden opportunity. The irony only deepens in that Israel was able to 'play' the situation – and perhaps even experience it – as the most mortal of critical extremities. In retrospect, 'Abd al-Nasir's *démarche* at Sharm al-Shaikh in the spring of 1967 virtually condemned the Palestinians to the tragic consequences from which the Oslo Accords in the 1990s have tenuous hope of saving them. It was the most signal occasion of political folly, virtually consigning the Palestinian cause to irreparable loss.

Explanation of the motive or the logic is not hard to seek and takes the enquirer directly to inter-Arab tensions. The collapse of the short-lived 'United Arab Republic' of Egypt, Syria and Yemen earlier in the 1960s had left much enmity and festering suspicion between the two former, while 'Abd al-Nasir's ill-starred intervention in the civil war in Yemen left him avid for prestige repair elsewhere. There is no doubt that what came to be known as 'Nasserism' at that point in time was a widespread indulgence by the Arab world of its collective pride and ardour for vindication. Israel was at once the major factor in its stimulus and the obvious target of its energies.

A complex of events and cross-currents of intrigue precipitated the June war of 1967 which presented Israel with a clear *casus belli* by which it contrived incredible 'correction of frontiers' – a goal which military activists had long had in mind – and with that *casus belli* a complete approving sanction on the part of international opinion in the West, if not also in the Third World. On both counts, i.e., political exoneration and military opportunity, Israel was presented with a situation fulfilling its wildest dreams and maximized it simply by letting its Arab adversaries contrive their own frustration by inept diplomacy and desperate blunder. Those futilities were made all the more evident by the contrast with Israeli sagacity, calculation and resourcefulness – qualities that lurked cunningly behind an appearance of extreme vulnerability fit to ensure the wondering admiration of wide approval as the crowning *fait accompli* to clinch all the others, past and yet to come. What logic could 'Abd al-Nasir conceivably have followed?

That it went so incredibly awry does not argue it feckless. It is clear that he did not expect, or wish, to do battle. The aim was diplomatic. The circumstances stemmed from 1956 when Israeli aggression, in connivance with Britain and France, had seized the Sinai peninsula. The intention had been to humble Egypt, as the major Arab power (given the circumstances created by the Suez crisis), and also to ensure the sea access to Israel's back door to Eilat via the Straits of Tiran and the Gulf of Sinai. Within three months President Eisenhower had required withdrawal by Israel, to the chagrin of Ben Gurion. The USA was never again to react with such forthrightness. A United Nations Emergency Force was set up on the borders and, by a tacit agreement, Israeli shipping was allowed through the Egyptian waters of Tiran while carrying a non-Israeli flag, thus preserving a required protocol.

'Abd al-Nasir's tactics called for a partial withdrawal of the UNEF from Egypt's side of the border (though not from the Gaza Strip nor from Tiran), the aim being to establish a counter, in diplomacy, as a means of responding to a situation sharply affecting his prestige on the Syrian borders. It is evident that he did not intend warfare and had made no preparations for it. But when the UN indicated that partial withdrawal was impossible, he was out on a limb and beginning to lose control of his strategy.

The issues in the north had to do with long-simmering border conflicts between Israel and Syria over the demilitarized zones surviving from the 1948–49 conflicts, which Israel had taken over and which had crucial relevance to water resources. Israel's capacity to make unsettling raids into border territory had been sharply emphasized in the Hebron area in the (then) Jordanian-held 'West Bank' in 1961 and shown the utility of such raids in engendering anger and recrimination between Arab states and the developing militancy of Palestinians within them. The early spring and summer of 1967 were marked by rumours, and some evidence of Israeli military intentions against Syria. Given the Arab emotions, which still centred on 'Nasserism', and the political instincts of their *Qutb* to fulfil them,[1] it was all a ripe field for gibe and passion as long as Egypt was sheltered by UN forces and Arab solidarity lay under test.

The perennial tangle of Israeli security from 'provocation' and the perpetual 'provocation' it engendered had acute phases in the pre-June exchanges of 1967. Israeli counsels were ostensibly divided – though ends were fostered, as was normally the case, rather than crippled by the fact. Prime Minister Eshkol and Chief of Staff Rabin warned Syria that rapid retaliation would be inflicted on any incursions, though others thought that these, while being a nuisance, were no cause for war. However, the postures against Syria were threatening and 'Abd al-Nasir was made, or allowed, to think so, thus creating a context of crisis calling for him to make good his pan-Arab role of leadership, while Israel still wore the mantle of the really threatened people. Moreover, were Syria to be invaded and neutralized, Egypt would have been in jeopardy.

The diplomacy that aimed to relieve Syria via bargains on Sharm al-Shaikh collapsed into a scenario where vigorous Israeli attack on the morning of 5 June 1967 set in train a totally humiliating defeat for the entire Arab forces, withal enjoying the warrant – in international eyes – of legitimate self-defence.[2]

Deploying successive raids the first morning on Egyptian air-strips on the whole front, the Israeli air force destroyed the entire air-cover of the Egyptian ground forces, consigning them to steady elimination in succeeding days and virtually excluding Egypt from the equation. Badly co-ordinated, the Syrian and Jordanian land forces could be severally dealt with by the prowess and superb competence of the Israelis. Once war had been joined by that pre-emptive strike and its immediate success, it was impossible for Jordan to hold aloof, prudent as neutrality would have been. Israel took occasion to resolve its long problem in the north-east by occupying the Golan Heights and a large swathe of Syrian territory towards Damascus. Most emphatically of all, it secured the ultimate prize of Jerusalem Old City and with it the entire 'west bank' as far as the river. There its valour had been most costly and its rewards ecstatic.

'Abd al-Nasir, it is fair to say, never really recovered from the trauma of the June war and the inept miscalculations that had led to it. Popular emotions came to his aid on his gesture of deserved forfeiture of power, but the renewal of his tenure saw the steady demise of Nasserism until he himself passed from the scene three years later, after his Chief of Staff had committed suicide. King Husain of Jordan suffered the truncation of his kingdom, the Israelis insisting that only his own folly made him a party to the conflict, while gratefully redeeming the occasion it had afforded them. 'Are we to be reproached for winning?' – their obviously legitimate stance – continued long to be the acid in the etching of the total Arab catastrophe.

As for the Palestinians, they paid the heaviest price of all in the bitter renewal and enlargement of refugeedom, the forfeiture of territory essential to their political survival, the besetting fear of an exile time would never repair, and the anguish of an Arab bungling and betrayal of the very shape of hope. Nowhere did Arabism more desperately gamble with its meaning than in the tragedy of 1967. The Palestinians bore the penalty, but not the shame, of its ineptitude, its treason to itself.

III

Sadly, the June war was only the most signal of occasions to have the measure of their destinies. The significance of its drama and its sequel justified its being taken here in precedence over earlier times in which Palestinian fates were at the mercy of fellow-Arabs. In the earliest days, it would seem that Arab minds were too trustful of Jewish intentions. They could not, of course, have foreseen in the 1920s the enormous implications that would flow in the next two decades from the rise of Hitler. No Zionist at that time was yet aware of the desperate urgency Nazism would give to what was a still modest quest for territorial repossession.[3] We have noted earlier how well ambivalence served not to arouse undue unease or suspicion. Egypt in

1925 gave formal recognition to the British Mandate over Palestine and Trans-Jordan, and made no reservations concerning the Jewish National Home the Mandate 'required' the Mandatory power to facilitate. It was only concerned that the border agreed with the Ottomans in 1906 should remain.[4]

This was in spite of several visits from Al-Hajj Amin al-Hussaini, Grand Mufti of Jerusalem, to Cairo to plead more circumspection. He found the Egyptian Press largely quiescent or acquiescent,[5] the issues far in the margin of Cairene concern. Neither the national leader Sa'd Zaghlul nor King Fu'ad made gestures of serious interest, and lesser politicians showed Zionist sympathies and stressed conciliation. Inter-Arab factors no doubt contributed. King Fu'ad aspired to the Caliphate and Al-Hussaini opposed that ambition. Trans-Jordanian opinion had the favouring constraints of its own anticipation of separate status. Syrian minds, which had been in the forefront of Arab 'liberation', had their own preoccupations with the frustrating betrayal they were undergoing in the French Mandate. Iraq would emerge from mandatory control only in 1930 and then with a penchant for continuing British *politique*.

It was after the disturbances of 1929 that Arabs at large – religious emotions and common folk rather than official governments – became restive as suspicion grew over the ultimate designs of Zionist ambition and the steady influx of settlers. In Egypt the tripartite subtleties of the Crown, the Wafd and the British cared more about the disruptive dangers of religious passions aroused around Jerusalem than for the ultimate destiny of the Palestinian population. With the British and French effectively in military control of the area from the Sudan to Aleppo, Arab nationalism had only modest potential for intellectual or practical response to the progress of Zionist purpose.

The Arab revolt of 1936 in Palestine saw the first international action by Arab states. The 'League of Arab States', precursor of the larger 'Arab League' of the 1940s and onwards and composed of seven members, was recognized by major powers as having the right to act in concert on the Palestine issue. Its representatives participated in the London 'Round Table' Conference of 1939. The League's seventh Article laid down the principle of unanimity but vitiated it by allowing majority decisions to be binding only on the states accepting them. Further, even decisions agreed by accepting states were to be enforced in them only in accordance with the basic laws obtaining in each.

The result was no more than a satisfying gesture that sanctified the *status quo* of competitive self-interest. Arabs could not hope to escape the tensions evident enough in the eighteenth-century making and retaining of American union, and those besetting European union more recently. They had several consultations in the early 1940s with a view to post-war situations but the League made no judicial provision for the definitive interpretation of its rules. A state could withdraw without obligation legally to explain its reasons. No authority was devised, still less effectuated, to establish any legal priority over separate jurisdictions, civil or political. The fragility of its intentions was grimly revealed when, beyond much verbal bluster, it miserably failed in 1948 to create any overall military command of armed forces. Its secretariat had no authentic supranational powers capable of disciplining sectional interests. Even cultural and economic co-operation failed to yield any lasting progressive unifying of political purposes. There would seem to be a special Arab dimension of the obduracies attending on human collectives.

Juridically the League held that Palestine had become an autonomous entity by its post-1919 detachment from the Ottoman Empire. It argued that the League of Nations Mandate, for all its pledge of encouragement to Jewish immigration, conceded, indeed required, the ultimate statehood of the people under it. At least in terms of Wilsonian idealism, it was in no sense a 'colony' but a 'trusteeship'. The British might sadly be caught in an impossible reconciliation of contrary obligations, but the very vehemence of the Jewish Agency's arrogation of the Mandate to its own ends proved how actual was the mandatory obligation to an eventually autonomous Palestine.

To their cost, the Arab states lacked any comparable tenacity in stating and asserting their protégé's legal stake in the Mandate and its meaning. The *de jure* situation within the League of Nations was incontrovertible, the Balfour Declaration in itself having absolutely no juridical value prior to its incorporation into the League's Mandate to Britain. Lacking the foresight of realism about the potential of Zionist purposes, the League of Arab States, at the time of the Peel Commission and the beginnings of 'partition' logic, could only join the Palestinian chorus of emotion about indivisible territory and absolute right. These doubtless had their valid urgency – for Palestinians most of all, for theirs were the farms and the homesteads under creeping threat of deprivation. Arab powers, at physical if not emotional remove, might have been expected to calculate more discerningly what, as resistance, offered the best hope of being significant, all odds considered. The League, however, lacked the political cohesion and the spiritual perception to prove more than feeble counsellors and barren allies. Zionists could out-think and out-manoeuvre them at every turn.

There was one unhappy aspect of the League of Arab States' inability to adopt effective Palestinian protection. It had to do with the purchase of land by Jewish Land Fund activity from, in many cases, absentee Arab landowners, some of them wealthy residents in Lebanon. Villagers were thus steadily deprived of agricultural holdings, while Jewish enterprise was afforded the legitimate alibi that land had been fairly acquired. Later the notion of a 'purchased' Yishuv would take ample place in Jewish apologetic, while ignoring the hardship entailing on Palestinian peasantry. Arab states were short-sightedly mindless of this process of legitimate land attrition, or too effete to counter it effectively by concerted action. For lack of it, 'Israelis' (for such they were even then steadily becoming) could often duly plead that their 'interest' in land enabled the owners to become exorbitant, extracting higher and higher prices, sacrificing political wisdom to private greed, and building vicarious tombs. When in due course partition came, linking up isolated pieces played a major part in map-devising.

IV

The *nakbah*, or 'disaster', as Arabs came to call it, of 1947–49, if more readily explicable, was hardly less catastrophic than that of 1967. Aspects of the encounter have concerned most previous chapters here. The inner Palestinian issues belong in the chapter to follow. Those occupying the territory could be forgiven for being in no emotional case to distinguish between the wisdom of 'containment' and the legitimacy of indignation. Three decades later the Likud mentors had taught their partisans to swear the eternal indivisibility of the land, defying all and sundry to dare to 'partition our country'. Palestinians had even better right, *de facto*, to think likewise and with equal passion in 1947. But Arab statesmen at large might have been expected to anticipate the likely future with more circumspection.

Had they observed the fact, which the Israelis-to-be had realized, in time and sagaciously, they would have seen that partition was a likelihood they would do well to reckon with intelligently. The Jews had discussed it diligently, considering how to preserve the ideology of an indivisibly Jewish 'holy land' and yet secure pragmatically whatever might be currently feasible. Only in hindsight did Arab intellectuals argue the merits of a policy of 'containment' of Israel against the passion of an 'all-or-nothing' confrontation. Given the diplomatic finesse of Jewish personnel like Abba Eban at the United Nations, and the Jewish leverage in US politics, the Arab states were at an acute disadvantage in the crucial vote in November 1947. It is no comfort to reflect that after its later enlargements the UN would never have voted the partition.

Once it had been resolved, acceptance – however galling – could arguably have contrived to hold the Israeli state within the 52 per cent dimensions it was allowed. Never since has the possibility of a genuinely viable Palestinian state been so desirably real or so really attainable. The logic, within Palestinianism, will be explored in Chapter 8. In 1947, however, Palestinians in the world arena had no status beyond what their Arab sponsors, the three neighbouring states, could command.

The sorry tale of their futility is well known. Their angry, inflated rhetoric only served to give semblance to the Zionist legend of a hapless 'David' ringed around with massively crushing enemies, wrong-footing their cause in the news arena. Their military preparations were uncoordinated and prey, especially on the Egyptian front, to long-standing corruption and incompetence in the body politic. Israel had the advantage of fighting on interior lines, albeit on three fronts, and of an *élan* born of desperate urgency and inner fervour. In the throes of birth the new state had skilfully manipulated the circumstances attending the withdrawal of the Mandatory. Above all, it was served by resolute and unrelenting leadership. Even the ugly tensions between the Haganah and the Irgun could be uneasily fused into the single goal of survival and victory, the excesses of the Irgun – as in the massacre of Dair Yasin[6] – serving the common ends while subject to the image-caring reprobation of the wily Haganah. The vigour – and the anguish – of interior discipline in Jewish arms and politics, demonstrated, for example, in the sinking of the *Altalena*,[7] had no counterpart in the story of Arab war-making during the decisive months before and between the truces of 1948–49.

There were heroic episodes on the southern front and notably in the salient west of Jerusalem and the 'corridor' to it. The net result of Arab intervention in the Palestinian cause was irreversibly to reduce the territorial prospect of a viable Palestinianism from the near half-and-half measure of 1947 to the mere fifth that remained when the truces were sealed – and only for a bare eighteen years until 1967 supervened. What diplomacy might have clinched in 1947 and arguably have finalized,[8] fatal confrontation had, as it proved, irrevocably forfeited. All the classic elements of tragedy were present. The inter-Arabizing of the Palestine issue, if we may employ the phrase, was, on every count of Arab feeling and of Palestinian realism, inevitable. The inevitable proved to be the disastrous. There was the cruellest irony in the steady Israeli insistence that Palestinians were Arabs and that their only refuge was among them.

V

The period between the débâcle of 1948–49 and the ensuing one in 1967 laid a searching responsibility towards the Palestinians on the conscience and the politics of the Arab world. There was the bitter onus of the Arab failure either to realize the strategy of containing Israel or to succeed in forcibly defeating it. With that onus was the desperate business of under-taking the flood of refugees into camps in what remained of Palestine and in Jordan, Lebanon and, minimally, Syria. What could, what should, be the politics of this new diaspora – a diaspora due in part, or in whole, to inter-Arab bungling and ineptitude?

A strange parallel emerged with Jewry itself. In the 'Enlightenment' time, diaspora Jewry had been striving to 'establish a natural right to exist unquestioned in the lands of their birth'.[9] Deciding they were fated to fail, the Zionists among them opted for a nationalism of their own, exhorted by their Pinskers, Herzls, Nordaus and Jabotinskys. Palestinians (the theme of Chapter 8) came to do the same but with a subtle difference. The 'natural right to exist unquestioned in the land [singular] of their birth' had been vetoed, partially, by the feat of Zionist arms in 1948. This was the more galling inasmuch as, unlike the long Judaic diaspora, theirs was an indigen-ous dispersion. The nationalism they developed was simply an intensified form of a native quality. The story belongs elsewhere.

The present concern is with the inter-Arab aspects of their unquestioned right to the land of their birth, the right now requiring the 'nationalism' of exile from it. A refugee is bitterly such *de facto*. What of *de jure*? In one sense, a *de jure* refugee is a contradiction in terms. The ultimate aim of Zionist policy was to end that contradiction, i.e., to make the Palestinian exodus, as far as it had been contrived or had usefully occurred, a permanent reality. It therefore seemed to Arab counsels a proper policy to perceive Palestinian refugeedom as a temporary condition. Hence the long persisting misery of the camps, subsisting by the ministrations of the United Nations Relief Works Agency (UNRWA). It was argued that 'resettlement' in Arab lands would compromise the demand for 'repatriation'. Only in Jordan were Palestinians allowed access to citizenship. Elsewhere the Arab world withheld that privilege, except in rare cases. Jordan had taken over the West Bank territory and Palestinians came to comprise a large segment of its people.

When, or if, the shape of the future is unclear, we act by near-sightedness which, in the event, turns into short-sightedness if maintained when time has receded. The dilemma was a cruel one. Permanent resettlement of refugees would have played into the hands of Israeli policy, the logic of which had always been that extra-Palestinian lands were the right place for Palestinian Arabs. Yet holding on to the miseries of refugeedom in the name of eventual repatriation played no less into the hands of Israeli propaganda as being heartless, inhuman, a sacrifice of pity to politics. Why could not Arabs emulate the resourceful, compassionate energies of Jewry in the repair of human tragedy? The Arab states could be made to seem heartless bigots trading on human wretchedness to satisfy political obstinacy. Lapsing years did nothing to diminish the indictment.

If not Arab recalcitrance then Arab disunity perpetuated Palestinian refugeedom. Not to have seen the original merit of containment of Israel was matched by failure to act on the evident indices available through those two decades. In the event, Palestinians realized that self-help would have to be their main, if not their sole, hope of salvation, though still one cruelly beholden to inter-Arab mercies. Already, in 1956, the Suez crisis and Israeli invasion of Sinai demonstrated the latent pugnacity of Israel, its seizure of any occasion presented to its incessant preoccupation with security. Could there have been any viable Arab *politique* at that juncture that might have contained that explicit anti-Arab belligerence, reassured its neurosis about jeopardy and encouraged it to think in terms of the ultimate security of the right 'neighbourhood' it takes 'neighbours' to achieve? The answer is 'Probably not'. In any event, no such *politique* was forthcoming. Even temperate Arab counsels had no reason to hope that Israel, on its own terms, would ever prove compatible within the region as Arab history identified it.

So the Palestinians remained in their camps, cherishing forlorn hopes, while Nasserism consoled Arab pride and indulged political illusions until the explosion of 1967. In its very intensity it captured in one drama the stultifying of Arab vision through all the years that led to it. The aftermath of 1967 would test that vision in still more vexing terms, while yielding yet more evidence – if some exoneration – of how intractable the whole equation cumulatively proved to be.

If Nasserism prior to 1967 was the central Arab resource, both about power and in the psyche, it was because Syria was beset with instability and sharp feuding around the Ba'th idea. The Asad regime was in part the delayed sequel in Syria to 1967. The original visionaries of the Ba'th or 'resurrection' ideology, Michel Aflaq and Salah al-Din al-Bitar, had focused their concept on a 'unity' of the Fertile Crescent, Syria, Lebanon and Iraq, with an exotic wave of sentiment towards Cyprus. Lebanon, as already noted in the context of 1982, was ever 'a special case', of close relevance to Syrian perceptions of Syria. How well, or how far, Ba'th perspectives could have stretched to genuine Palestinian inclusion, debatable in itself, was precluded by a tragic subjugation of the ideologues to the fratricidal conflicts of the men of power. Israel had no difficulty in outlasting the serial struggles in Damascus. Lebanon, as Lebanon, was dependably innocuous until after the next violent episode in the inter-Arab entanglement of the Palestinian cause.

VI

That entanglement bears the name of 'Black September'. The year was 1970. The events of that summer were a further dire expression of the dilemma besetting inter-Arab action and of total failure to surmount it. It had to do with the steady development, by Palestinians, of their own active 'resistance' in a militancy of their own. The impulse had grown in the early 1960s but came into determined shape after the tragedy of 1967. The weary years of refugee status, awaiting the vaunted all-Arab salvation, had endured the bitter lesson of hope deferred and, finally, denied. The initiation of an autonomous militancy by Al-Fatah and other groups, later merged into the Palestine Liberation Organization, signalled a despair about the pan-Arab aegis in the form of ardent 'self-help'.

Its tragedy was that there was no 'autonomy' to be had. It might be willed in emotional terms; it could not be had in military terms. The Arab 'neighbourhood' or hinterland, which had cruelly blundered in riding to the rescue in 1948 and 1967, controlled the terrain from which Palestinian militancy could operate. After 1967 Israel was in effective control of the West Bank where no large-scale, significant military resistance could be mounted. Jordan, Syria and Lebanon, if at all, must furnish, and sustain, occasion for Palestinian action. Doing so in terms that Palestinian ardour and extremity required meant a certain fusion of host-nation sovereignty and Palestinian autonomy – a situation which called for strong political skill and negotiation. These, in the event, proved sadly wanting.

Jordan, with its large concentration of Palestinian émigrés within its borders, still cherished a sense of Jordanian identity and a pride in an independence it was unwilling to compromise, still more to forfeit, in response to the exigencies of Palestinian action. Moreover, operations against Israel, however modest, engendered sharp retaliatory raids that endangered life and limb in Jordan. The refugee camps were an obvious arena for the recruitment, training and deployment of resisters. As such, what of Jordanian control and policing? Could they be allowed to develop into bits of Palestinian extra-territoriality within Jordan? 'Palestine' might be a 'sovereignty' other Arabs were ready to 'recognize' in vague terms but not one to be accorded rights outside the only area in which they were relevant – and impossible.

The conflict implicit in the desire of Palestinian resisters to exercise a free Palestinian hand on Jordanian soil came to a head in the third summer of its incidence in Jordan in the form of 'Black September'. Despite the broad hospitality to emigrants from Palestine, the state of Jordan was in no mood to tolerate any action, implied or demanded, that refused Jordanian control and impugned Jordanian sovereignty. The emerging PLO saw liberty of action as crucial to their hopes. The inter-Arab mind found no agreed solution, for all the elusive talk of total solidarity. King Husain decided on the complete expulsion of Palestinian militants in what came to be known as 'the battle of Beds and Feds'. He used the same Jordanian army that had battled valiantly, if unsuccessfully, in 1967 to hold Arab Jerusalem, to expel erstwhile comrades. That army had its core traditions from the 'bedouin' Jordanians, i.e. 'Beds', now bitterly engaged with the *fida'iyyun* ('Feds') from the PLO, who resisted strongly.

It was a desperate chapter in the inter-Arab story, leaving a long legacy of enmity between the parties and mutual suspicion. Whether King Husain could ever have fully made the Palestinian cause his own in terms of state sovereignty, or whether the Palestinians would have allowed the fusion, historians can only surmise. It may be evident that Israeli power did the utmost to ensure, by reprisal raids and other diplomatic means, that no such fusion should transpire. The issue was further complicated by international factors, the nature of the Jordanian economy and long-standing tensions in the psyche of differing regions of a common Arabness.

Worse was to follow in the pawn experience of a Palestinianism seeking in vain to be a 'sovereignty' with no territorial base ensured by common Arab will. For 'Black September' simply transferred the dilemma to the fragility of Lebanon, where – unchanged in its basics but tragically aggravated by Lebanese factors – it would precipitate civil strife within four anxious years. With all its complexities, Lebanon would prove the most anguished symbol of inter-Arab conflict betraying inter-Arab ideology.

Syria, now at the beginning of the Asad regime which was to prove the most durable in its modern story, was in no mood to harbour the problem, its Palestinian elements being few and under rigorous control. Instead it relayed it into the potential disintegration of Lebanon – a sequel which duly followed. Its inevitability could have been foreseen. Perhaps it was ignored as being insuperably vexing for separate Arab interests, ambitions and intrigues.

The elements in the situation were evident enough. Syria had long assumed a special role in Lebanon. Large Lebanese areas in the far south and far north had been detached from Syria by the French, for reasons of their own, at the outset of the Mandate. Resented by the Syrians, this had diversified still further the chronic, still largely feudal, divisions of Lebanese society, making more difficult any sustained national Lebanese identity which the Maronite Christian core sought, despite the enlarged frontiers, to confine to its own emotions and its own ends. The vexing question 'Who are the Lebanese?' would become steadily more vexed after the Palestinian would-be armed presence arrived.

The situation had been viable in immediate post-Mandate years thanks to the sanctions of trade – always significant to the Lebanese – and to the concordat between the Maronites and the Sunni Muslims. Palestinian refugees, only second in number to those in Jordan, had been in Lebanon from 1948. Hospitality to them as refugees was generously given or obtained. They remained pitifully innocuous in numbers that grew with the years. With very few exceptions there was no acquiring of citizenship. The camps were assumed to be waiting forlornly for 'repatriation', the misery of their presence, for all parties, accentuating with time.

With the advent of the PLO and other elements, all the issues emerged which had bedevilled the far more homogeneous state and society of Jordan. Lebanon was in no shape to resolve them. In due course precisely the same question arose: 'Who is master in Lebanon?' It could in no way be answered forthrightly as it had been in Amman. The Lebanese were at odds about the same question and were coming to be more so precisely because Palestinianism raised it so sharply. It could no longer remain tacit or implicit. The question hid a further one: 'Who is to say?'

Answering both questions unleashed a multiple schism in the fabric of the country. Its constitution provided for a confessional make-up of Parliament and government according to the relative size of the religious communities, based on a long-obsolete census. The several Muslim, Christian and Druze sects were characterized by tribal and local family dynasties reflecting, in part, the old feuds and legends of the land. The whole order of things proved tragically precarious with the coming of the fall-out from 'Black September'. For it faced Lebanon with a radical decision about its very identity in urgent, potentially violent terms – a decision which, the Palestinians apart, *might* have been indefinitely deferred or resolved by intelligent neglect. Was Lebanon, by broadly Christian tradition essentially Mediterranean, only Arab as – at most – a bridge from Europe into Arabism? Syria, of course, could have none of this, being its ineluctable bond into the hinterland. Nor, for the most part, could Lebanese Muslims, already relenting from their fascination with Nasserism but looking for some other shape of effective Arab pride.

If ever there was a decisive vocation for Arab political genius it lay here in Lebanon. None was forthcoming. The elements first of tension, then of fracture and violence, proved untameable. There had been a brief pre-run back in 1958 which, in that milder form, had been weathered by the sagacity of General Shihab.[10] By the mid-1970s passions would be implacable. Were the Palestinian camps to become training grounds and action posts for raids on Israel? Reprisal sufferings apart, sanctioning such would draw Lebanon into a form of Arabism incompatible with Maronite dreams. Refusing the Palestinians their liberty would be to repeat the treachery of King Husain to the inclusive Arab cause. On the one view, a Lebanon sucked into antagonism to Israel would no longer be the Lebanon of Phoenician ideals. On the other, a Lebanon absconding from the urgent demands of Arabness as Palestinianism required them would be denying its true identity.

There were confusing intermediate positions, an urge for *status quos* of trade and peace. Nor was Israel a negligible dimension in the domestic issue. Going the pan-Arab way would invite her fist and clout in menacing power as long as Palestinians were harboured other than as refugees. Permanency in refugeedom, with which Maronite Lebanese would have connived all too readily, was just the anathema the PLO was avid to resist. A Maronite-style Lebanon would not only inhibit Palestinianism, it would negate its whole *raison d'être*. For some Lebanese it could even transpire that Israel would tacitly or openly suggest an emulation of itself, conspiring with some Lebanese to realize the common Arab 'enemy' and envisage a Lebanon, client to Israel and emulating Israeli resourcefulness in self-assertion and some conceivable alliance. The least suspicion of such a scenario was further fuel to inter-Lebanese enmity.

All these factors combine to explain the internecine hatred that developed between some Lebanese and the Palestinian elements, the massacres of Tell Zatar, Chatila and Sabra, and Palestinian devastation at places like Damour. The enmity became implacable. Moreover, the tangle of refugees and militants meant that the former were drawn into tragic suffering by the very violence intended to bring them final rescue.

The entire story is of relentless tragedy as Lebanon sank into chaos and angry confusion lasting some fifteen years in blood and destruction.[11] What matters here is the utter bankruptcy of the Arab League, stressed and stymied by quarrelsome sovereignties and inter-Arab intrigue. Syria played its own game, shifting fronts from time to time, consistent only in a will to ensure that, in whatever eventuality, Lebanon remained firmly within its control, bargaining with Lebanese factions with the card of an 'eventual withdrawal' that was never 'on the cards'. In the early years of the long tragedy, Egypt under Sadat made its own peace with Israel, purporting – Israeli ambivalence allowing – to achieve Palestinian autonomy by 'linkage' in the Camp David agreement. That Begin had different intentions we saw in Chapter 4. Egypt's expulsion from the Arab League, which lasted for ten years, ensured her exclusion from the Lebanese issue, but also freed Israel, in her response to the northern imbroglio, from urgent preoccupations in the south. The net result was that Palestinian will to autonomy was doomed to increasing futility with desperate victimization.

It was not until 1988 that counsels by the Arab states achieved in Jiddah the plan which, after further delay and facilitated by sheer war-weariness, brought a *de facto* end to Lebanese warring, though not yet to the factions *de jure*. We take stock in Chapter 9 of the American factor in the prolonged crisis of inter-Arab tensions and the Lebanese civil war. For the more domestic Arab ones, it may be that no regional diplomacy could have resolved its tensions or allayed its passions. It had many Balkan-style aspects of intractability, reaching back into the memory of the Ottoman era. The whole truth in any history is never told. Yet a solidarity that could proclaim itself so fondly in rhetoric as Arabic could was deviously barren in the throes of its most acute political test.

VII

When Israel invaded Lebanon in 1982 it desperately intensified the tragedy but also, in ghastly terms, grimly satirized the failure, insisting, as it were, that Israel would resolve Lebanon's problem decisively where vacillation and intrigue had bedevilled it. By that time the antagonism within Lebanon had intensified, providing Israel with both an alibi and an occasion for intervention more emphatic than the trial run of 1978. By engineering recruitment of Lebanese factions for its own ends, Israel found a pretext for escalating its border problems into a full-scale invasion as far as Beirut and beyond, to expel Palestinianism for ever from its northern neighbour.

The element of revenge has concerned us elsewhere. There was also the dark possibility of exploiting the situation to the point of aligning the Maronite version of Lebanese nationalism with its own animosity to the Palestinians, making allies in the same ends. If there could be Major Haddad's client buffer 'army' on the northern border, why not a larger enclave of a Maronite expression, tributary to its Israeli sponsor, by the partitioning of a country demonstrably incapable of affirming its own unity? This was the dastardly potential of the 1982 invasion. That there were Lebanese minded to be inveigled that way is proved even by the hesitancy that balked at the prospect. The whole scenario was the ultimate measure of the bankruptcy that allowed it to be conceivable.

These several chronic aspects of inter-Arab postures and counsels around the vicissitudes and agonies of their Palestinian 'brothers', and the bitter experience of those refugees and militants from Palestine, belong with Chapter 8. Right from the first, when the Palestinians had been operating on their own soil in the truce period and post-1949 in the confusion of partial exile, before and after the catastrophe of 1967, through the Jordanian quarrel and expulsion, and in the fragility of Lebanon descending into anarchy, Palestinian interests had been prey to, or a pawn in, the politics of the neighbouring states. These had used and ill-used them in the pursuit of separate interests, accentuating potential or actual divisions among Palestinian groups and contriving that they should not become too autonomous and cease to be amenable to manipulation.

In these unhappy circumstances, what strikes the observer is the ineptness of the Arab League, manoeuvring to meet or not to meet as private advantage required, lacking bold clinching initiatives in repeated crises, meeting without effective decisions or deferring vital issues until they passed out of reckoning. There was no perceptive, united leadership in the aftermath of 1967, when there was a brief 'window of opportunity' to maximize on the thinking in Israel that advocated a generous 'land for peace' exchange. The famous UN Resolution 242 about 'territories occupied' that were to be relinquished was not pursued, though often cited. Its deliberate ambiguity was not recruited for Arab rather than Israeli ends.[12]

To be sure, the trauma of humiliation and defeat in 1967 required hero-ically perceptive leadership to make good the Arab potential in the genuine Israeli case for negotiation within Resolution 242. There was the intense desire for Jewish homogeneity; the unease – for Zionist idealists – in the prospect of a 'police state' enclosing a mass of non-Jewish, legitimately disaffected population; the fear of that population later outstripping the Jewish one; and the profitable bargain of dispensable territory for the inestimable final boon of peace. The case was genuinely made by some in Israel and could have been taken forward by resolute and unified Arab diplomatic initiative.

It was not to be, and maybe might never have availed. The window closed. Harder logic developed in Israel, maximizing not forgoing territory and aiming to resolve future issues about the homogeneity of the Jewish state in more brutal ways by the slow attrition of Palestinian will. Maybe also Egypt, the major party, needed to recover its sense of pride and capacity by the battles of 1973. By then Israel was less 'negotiable', thanks *inter alia* to the shock of that war; and in the ultimate event Egypt made its own extrication from the Palestine equation. It had every reason for doing so – retrieving its own 'home refugees' (no less than half the total of all Palestinian ones) out of Sinai and the Canal Zone, and recovering the Canal for the help of its economy.

It remains a measure of inter-Arab perceptions that Sadat's policy was read as treachery, despite his genuine hope of 'linkage' with a Palestine autonomy, because it relieved Israel of anxiety about its southern frontier. Israel was already mastering the northern and eastern frontiers readily enough. With US encouragement, it had long been Israeli policy to insist on Arabizing the Palestinian issue,[13] and on dealing separately with neighbouring Arab states. On both counts, Arab attitudes and action thoroughly vindicated that Israeli wisdom and at length played into its hands. There could be no clearer commentary on the illusion of Arab unity.

Other aspects of the whole history belong elsewhere in these chapters. It remains to raise one final query that must be remitted to Chapter 10. Is there something in the Arab soul, its instincts about language and its perception of identity, that explains what history tells? Ethnicity is a hazardous conjecture in the comprehension of events. Yet it may be said of history, as it has been noted of biography, that the past is never simply the past but a kind of prism through which is filtered the subject's own image. Historians, however, cannot presume that they have rightly seen it.

Notes

1 *Qutb*, as 'axis' or 'pivot' or – in politics – 'leading personality', was a familiar concept for Muslim Arabs as a focus where symbol musters emotions and hopes.

2 I have a vivid memory of a broadcast at noon that Monday, 7 June, by Michael Elkins, a BBC correspondent in Jerusalem, confidently telling the world that the war was already virtually over. He knew of the redoubtable strikes that had eliminated the Egyptian air force by confining it uselessly on runways and then serially destroying all its planes. Israeli tanks in Sinai would then have a walk-over. When he spoke, Jordan had not yet entered the fray but Israeli confidence about the south certainly aided the sharp battles for Jerusalem.

3 It is important to realize how long political Zionism remained a small minority movement in world Jewry. Without Nazism it might have remained a wistful rather than an undeniable cause.

4 Out of concern lest the British might be intending to bring Sinai within the territory of the Mandate.

5 *Al-Ahram* gave ready coverage to the activities of the Jewish Yishuv. Only *Al-Balagh* opposed the Zionist idea. The eminent Egyptian writer Ahmad Lutfi al-Sayyid was sent officially to represent Egypt at the inauguration of the Hebrew University in Jerusalem in

1925. See further Israel Gershoni and J. P. Jankowski, *Egypt, Islam and the Arabs, 1900–1930* (Oxford, 1986).

6 Bitter controversy and pseudo-exoneration have clouded the tragic story. The narrow extended corridor to west Jerusalem was the scene of desperate engagements in which there were atrocities on both sides. The symbolically infamous one occurred at the Palestinian village of Dair Yasin, in which the Irgun Zvi Leumi killed 254 unarmed villagers, men, women and children. Its leader Menahem Begin, thirty years later Prime Minister of Israel, denied he was ever a 'terrorist', but news of the slaughter, from which Haganah distanced itself, helped to precipitate the frightened exodus of Palestinian peasantry which, deliberately or otherwise, served well the Zionist policy. Mutual acts of outrage followed around Jerusalem.

7 The supply ship of the Irgun, laden with arms which Haganah wished to block during a truce in the summer of 1948 about the import of arms. When Begin, aboard the vessel, persisted, shore batteries sank the ship. Begin escaped. The incident sharpened the tension between the two participants in the Jewish war against the Palestinians. See further Chapter 6, note 6.

8 'Finalized' is a conjectural word, seeing that Zionist policy and diplomacy might well have escaped from any Arab strategy of 'containment' even if the Arabs had accepted partition. Israeli consent to come into being via a partition in no way abandoned the ideology of an indivisible 'holy land' or the purpose to attain it.

9 Saul Bellew, *To Jerusalem and Back* (London, 1976), p. 26.

10 General Shihab, a trusted Maronite from a family that decades earlier had been Muslim, had the *sagesse* and esteem to pacify the quarrels of that year. President Eisenhower's intervention also helped. There was no Shihab available in the mid-1970s.

11 For vivid documentation see Robert Fisk, *Pity the Nation: Lebanon at War* (Oxford, 1991).

12 The different interpretations that could be read in the Resolution (which may well have ensured its adoption) had to do with whether *all* or *some* of the 'territories occupied' were to be returned. If that was at issue, then endless negotiation would be possible, delaying tactics and prevarication. In the event, the Resolution was made to underwrite prolonged irresolution of its meaning, to the frustration of one party and the 'book' of the other.

13 By regarding it as belonging with Arabness at large and not as having to do with a 'local' nation existing in separate validity or credibility. Arab rhetoric itself might be cited for that view, though a genuine 'Palestinian' identity was to prove and authenticate itself in the very throes of its encounter with Zionism.

8
The politics of realization

I

The fault, dear Brutus, is not in our stars
But in ourselves that we are underlings.[1]

We will meet later the Brutuses in Palestinianism. For they had many occasions for such sentiment against self-excuse. Yet things reviewed in previous chapters would reasonably have us disputing with Cassius in Shakespeare's play were he on the stage of Palestinian history these scores of years. 'The fault' was grimly in 'their stars' – the array of adverse factors set against their hopes and aims. The list is formidable: a fated geographical location; the enormous burden of seeming to impede a modest reparation for the Holocaust – that deep alibi on which Zionism could rely; the steady bias of the United States in monitoring the issues; the ineptitude and blundering of Arab partners. 'Men at some time are masters of their fates' – and sometime not.

'Underlings' among things imponderable or seemingly incorrigible Palestinians too often were. That experience is where 'realization' begins, meaning that identity and the struggle to possess it are the very context in which its elements are known. Being and becoming belong together. Identity is known in the action it generates. It has been so with Zionists themselves. Palestinianism knows itself in what it endures. Its definition is its story, its story the theme of its definition. Self-realization is active as a struggle with circumstance, passive as a wakening to awareness. The two are one experience.

It is this that we mean in the chapter's title: the politics of identity, striven for and known. Chapter 10 has the poetry and literature of the story; here the concern is with the episodes and manoeuvres of the minders on the bridge. Previous chapters have measured how crippling and daunting the stresses were: the sheer fact of wide diaspora; the lack of any territory from which to retrieve dispersion; the obstacles to any real autonomy in policy; and the perceptions of pity rather than of justice which for too long dominated the world community. There was the actual or potential atrophy even of pity itself in the welter of propaganda concerning how everything had eventuated.

Things 'coming to grief' had to be countered by a 'coming from grief' with whatever resilience there might be. The struggle was for the recognition of identity in 'people terms': recognition from within the surrounding Arabism, recognition in the perceptions of the world at large, and – most grievously – recognition from the very Zionism that disowned it.

It might be said that a proximate attainment in this task came in the speech of the leader of the Palestinian delegation to the Madrid Conference in 1990, Dr Haidar 'Abd al-Shafi. He said:

> We the people of Palestine stand before you in the fulness of our pain, our pride and our anticipation, for we long harboured a yearning for peace and a dream of justice and freedom. For too long, the Palestinian people have gone unheeded, silenced and denied. Our identity negated by political expediency; our right for struggle against injustice maligned; and our present existence subdued by the past tragedy of another people. For the greater part of this century we have been victimized by the myth of a land without a people and described with impunity as the invisible Palestinians. Before such wilful blindness we refused to disappear or to accept a distorted identity. Our Intifadah is a testimony to our perseverance and resilience waged in a just struggle to regain our rights. It is time for us to narrate our own story, to stand witness as advocates of truth which has long lain buried in the consciousness and conscience of the world. We do not stand before you as suppliants, but rather as the torch-bearers who know that, in our world of today, ignorance can never be an excuse. We seek neither an admission of guilt after the fact, nor vengeance for past inequities, but rather an act of will that would make a just peace a reality.[2]

It had taken strenuous and desperate years to reach such a forum, to find such articulate language and to offer such magnanimity. Madrid left so much unresolved but it was a register of clarity and controlled passion culminating decades of groping stress and angry dismay. It stands as a climax to the realization of political destiny out of antecedents full of adverse odds without and within.

II

It is a far cry back to the 'Arab Ottomanism' where all things relevant began. The Arabs of the (then) Near East were in no way exempt from the stirrings and strivings of growing people-consciousness which drew Jewish writers like Leo Pinsker to write of 'Auto-Emancipation' and Moses Hess of 'Rome and Jerusalem'.[3] In their European case, however, the paradigm was Italian unification – a people repairing the fragmentation of Italy so that it might become again a single unity, one people for a whole land, a land as one people. In the Arab case, nationalism meant the exchange of a spreading imperial allegiance for its geographically diverse expressions, peoples affirming themselves *out* of a Caliphate rather than a people repairing their divisions.

The contrast was significant and the decisions more complex. There was a vigorous Arab Ottomanism lasting, for some, until the defeat of Turkey in 1918 made it irrelevant. Ought Arabs, as predominantly Muslims, to rebel against a hallowed Islamic submission such as the Caliphate demanded and deserved by its religious prestige? But did it deserve Arab fidelity? The dubiety turned partly on Ottoman attitudes. Were they genuine in offers of an Arab provincialism with secure autonomy on dependable terms? If so, loyalty should prevail. When, however, tyranny ruled, harsh and ruthless, an Arab Ottomanism seemed a craven humiliation, properly kindling a passionate rejection.

The issue was prolonged through many vicissitudes. Other factors entered in: European power-intrigue, economics and cultural tensions. The logic of prestige, passion and pride in the Arab Revolt and the victory of Allied Forces consigned Arab Ottomanism to history.[4] For a time, and for some activists, this emerging situation in the second decade of the twentieth century posed an unresolved question, namely, how unitary or how separated this new-found Arabism-in-opportunity would be. The Arabism, in struggle, had been composite – Syrians, Lebanese, Palestinians co-operating in its counsels and its risks and affording its martyrs. What form should their autonomy or autonomies assume? In effect, the Western powers, France and Britain, decided for them, American Wilsonian idealism being (as we note in Chapter 9) in eclipse. The Mandates took over, that in Syria abruptly imposed on a short-lived Hashimite crown, that in Iraq changed into a

Hashimite monarchy after a dozen years. There was no doubt about the geographical character of Lebanon, though the French drastically amended and enlarged it to the abiding disquiet of the Syrians.[5] What of Palestine?

The British quickly confirmed it as a west of Jordan entity and made the trans-Jordan territory into an Emirate with that name. Old maps still had Syria extending as far as Gaza and Beersheba a Syrian town. Indeed, the Ottoman Vilayat of Beirut extended southwards well beyond Nablus, while the Sanjaq of Jerusalem stretched from around Ramallah to Aqabah. The Caliphal administrative divisions have sometimes been invoked to show that there never was a 'Palestine' as a political or national identity.

True once, but only in Ottoman terms of administration. Davidic monarchy, not to say Zionist aspiration, had bestowed a discernible status and description on the territory so denoted. Was there not the Palestinian Talmud (otherwise the Jerusalem one)? Balfour had said where the 'favour with which he viewed it' was located and had named it by its name. And prior to these there was old Philistia of which the psalmist made satirical play. Zionism could hardly be itself and disavow a Palestine, even if it only thought of it as the place of Yahweh's 'real estate'.

The early 'politics of realization' had to do painfully with the odd necessity of having to insist 'we are we' and 'we are here', the strange onus of affirming the entity to be one. The decision out of Ottomanism, Arab-wise, had done that. Long-range and immediate factors ensured that Palestine possessed and required the right of recognition, by ancient heritage and immediate events. These had effectively politicized it in a delimited territory which was not Egypt, not Lebanon, not Syria and not Trans-Jordan. We have to add, without malice, 'not yet Israel'. For, that truth apart, there need have been no Zionism. The reality of Palestine could not, and would not, *per se* elide the Israeli confidence that the same land was eternally Jewish. Otherwise, there need have been no conflict. One cannot interpret the whole story as about a non-issue. The very vision and violence and version of land claim by Zionists underwrote the reality of Palestinianism. Neither side could find itself in strife if it pretended that the right of the other was something the other neither believed nor claimed and breathed and lived. Yet it took a *Palestina Agonistes* to be acknowledged as a Palestine at all.

The supreme irony is that the inner secret, the people–place fusion, was common to both. Palestinians, too, thought in their minds and felt in their souls the same nexus, 'the land as ours and we the land's', if without the kind of sanction Judaism perceived as unique to itself. The case made by an Israel-in-process is well analysed by Yossi Beilin:

To define the Arabs living in Palestine – and later Israel – as a nation leads to the necessary conclusion that they deserve the same right of self-determination demanded and received by Jews. Only by defining them as an entity that does not constitute a nation can one explain why they are not entitled to self-determination.

He goes on to cite Ber Borochov, an eminent Russian Zionist, with Moshe Beilinson in Israel, distinguishing between 'a people' and 'fragments of a people'. Returning, in effect, to the Ottoman situation, they claim that as 'fragments' Palestinians are not included in the otherwise legitimate nationalism of Arabs at large. The verdict is useful to Zion.[6] The 'fragment' had to assert its non-fragment quality and the task proved long and arduous. It was made all the harder because, as noted in Chapter 7, the 'legitimate' Arab nationalisms made the 'fragmentary' one so hapless.

III

It follows that what might be called 'Palestinizing' the situation was the prior task, vis-à-vis the Jewish disavowal of any Palestinian dimension to it by the insistent 'Arabization' of their Zionist encounter; and also vis-à-vis the Arab states around. The former was a misery that persisted right up to Madrid in 1990; the latter would prove a constant imponderable in the whole equation. Palestinianism underwent many self-inflicted wounds as well as undeserved adversities in this entire complex of emotions and factors.

Keeping in mind the areas reviewed in Chapters 4 and 7, it might be useful to ask at the outset whether the whole encounter need have been politicized at all, if only to underline how inescapable a political captivity was. In the abstract, it might be argued that, but for the mutual fascination with sovereignty, an economic co-existence could have been devised. Water would be a vital concern of both parties. There is no doubt that Jewish incoming greatly stimulated the local economy, providing work for the Arabs, increasing the sale value of their holdings and helping to retrieve the post-war impoverishments. There was industrial stimulus arising from a quickened agricultural base. As a meeting of two cultures as well as of two peoples, potentially mutual benefits abounded.[7]

Only angelic agencies, however, could have substantiated such dreams. Arab labour might be cheap and plentiful and, by that measure, attractive to the Jewish developers. But exclusively Jewish labour was their objective. Weizmann warned that using local peasants might 'endear' the locals unduly to their soil and so prejudice its Jewish acquisition.[8] Herzl's

Zionism, and Weizmann's, had emphatically rejected the purely agri-cultural version of the Bilu pioneers, of Rothschild and Moses Montefiore,[9] as too vulnerable and idealist. Political Zionism's logic pursued and demanded statehood by its every reading of diaspora and the 'Gentile' world. It was a logic requiring time and evolution but these were not meant to obscure its ultimate necessity. So much we have seen elsewhere.

In turn, the slow self-realization of the Palestinians had to hinge, by all their lights also, on politicization. How could it be otherwise, once an Ottoman federalism had been excluded and Arab states were forming east and north? The same Mandate under which Zionists found warrant was also entrusted with the development of Arab nationhood. The very rules, so to speak, of the confrontation were in national terms and it had, as we have seen, by its very location and its emotion 'Palestinized' its programme in political form. There could be no indigenous escape – or will to it – from political assumptions.

That being so, Palestine's political ends and means would be enmeshed in co-Arab tangles. Through vital periods it was no free agent at all and suffered massively from resulting helplessness. Even after 1967, when despair kindled more avowed self-help, its purposes were dismally hobbled and shackled from outside. Circumstances and connections were always conspiring against an autonomous will or engendering factions within it.

There was an early instance of how it might be in an episode now long forgotten. In the summer of 1918, while the British military were still in charge of the area, Faisal, son of the Sharif of Mecca and a leader in the Arab Revolt, met Weizmann, fresh from a Zionist conference in London. Jewish support could be welcome to Faisal's 'kingdom' hopes in Damascus, whither he was bound. The two later agreed on a vague document which acknowledged the Balfour Declaration, approved rapid Jewish immigration into Palestine, and pledged Zionist co-operation 'in the development of the Arab State and Palestine'. The 'and' was elusive and there was no reference to Jewish statehood.

It was soon overtaken by the débâcle in Damascus, while it angered Palestinians despite Faisal's condition about 'Arab independence'. They did not relish his consent in their name to the immigration they were already identifying as the crucial point of suspicion. Their resentment soon found what would prove to be disadvantageous leadership in the person of Al-Hajj Amin al-Hussaini, for whom Herbert Samuel secured the office of Grand Mufti of Jerusalem in 1921. The High Commissioner may have been intending to demonstrate a counter-bias to his own Jewishness but the choice was unhappy. It brought a pointed Islamic dimension into the resistance to Zionism – one that later the PLO tried strongly to avoid. More importantly, it involved the local Palestinianism in a leadership of problematic credentials and a verbally violent personality, about whom the Jewish side had reason to be alarmed. The early 1920s were inevitably a time of embroilment in the interpretation of 'the national home', the nature, limits and goals of Jewish immigration, the avoidance of coercion and the impasse of endless discussions, soundings and 'statements' on them all. As one historian had it at that point:

> Moderation in nationalism is only practised and perhaps only can be practised by people who have experienced independence for a long time.[10]

No one had, and each was the more apprehensive about the other.

Resenting Emir Faisal's parley with Weizmann, Amin al-Hussaini and his followers entered on a policy of agitation leading to uprisings and armed demonstrations against the liberty of Zionist immigration. Relieving deep emotions nourished on unallayed suspicions and fears, the reaction was understandable enough. However, in its haphazard quality and its impulsiveness devoid of long-range vision, it only served to militarize the immigrants themselves and to stimulate vigilantes in protection of their settlements which, in the 1920s, were isolated and exposed. Palestinian risings thus paved the way for what would become the Haganah, the Irgun and the Stern Gang – their most inveterate and ruthless foes.

It may be argued that, instinctive as it was and, for some, temperamentally congenial, this sporadic and ill-contrived violence during the 1920s was the only option resisters had. The Mandatory power, having vexed itself with an irreconcilable conflict, sought in the primary sense to prevent the two parties squaring up against each other, Jew against Arab, kibbutznik against villager and Zion against Palestine. Yet, inevitably, this is what ensued – the nemesis on the political folly which in 1917 had set up the scenario. If there was gathering futility in the steady Palestinian gravitation towards mutual embitterment physically transacted, the built-in provocation inherent in the situation was sufficient reason – irrational as the outcome was. The Mandate had virtually created a triangular fiasco. Zionist immigration could neither be terminated nor tolerated. Either party's satisfaction meant the other party's distraint. Merely holding the ring for confrontation contented neither. For the referee had no rules except the very ones that had created the contention. That being the case, the holding of the ring only embroiled the contestants the more.

There is no need here for the tangled narrative of those inter-war years:

the Arab disturbances of 1921, 1928, 1929 and 1936; the steady element of belligerence among the Jewish partisans, in the spirit of Jabotinsky; numerous delegations to London; divided counsels in both camps and the conflict tending to embitterment within, as well as between, them both. There were also intense arguments about 'the spirit of the Covenant' of the League concerning 'self-realization' for all, and the precise intention and interpretation of the Mandate. If in no other conclusive sense, through those years Palestinian 'realization' was happening, painfully and bewilderingly, as an education in the elusive relation between being and becoming a people.

Abetting that elusiveness was the futurist, prospective accent in the warrant of the Mandate. It was supposedly presiding over the 'development' to 'independence'. But when was the process due and what was its end measure? As early as 1922, the first of many 'White Papers' from the British Colonial Office (sic), to which, under Winston Churchill, the Mandate was assigned, declared:

> When it is asked what is meant by the development of the Jewish National Home in Palestine, it may be [sic] answered that it is not the imposition of a Jewish nationality upon the inhabitants of Palestine as a whole [sic; partition one day maybe?] but the further development of the existing Jewish community with the help of Jews in other parts of the world in order that they may become a centre in which the Jewish people as a whole may take, on the grounds of religion and race [not statehood?], an interest and pride . . . It should know that it is in Palestine as of right and not on sufferance.[11]

How better could Palestinians have played their cards – having so few – in this studied official evasion in definition, of definition in evasion? They had little experience of what political finesse entails.

There is one interesting feature of this process, namely the feeling generated in the ranks of those actually operating the Mandate. It was a feeling that there had been much that was devious in Balfour, in the Sykes–Picot correspondence and the exchanges of the MacMahon Letters, about the pledges supposedly being 'processed', and that Palestinians had been cheated or betrayed. The conscience debate also extended into successive British Cabinets and parties. The Palestinians were not well placed to capitalize on this but it had two consequences. The one was a heightened Zionist prejudice against, or heightened vigilance about, the Mandate. The other was a perceptible loss of conviction about the Mandate on the part of those who administered and policed it, a sense of dogged and costly endurance under its compromising pain. The analogy of being 'in Pilate's seat' came to not a few minds.[12] The Palestinians were not alone – nor were the Zionists – in learning hard ways.

IV

Too often, with them, there was costly lack of realization of what a wise strategy required. They had no Weizmann to impress sagacity and calculating patience on their attitudes. The Mufti Al-Hussaini was not lacking in forceful gifts of mind and reason but his personality evoked divisive passions. Palestinians had earlier rejected the offer of a Legislative Assembly on the ground of non-co-operation with Zionists. They failed to build on the brief waning in the mid-1920s of Jewish immigration and to deal effectively with the Sursoks and others in the land sales that weakened their cause both materially and logically. The 1929 disturbances were stained by massacres of Jews in Hebron and Safad,[13] serving sharply to intensify the Jewish case for intransigence, and to darken the situation coincident with the arrival of a new High Commissioner.[14] Al-Hussaini emerged more clearly as a man moved by deep bigotry against Jewry, to the sad prejudice of any judicious Palestinian case.

In the post-1929–30 appraisals, with the coming to be routine conferences and 'Papers' in London, the Palestinians again preferred boycott to negotiation and refused the invitation to discussion on the constitutional debate; six years later they were faced with the Peel Commission. They proved unable to surmount the adamant, but pragmatically flawed, conviction of the categorical nature of their 'land right'. The 'Paper' from which they excluded themselves did 'recognize' their national rights but proved only another hiatus in the process of their attainment.

That hiatus, in deepening tension, brought on the Peel Commission of 1936 which opted for partition in its Report in 1937. While Weizmann sedulously cultivated the main case-maker on it, Reginald Coupland, Al-Hussaini botched his strong brief by extravagant imaging of Jewish intentions around Temple building and demolition of mosques, also demanding complete cessation of immigration and the relinquishment by Britain of its Mandate. Some of the Commissioners had inclined to a Swiss-style idea of 'cantons', but the Weizmann–Coupland axis turned their decision to partition, entailing on the Palestinian mind the still sharper test of the ultimate crunch.

Once again, obduracy they would never have called such, prevailed. Whereas the Zionist mind had come to terms with itself, after long ideological musings, concerning the necessary tactic in partition acceptance, the Palestinian will allowed itself no compromise. Its territorial nationalism was not negotiable. Pragmatism had no place in its innate dogmatism and legitimacy. Had there been also a latent Islamic dimension in this decision, tending to inject into a valid anti-Zionism a degree of anti-Semitism, religiously tragic and politically inept? The bearing of Islam on Palestinianism concerns a final Chapter 12. The careful 'secularity' of the later Palestine National Charter was in sharp contrast to the Mufti's stance.

The heightening impasse in 'the politics of realization' after the Peel Report was followed by the exigencies of the Second World War in 1939. It imposed a sort of uneasy moratorium on conflict and debate in Palestine by virtue of the larger preoccupations of the global scene. But it served to rid Palestinianism of the handicap, if not the legacy, of the Mufti's contribution.[15] The most significant fact about 1939–45 in Palestine is that the Western Desert victory saved the future Israel from the entire elimination Nazism would have brought. Realism, if not gratitude, conduced to a Jewish effort at a degree of ingratiation *vis-à-vis* the British, wary as these were of arming Palmach and other Jewish units lest arms and skills at some later point would be turned against them. This Jewish pragmatism was in spite of sharp resentment at the MacDonald decision to limit Jewish immigration for a five-year period to 15,000 a year. There were loud protests that the Mandate had been betrayed, Arabs placated and obligations renounced.

The British argued war necessity, but while the Palestinians stood to gain from the thinking behind the decision, they quite failed to emulate the Jewish stance towards the Mandatory. Some rather saw in the Germans a common 'foe' of Jewry and found a devious fellow-feeling in doing so, while the Mufti betook himself into the embrace of the Nazis. They found themselves seriously wrong-footed at the war's end in 1945, despite having remained quiescent. They could not have known, in 1939, that their satisfaction with the curb on immigration would be grimly outdated by the revealing of the Holocaust's enormity and by the shift in global politics. The emergence of the United States to the world centre-stage would prove deeply prejudicial to Palestinian hopes, yet their antennae had done little to detect what was impending or to anticipate what, politically, it would require of them against the odds it reared.

V

The pace quickened. The MacDonald curbs were swept away. The Mandate ended with the partition vote, with the Peel solution internationalized by

UN decision and significantly more than doubled in Zionist favour on the map. The Arab disadvantage in the UN has been noted elsewhere and, on the ground, the Arab disarray, bombast and collapse (the Jordanian forces excepted) that turned Palestinian ideology of statehood into the poverty of exile. In New York, again, they had no Weizmann, on the ground no Saladin.[16] Phrased that way, it could be said that their very predicament exonerated them. For they had no chance of either in their counsels or their armoury.

The consequences of any Palestinian–Arab acceptance of the UN partition have long been debated. It has been argued that they could have gained, and retained, almost half the whole, more than half the pittance of 'the occupied territories' that are now their limited and precarious aspiration. The essential drive of Zionism might well have amended 1947 in ways it is useless to surmise. Hypotheses apart, it would have taken a sternly disciplined authority of will to have seen the wisdom of compromise on so spiritually 'compromising' a decision and to have sustained it in popular implementation. Such an act of hard choice was probably beyond the set of a culture's soul. There are times and places where even pragmatism collapses on itself, like an overweighted cart. Hindsight is always too late, while foresight always lacks its evidences. The realization we are studying was an education into might have beens.

What followed 1949 in Palestinian experience takes us to Chapter 10 in its deepest human terms. Here it tells of political limbo-izing in that, until almost the early 1960s, all has to do with refugees. Local armed units in the 1948–49 fighting had been overtaken by the Arab forces. The world saw Palestinianism hardly at all as such, but rather as an issue of homelessness and dispersion, regrettable no doubt but largely self-induced (so the propaganda ran) and deserving merely of compassion. UNWRA came into being and was perpetuated because of non-return either as an option or a policy. The new Israel was in the full flush of pride in its extended size, including the salient, so hard fought for, up to the western rim of Old Jerusalem. Palestine was a dazed, truncated, partially depopulated expression, crowded in its remnant with houseless families all dispossessed.

There began the long and weary struggle towards recognition as a political identity. The Jordan dimension at once took over – an economic and administrative necessity, but raising tensions and misgivings as old as 1916. With refugees languishing – and multiplying – under UN care, some fifteen years were to elapse before Palestinianism was repoliticized. There was a sort of stalemate of bewildered inaction. 1956 came and went with the occupation and evacuation of Sinai, a three-nation conspiracy of no relevance to Palestinian anxieties. Hapless among their proxies, their education into real autonomy was slow and fitful, and it was, one might say, necessarily violent. Formed in 1964, the Palestine Liberation Organization was greatly boosted by the trauma of 1967 and the growing perception of urgent self-help amid all the tokens of the near futility of Arab links.

The PLO beginnings go back to a small group in Cairo, with Yassir Arafat their leading pioneer. The doctrine of 'armed struggle' was invoked, Israel perceived as a colonialist power needing to be disqualified, however remote the odds, by Frantz Fanon-style invocation of anger as, in itself, a psychic liberation and, in context, the only remaining option, the political identity being disallowed by nations at large and ill-served by Arab neighbours. These Palestinian militants could hardly be aware of the source but certainly shared the sentiment of a speaker in 1949, addressing the Rabbinical Assembly of America:

> Though soil cannot be stolen, a man may forfeit his right to this soil by giving up hope of ever regaining it.[17]

Arafat and his lieutenants had no intention of renouncing the land by default of the will. To cease to will is to deserve to fail.

It was a beginning of ambition to autonomy different in kind from the Mandate time. It had no solution for refugee camps except recruitment from them of volunteers suited to its ends. Needing havens in 'host areas', its manoeuvres were desultory and conspiratorial until the débâcle of 1967 gave a strong thrust to its philosophy and its activity – witness, within three years, its show-down with Jordanian sovereignty. Fragmented in ways similar to the militant groups in Israel's story because of personal tensions and the sheer strains of violence itself, it had a radically different *mise-en-scène*. The Israeli groups were based throughout on the territory of their concern, fighting a very exposed 'oppression' (as they saw it) and claiming legitimacy as 'freedom fighters' not 'terrorists'.[18] Armed Palestinian resistance had a much less feasible goal, against not a Mandatory caught in insoluble ambiguity but a resolute, newly forged nation fighting from within its *élan vital* and strongly denying toehold to internal subversion, and consigning resisters to the perimeter beyond their borders where, if need be, they could be ruthlessly pursued.

These circumstances may explain, though not exonerate, the sometimes bizarre acts of violence by which Fatah and others strove to make their point with the world that would otherwise ignore their 'rights' or merely pity them as refugees. Violence, by all moral criteria, stains its own ideals, contradicts in others the humanity it pleads for itself, and undeserves its own deservings. Yet thereby the Kenyattas, the Begins, the Shamirs of this world can finally attain to be Prime Ministers and Heads of State, just as Arafat, at long last, can make it to an audience at the White House.

Palestinian 'resistance' could base its logic not only on the precedent of militant Zionism but on the actuality of the situation within Israel after 1948. To its glory, Israel accorded citizen rights to the local population that remained. But the solution that came to be embodied in the personality and significance of Emile Habibi[19] was necessarily an option only for a limited minority, based on the assumption of the non-repatriation of departees, the concept of the uncompromised Jewishness of the state and the essential minority status of such remaining Palestinians. Being Palestinian *qua* a remnant within juridical Israel entailed a permanent renunciation of Palestinian identity. It constituted a virtual acknowledgement of Golda Meir's view that Palestinians did not, politically, exist. The fact that those remaining in Israel after 1948, despite the dubious fortunes they would experience, could never represent or achieve Palestinian destiny served to confirm the necessity of asserting that destiny at any cost as 'liberators' saw it. Would Zionists have been content with permanent minority status in a political expression they did not dominate? That *they* could never have done so justified a comparable verdict on the part of the PLO.

It did not justify the wildness with which the various fighters in fact proceeded. Hijackings, Olympic killings, the *Achille Lauro* raid, an ambassador's murder in London – all these were more manifestations of angry frustration than the hard-nosed efficiency of the Israeli raid at Entebbe. They alienated the international community and drew down on their perpetrators the image of near insanity. The operations were no less, perhaps even more, divided internally than were the Jewish Haganah, Stern Gang and Irgun Zvi Leumi. Desperate causes always generate passionate inner contentions around personalities and means to ends. Palestinianism sowed much madness and reaped much futility.

Yet they knew desperate provocation. Lebanon was the tragic arena of all three. There is no doubt that the Palestinian presence there from 1970[20] greatly abused the hospitality it forcefully assumed to be its right. Sober reason would have known how fraught the issue of sovereignty could be. Experience in Jordan from 1967 to 1970 had swiftly demonstrated that. Imaginative reason, further, could have perceived how differently contrived the Lebanese situation was, so direly in contrast with the royal hold in Jordan on the conditions of its tolerance of the Palestinian presence and its will to be belligerent against Israel from local soil. Lebanon, with its uneasy confessional set-up, its subtle liability to fractiousness, its role as suffering the tension between Mediterranean, Christian 'westwardness' and Muslim, Arab 'eastwardness', was in no position to admit an ardent active Palestinianism ruining that delicate equilibrium.

Sane compunction about guest status, however, has no place in urgent belligerence. Palestinian fighters took the unhindered right to operate violently against Israel, so generating a mutual hatred between themselves and those Lebanese who most traditionally wanted to repudiate the costly pan-Arabism which such militancy implied. Hence the murderous enmity that developed between some Maronite Lebanese and the Palestinian presence. Mutual massacres ensued, abetting reciprocal passions. The dark tragedy of Sabra and Chatila camps in 1982 recorded how wretchedly Palestinian 'liberation' had imperilled its own innocent refugees, the helpless thousands whose sanctuary became a killing field. The crime was retaliation for atrocities Palestinian fighters had committed against 'obstructive' Lebanese whose version of Lebanese patriotism impeded their sacred cause.

Palestinian activity in Lebanon occasioned, though in no way deserved, the vehemence characterizing the Israeli invasion of Lebanon in the summer of 1982. That angry venture derived from the ambivalence studied in Chapter 4 and the nemesis theme explored in Chapter 6. As there noted, it had in mind long-standing notions of creating some sort of client state in Lebanon based on a common anti-Arabism.[21] Palestinians might have played into their hands by cruelly provoking Maronite Lebanese to think, however conjecturally, in such terms. It was, in the event, too illusory to happen. Could Palestinians be blamed for contributing to the possibility? Yet were they not in measure responsible for what Israeli venom against them caused to the Lebanese economy, ethos and population in 1982? For the Israeli aim had been to eliminate them from Lebanon in sequel to the manner of their presence there. Yet there would have been no such presence had not their landlessness necessitated their haven there. Was it not Israel, as the Israel it was, that explained their landlessness? That which most incriminated the fighting Palestinians in Lebanon was strangely requited in 1982 by the guilt of Israel. So are the ways of human history.

VI

The bitter expulsion of the PLO from Lebanon and its still defiant migration to Tunis left encamped Palestinian refugees – many of them in family linkage with the fighters – to total jeopardy. The added catastrophe in the massacre only intensified the will to sustain the struggle in more distant exile. There was also another heavy consequence, namely the division between Palestinians still in 'the territories' and the leadership in distant exile. The problem had been there during earlier sojourns in Jordan and Lebanon. Now it was intensified.

Israeli resistance to resistance was able to maximize on the distinction between the two segments of Palestinianism and develop the illusion between 'real' and 'unreal', or 'resident' and 'banished'. Thence came the slow struggle to establish the PLO as 'the sole representative' of the Palestinian people. The effort was no little part of the task of 'realization' we are studying. The Weizmanns, Ben Gurions, Jabotinskys, Sharons and Dayans of Israel could have appreciated the question 'Who speaks for Israel?' or known the nuisance of those who thought no one could.

Slowly, however, through the early 1980s in the aftermath of the Lebanese disaster, the wilful fiction of a disparate Palestinianism was disproved. The territories, without electoral opportunity, showed the resilience of a common cause, refusing to admit the political nullification of the PLO and other groups. Arafat had appeared before the UN in 1974 armed with olive branch and hand weapon conspicuous in its holster. He continued to appear in military fatigues. Slowly international violence diminished and the blurred image of a 'nation' began to emerge and clarify an unblurred quality. 1988 brought the declaration of readiness to acknowledge Israel as an abiding political reality – the boundaries being peaceably determined.

The Israeli government then in control, vexed in its own ambivalence, dismissed the gesture as an idle, empty one and continued to insist that it alone would decide which, if any, Palestinians, probably none, were to be deemed politically acceptable. The charade continued until, more perceptive than most US governments, President Bush and his Secretary of State James Baker began to relent somewhat about Palestinian negotiability and the stony road to the Madrid Conference was under way.

That development owed everything to the tenacity displayed in the Intifadah of those years, a spontaneous uprising within the territories, enshrining a unified solidarity of the local with the distant, and persuading enough Israelis that a Zion and a Palestine, in some sense, would have to co-exist if the former was to be in any sense democratic and duly Jewish.

The Intifadah, at long last, showed a different form of resistance, not wild and wayward and obscene, but local, dignified and heroic and, therefore, somehow undeniably authentic. Folk in the West Bank had, as it were, realized themselves as at least autonomous in will, if not yet in fact. It was as if Israel could not be conceded in their politics until it had been mastered in their souls. They were no longer Arab alibis, protégés of self-serving sponsors, nor even simply a people hanging on the ventures of their fighting partisans beyond. They were valiant in themselves and slowly the world began to take in the fact of them. The battle for international recognition was being painfully won. The PLO in broad terms could ride to negotiable status in the aura of an unequivocal popular will to have it so.

The charade of who was, negotiably, who would persist into and beyond the Madrid Conference – non-Jerusalem Palestinians, first vetted or then not vetted by Israel, and no 'Tunisians', then a blind eye to 'Tunisians' and locals coinciding their counsels. These were the necessary subterfuges of the Israeli reluctances only patiently forgone. Unhappily, it was those hesitancies and the ancient misgivings they warranted which engendered the Hamas movement, even if, oddly, Israelis had secretly fostered it initially in order to compromise the Palestinians in general.

Hamas's scepticism about the PLO's 'peace process' stems partly from its many delays and ambiguities, but it is also more avowedly Islamic in contrast to the studied 'secularity' of the PLO. It is, therefore, a pointed commentary on the perceptions and the slow speed of peace-making and the sharp impediment that the continuing settlements threaten to its integrity. Hamas thus measures how far PLO Palestinianism has had to come and the travail of the realization it has achieved. The year-long expulsion of Hamas personnel, including many intellectuals, in 1992 by Yitzhak Rabin to a sort of limbo on the edge of Lebanon demonstrated a different sort of embarrassment to the PLO when 'credibilizing' its gathering momentum towards agreements with Israel. This was the more so in view of the dignity with which, as media attention informed the world, the banished were able to conduct themselves perched on the hillsides in the winter winds.

There was a quite contrasted and potentially lethal self-embarrassment of the Palestine leadership in the PLO's approving of the aggression of Saddam Husain of Iraq against Kuwait. It threatened seriously to set back the clock envisaged at Madrid and could have proved a desperate miscalculation. Emotions ran high. In Arabism at large impulsive passions have often over-ridden or denied cold reason. In different terms, the Hashimites in Jordan were in the same dilemma. Saddamism – if we may so speak – seemed to some a latter-day Nasserism, this time from that other ancient river valley of the Arab east. Did not successful absorption of Kuwait into Iraq, together with its leverage of oil and oil money, promise illusory hope, at long last, of some Arab adequacy against Israel? Something of the old inveterate enemy image of Israel came again as a foe perhaps now in unusual presumptive jeopardy.

The misreading was short-lived. US and other interests doomed such an eventuality and succeeded in restraining Israel from the sort of unilateral action that would have endangered the Saudi–American alliance and truly made the conflict one between Arabs and Israel. For the PLO the blunder cost dearly in the forfeiture of Saudi funding and the expulsion of Palestinians from the Gulf oil bonanza so vital to their livelihoods. Saddam had precipitated a serious miscarriage in Palestinian counsels from which other dynamics and their own resilience have partly rescued them. Hazards had always been their stock-in-trade. Israel could justifiably read the episode as warranting the Likud-style assessment of Palestinians being fit only for rejection. Zionism has known times when it needed to show itself redeemable from within when its wiser minds were embarrassed by the more impetuous.

VII

The 'realization' with which this chapter has been concerned relates to inter-Arab, USA and world perceptions of the Palestinians in prolonged and arduous engagement with the enterprise of Zionism. It relates also to their perceptions of themselves in the throes of that encounter. It remains here to ask whether there might have been a more articulate leadership emerging, responsive to the entire situation in all its harsh proportions, a leadership at once politic in its realism and visionary in its passion. No such leadership emerged.

It is noteworthy how Zionism somehow contrived to produce the personalities it needed at every juncture of its story. Herzl and Weizmann are on record that they were ready, and able, virtually to steer their cause by its total identity with their mind and will.[22] Ben Gurion, Dayan, Meir, Begin were masters of their mind, capable of relentless goal-pursuit allied with almost mystical intensity. The Palestinian side produced no Lincolns for its crisis, no Churchills for its rescue. Was it that there was a short-sightedness concerning what the prospects were, what the panorama held before them? How religions belonged for good or ill with the *mise-en-scène* is the enquiry of Chapter 12. That the odds were enormous was never in doubt. If we can imagine roles reversed and a local Jewish population faced with a God-warranted but virile secular identity arriving on stage, in fitful waves of a steady tide and with strong Western assets, they might well have fared no better.

Was Zionism ever negotiable had there been a disciplined, clear-eyed, tenacious leadership to concert a mutual existence, tentatively while the

Mandate lasted, definitively thereafter? The story of Fawzi al-Hussaini and the *Falastin al-Jadid* initiative in 1946 yields the tragically negative answer. That vital year Fawzi al-Hussaini, a cousin of the ill-fated Grand Mufti, signed an agreement on co-operation and mutual assistance with the League for Jewish–Arab Rapprochement and Co-operation, led by Judah Magnes and Martin Buber. It provided for a Jewish–Arab Palestine with political equality after the Mandate's end. Further Jewish immigration would be 'according to absorptive capacity'. Future affiliation of a Jewish–Arab Palestine with neighbouring countries was to be explored.

Al-Hussaini promoted the theme of a joint state in public meetings, explaining that having taken part, as a youth in his late twenties, in the 1929 anti-Jewish disturbances, he saw the futility of antagonism, a disaster for both peoples. In November 1946 he was murdered by assassins who were never found (like those of Count Bernadotte). Though some of his associates were ready to continue, Buber told them to go home as it was too late. He would not take on himself the burden of asking them to risk their lives further. Partition was voted at the UN a year later and war ensued.[23]

That 'go home' has a ring of pathos. Now long forgotten, the plan was anyway utterly forlorn. Separate statehoods cannot cohabit, and separate statehoods, given the strong illusions about the bearing of sovereignty on life, must be incompatible. When asked if he could see any possible accommodation with a State of Israel, Faisal had replied: 'None that is compatible with its [state] existence.'[24] Yet to be its own state was the implacable purpose of the Zionists.

Given the intractable quality of the stakes, it would have been the wisdom of Palestinianism to have clinched in 1947 what partition might have afforded. To have reconciled the population to that essential humiliation of their identity would have required consummate leadership both to make the realist case and to guide an angry repudiation to a change of mind. It was not forthcoming. The lack of realization meant that a long and weary toil towards the salvages of failure would be their destiny. Since they never came to their Biltmore, they would learn the sharp irony of what Oslo 1993 called 'immediate empowerment'.[25]

The four-year sequel studied in Chapter 4, where it fitted the theme of 'ambivalence' most aptly, showed how ironical was that 'immediate', how partial and precarious that 'empowerment'. The periodic possessing of the findings of Oslo and their abrupt jeopardy in the wake of the May 1996 Israeli election provided the bitterest test of all for a Palestinian leadership embittered, bewildered and impaled by the volte-face of the Likud coalition government concerning both the meaning and the sincerity of the Oslo

Accords. Does the whole experience somehow spell the futility of any politics of Palestinian realization, leaving them only with the dream?

Notes

1 William Shakespeare, *Julius Caesar*, I.ii, lines 140–2.

2 Cited from Barbara Victor, *Hanan Ashrawi: A Passion for Peace* (London, 1995), pp. 174–5. It is assumed that the text was in fact the work of Hanan Ashrawi and betrays her literary hand and political spirit.

3 Hess's 'Rome' in his title did not mean the Papacy. It meant that 'Jerusalem' of the Jews should emulate the independence-seeking nationalism of Mazzini and Garibaldi.

4 It is important to realize how far-reaching this interior debate was, during and prior to the Arab Revolt. Life-style was highly Ottomanized. Turkish was still written in Arabic characters, 'Ya Effendi' a courtesy title, with Turkish authority or its local agents everywhere. The situation is usefully analysed in Hassan Saab, *The Arab Federalists of the Ottoman Empire* (Amsterdam, 1958). See also Chapter 3, note 9.

5 By adding to the nucleus of Mount Lebanon (mainly Maronite) extensive territories to the north beyond Tripoli and to the south beyond Sidon and in the hinterland of Tyre. These incorporated into a thus more diverse entity large Sunni or Alouite populations in the north and Shi'ah Muslims in the south. Was it a case of 'multiplying to rule'? Syria thought so and also resented the ceding of Alexandretta in the far north of Syria in 1939 to Turkey. Syria and Lebanon had a single currency and much other integration during the French Mandate.

6 Yossi Beilin, *Israel: A Concise Political History* (London, 1992), p. 111.

7 Judah Magnes, with his *Brith Shalom* or 'Covenant of Peace', pleaded with unswerving conviction for a bi-federal state – a vision intolerable to Zionists for whom *ab initio* statehood was an absolute goal. See Christopher Sykes, *Crossroads to Israel: Palestine from Balfour to Bevin* (London, 1965).

8 There was always an implicit tension in land-sale and land-acquisition. Arab landlords (sometimes absentees) read Zionism as materially enhancing their land-asset. For mere peasants land-acquisition by new – and strange – incoming developers could prove a deeply disturbing experience even when the new owners – for a while – employed them.

9 The *Bilu'im* (word formed from the Hebrew initials of 'House of Jacob, come let us walk') came late in 1882 from Russia to settle in agriculture and small trading. Baron de Rothschild supported them. They settled mainly in Gedera. The Montefiores were patrons and sponsors of such incomings to an as yet non-political *Hibbet Zion*, or 'Love of Zion'.

10 See Sykes, *Crossroads*, p. 65.

11 Quoted from ibid., p. 77.

12 E.g., John Marlowe, *The Seat of Pilate* (London, 1959), a study of Britain in Palestine. Cf. also Elizabeth Monroe, *Britain's Moment in the Middle East 1914–1971* (rev. edn; London, 1981).

13 Through the whole country in that conflict, official figures had 133 Jews killed and 339 wounded – all by Arab action – and 116 Arabs dead and 232 wounded, almost all by British action.

14 Sir John Chancellor, taking over from Lord Plumer.

15 The Mufti's later career as an exile from Palestine was a strong but finally futile courting of the Nazis. Perhaps it was in part the aridity of his leadership that led the PLO to avoid using pan-Islamic rhetoric and to pledge a Constitution open to Jews resident before partition.

16 Some have seen a striking resemblance between Israel and the Latin Kingdom of Jerusalem, without drawing any 'futurism' from what happened to the latter after eighty-odd years. Saladin's achievement was to unify the hinterland.

17 He was S. Lieberman: *Proceedings of the Rabbinical Assembly of America*, vol. 12 (1949); Kilayyim vii.31 a, ed. Krotoshin.

18 Menahem Begin always vehemently denied he was ever a 'terrorist', since he was fighting armed British forces, not innocent targets. See his *The Revolt*, rev. edn, trans. Samuel Katz (London, 1979). This would not cover the assassination in Cairo of the British envoy Lord Moyne, nor the brutal murder of Count Bernadotte of the UN by an associate of Ben Gurion who was never identified publicly or indicted.

19 A notable Israeli Palestinian (1922–96) who opted to remain in Haifa, his birthplace, and has the legend 'Remained in Haifa' as his epitaph on his tomb. It was perhaps his Communist sympathies which helped him to his version of 'patriotism' inside Israel. For Marxism had at times been seen as a bond between ethnicities that transcended political niceties about 'sovereignty' and 'national' fulfilment. Habibi began, late in his life, a literary career, producing *inter alia* an influential novel for which he coined the phrase 'pess-optimist' or 'optotrist'.

20 'From 1970' since the earlier 'presence' from 1948 had been in pathetic refugee status only and receiving, if not enthusiastic welcome, at least tolerance from the Lebanese while UN agencies carried the cost.

21 The dream had occurred from time to time in Israeli thinking of some viable, and useful, active common interests between the Zionist venture and a discernible Christian counterpart to the north. The connivance Israel was able to concert in south Lebanon, first with the proxy troops of the renegade Major Haddad and later in the 'occupied zone', indicated how relevant to Israel's protection of its northern area it had become in the context of Lebanese political chaos. But it was never practicable – either politically or militarily – for Israel to develop in Lebanon a complete cliency. For all its inner tensions, Lebanese identity was too loyal for such an eventuality.

22 Theodor Herzl, *Complete Diaries*, ed. and trans. M. Lowenthal (London, 1960), vol. 1, p. 41: 'I conduct the affairs of the Jews without their mandate, though I remain responsible to them for what I do.' By leadership, he understood 'an authority delegated by itself'. Chaim Weizmann wrote in a similar sense. See Chapter 2, note 28. Given the many strands of Palestinian politics and action, no single personality achieved or deserved such policy-making ascendancy.

23 See *New Outlook* (Jerusalem: September 1964).

24 Cited from Vincent Sheean, *Faisal: The King and His Kingdom* (London, 1975), p. 95.

25 The Biltmore decision was named after the hotel in New York where Zionists debated whether, in the event of its being 'on the cards', partition of 'the promised land' was acceptable. The idealists found it 'unthinkable', the pragmatists 'acceptable' as a beginning. The latter prevailed.

Unlike the Camp David understandings about Palestine, which set no timetable, the Oslo Accords required that when the Gaza–Jericho Israeli withdrawal happened, Palestinian control could follow at once. The Palestine National Covenant had 'rejected any solution that was a substitute for a complete liberation of Palestine'.

9

The odd-handedness of the USA

I

The White House lawn seems the coveted stage for the ceremonies of international relations, the due and proper theatre of symbolic transactions. The coveting seems mutual, with Presidents basking in congratulation and other leaders welcoming the glamour, though sometimes at the price of embarrassment. Washington is the apt venue for accords supposedly achieved there.

To be sure, successive US Secretaries of State have shuttled back and forth across the Middle East in energies of diplomacy, relaying ideas and hints and peradventures from capital to capital. Though the USA declined the Palestinian Mandate after the First World War, its diplomats and ambassadors have been tirelessly concerned with the area ever since the King–Crane Commission and the first murmurs of bi-federalism and partition.

Yet, with all these mediating offices, there has been a sorry lack of even-handedness in the American relationship to the Palestinian–Israeli equation from the beginning and sharply so since 1948. If it is permissible to have the usage 'even-handed' to denote an equal concern and a fair balance, then 'odd-handed' will convey the opposite. There have been many times in the post-Second World War scene when it hardly needed a cynic to conclude that the foreign policy of the USA in relation to Israel was 'made in Jerusalem'. The situation has left observers outside America to wonder how a state so powerful and almost 'regnant' in world affairs could be so far constrained by a small client in the Middle East. The puzzlement is the more sharp in that no less a person than George Washington himself, the paragon of all things American, had officially farewelled his Cabinet and people in 1796 with the warning that there should be 'no passionate attachment' in their international relations, just as there should be no 'inveterate hatred' of any peoples. He could not have known at the end of the eighteenth century how the attachments and hates he sought to preclude would entrench themselves so deeply in the population and the politics of his own nation. Of all the immigrants whom the Statue of Liberty welcomed to the Atlantic shores none would be so passionately attached beyond their new borders in coming generations than the American 'lovers of Zion'. Palestinians have been highly disadvantaged by the resulting factors within American politics which they had little or no possibility of transforming. No small part of their predicament and captivity hinges on the American factor. It therefore takes a necessary place in the story of *Palestina Agonistes* – one this chapter must explore.

II

The first American Consul in 1844 might be said to have set an intriguing precedent. Called Warder Cresson, he was accredited to Turkish Jerusalem and 'All the Holy Land'. Three years later in 1847 he embraced Judaism, taking the name of Michael Boaz Israel and founding an agricultural village, which he named 'God's Vineyard', near Jerusalem. Two hundred fellow-Americans joined him, of whom a quarter were of Jewish birth.

Americans of Jewish birth, as we must see, have played a constantly crucial part within the United States in the fortunes of Zionism and of Israel. They have done so, not by any numerous migration into the new state (apart from idealists) but by massive financial sponsorship and still more by the subtle political influence wielded in the Congress, banking and the media and throughout the structures of American society and economy. This extra-territorial Zionism within the United States makes intriguing irony of the last proviso of the Balfour Declaration of 1917, which noted that any 'national home' it 'favoured . . . for the Jewish people in Palestine' should not 'prejudice . . . the rights and political status enjoyed by Jews in any other country'. Such American 'political status enjoyed by Jews', far from being prejudiced, was enormously recruited to the immense gain of the projected 'national home'.

The point of the proviso, no doubt, was the fear – which most anti-Zionist Jews shared – that ideas of a potential 'state' for Jews in Palestine would query the good faith, and so the emotional and political loyalty and security, of diaspora Jews in commitment to genuine citizenship in 'Gentile' statehoods. As far as American Jewry was concerned, the 'prejudice' would be all the other way, with US policy too often incongruously made in Jerusalem in things pertaining to Zionist aims. There can be no comparable example of a superpower so readily manipulable at the hands of a client state.

In 1919, however, at the end of the First World War, that scenario of a Jerusalem–Washington axis lay some two decades ahead. The concept of 'mandates' stemmed from President Woodrow Wilson's ideals at Versailles of the full autonomy of 'national' peoples, even if a persisting imperialism by France and Britain still thought to utilize the concept in something like the old terms. Lip-service was at least paid to the idea of Arab independence but the deliberate ambiguity was left to European interpretation by the refusal of the United States to undertake the Mandate for Palestine.

It is intriguing to conjecture how the issue might have been had President Woodrow Wilson's ideology survived into the 'mandate' implementation. For him it genuinely represented an interim, if dubiously legitimate, implementation of the principle of national autonomy in respect of Arab peoples. To his partners at Versailles when the mandates were devised for the Treaty and Balfour's Declaration written into the British one for Palestine, it meant a disguise of necessary imperialism. It had, however, been British arms which had liberated Palestine from Ottoman power, while the USA – as Wilson noted when the intense discussions were proceeding prior to the Declaration – had not been in a state of war with Turkey. Any arguable pursuit of Wilsonian ideals, under American auspices, in the Middle East was forfeit to the tragic circumstances in which Wilson was overcome, within the USA, by physical and mental collapse amid his campaign to rally popular opinion to his vision. Adroit Republicans, led by Henry Cabot Lodge, ensured that America drew back from world commitments in Wilsonian terms. The 'mandate' concept, in turn, was forfeit to British power-designs relating to the Raj in India and the idea of a potentially client entity on the eastern as well as the western flank of the Suez Canal. The Wilsonian concepts, to which alone the Mandatories owed juridical sanction, were lost in the political ambiguities surrounding them.

At that point, too, American Jewry, despite the eminence of figures like Justice Brandeis and Rabbi Stephen Wise, was in junior, and sometimes uneasy, rapport with Chaim Weizmann, at the helm, almost single-handedly, of Zionist diplomacy and counsel. Those were the years of Eastern European dominance in the Zionist enterprise and Weizmann himself was zealously committed to what he called 'the British option'. In contrast to Zionists who had sedulously cultivated the Axis Powers before and during the First World War, Weizmann, on many counts, saw the British as the best and likeliest option. Balfour fully vindicated him. Writing in 1919, B. A. Rosenblatt explained why:

> The Jewish people ask for only one trustee to carry out the degree of justice in the creation of the Jewish Commonwealth. Having found 'a good and faithful servant', a nation that has proven itself the greatest and best colonizer in history, it is altogether fitting and proper that the Jewish people should select Great Britain as the trustee for its precious inheritance ... Excepting the Jews, the English are the most biblical of all the peoples of the earth and fate itself decrees that it shall stand as the guardian over the heritage of 'the people of the Book.'[1]

Sundry American visionaries, the novelist Herman Melville among them, with the USA as 'God's other chosen people', would have disputed the terms of this verdict. By the 1930s Zionists themselves were to reverse their perceptions around the ambiguities in and after Balfour, studied in Chapter 4.

Sentiment mattered little in 1919. 'National autonomy' in Palestine would be hostage to contradictions the Balfour Declaration had compounded, if only by studiedly eluding them. When they came home to vex the British Mandatory power, American attitudes would loom into the picture and by 1945 become, in effect if not in intention, 'the good and faithful servant' of the emergent Jewish state. The Zionist client by then was far less starry-eyed and docile and, in differing circumstances, more successfully manipulative of its 'guardian'.

Even so, it is instructive to ponder how American auspices might have operated had the Mandate been theirs, innocent of direct obligation for the Declaration (albeit phrased into the mandating of the League of Nations) and free of the cynical pledges given by Britain in prompting and aligning with the Arab Revolt. For it was those inherently inconsistent antecedents which bedevilled Britain in Palestine from the outset.

What that different aegis might have meant, had the calendar of international 'standings' given to the 1920s been those of the 1950s, was evident in the findings of the King–Crane Commission in the summer of 1919. These reflected the fund of local wisdom-*cum*-ideal nourished by American ventures in education and mission, symbolized in the American University of Beirut.[2] A sequence of fine personnel in the Wilsonian tradition had developed a strong, discreet and warm understanding of Arab affairs and earned a legacy of goodwill among the emerging leadership in Arab politics. Had the Palestine mind been able to ally with this potential fund of vision and realism, its response to the gathering impasse in Palestine could have been more intelligent and hopeful.

As it was, the King–Crane Commission, named after its two US members, was prescient enough in its reporting of the realities that would frustrate the British Mandate. Sent, against European demur, from the Peace Conference, they spent four months in the land. Before touring the whole area and gathering impressions, they had – as they said – 'minds predisposed in favour' of Zionist hopes. If Jews so understood themselves, why not a Jewish 'national autonomy'? Yet

> actual facts drove them to recommend a serious modification of the extreme Zionist program of unlimited immigration.

Their soundings convinced them, further, that if

> Zionists looked forward to a practically complete dispossession of the present non-Jewish population of Palestine . . . No British officer consulted believed that the Zionist program could be carried out except by force of arms . . . Not less than 50,000 soldiers would be required even to initiate the program.[3]

Costly subsequent British experience in the evolving story entirely justified the King–Crane finding that Zionism was inherently forcible or else necessarily impracticable.

Almost thirty years were to elapse before US policy would again be involved with the Palestinian issue, Britain jealously guarding its hegemony against intrusion until the Second World War radically transformed the international scene and brought the 1919 analysis, in its later logic, squarely into the purview of Washington and Wilson's fifth successor, Harry S. Truman. For time had proved how right the Commission had been in diagnosing the built-in paradox between Zionism's statehood and Shalom. The King–Crane Report could do little to help the Palestinians. Indeed, Jewish elements accused it of exacerbating the situation merely by under-lining its 'invariables'. The Report was shelved in Washington and kept back from publication until the Harding succession. By 1946 Britain's post-war *de facto* demotion in the world power equation made the US central to the issue. In the meantime, radical changes were under way in the stance and power of American Jewry.

III

Chaim Weizmann, as protagonist of Zionism in the 1920s, found his US counterparts sometimes inconvenient allies. Their perceptions of the private financing and modest objectives of resettlement in Palestine were at times at odds with his insistently political goals. Figures like Brandeis, Wise and Morgenthau were impressive allies but Weizmann was alarmed when the last-named seemed to take an independent line with the Ottomans about a Jewish tenure in Palestine. The core thrust was Eastern European, in any event, and though some American Jews shared the tangled overtures to the Balfour Declaration, Weizmann saw them as his accessories. They were a far cry from the thrusting Zionists of the current Israeli lobby.

Indeed, until the near-miracle of 1967 many in US Jewry were reticent about Judaic politicization and, like their UK counterparts, nervous about its implications for the *bona fides* of *Galut* or diaspora Jews. Far back in 1885 the Pittsburgh Platform of US Reform Rabbis had resolved:

> We consider ourselves no longer a nation but a religious community and, therefore, expect neither a return to Palestine nor a sacrificial worship under the sons of Aaron nor the restoration of any of the laws concerning the Jewish State.[4]

Readings of destiny were to change. It became less a matter of 'the sons of Aaron' as of the prowess of David. Jews in America could come to reconcile their abiding leverage in American public life with a lively 'Zionism at one remove', by vigorously championing the 'return to Zion' of those fellow-Jews in bleaker scenes for whom the nation-state was a salvation in which Americans, while absent from it (*pace* Ben Gurion),[5] could nevertheless take active pride.

The Shoah, though in no sense an originating factor in a Zionism launched half a century earlier, immensely fortified American Jewish responsibility and turned opinion round to yearning and straining actively for Jerusalem. Even so, the same Shoah demonstrated how self-enclosed American Jewry still remained even when the horror had become clear. The reproach so often held against European states, Britain and France, for failure to intercept Nazi genocide and frustrate it attaches no less to the negligence of Jewry on the far side of the Atlantic. Unlike the Vietnam protests later, there were no sustained rallies or appeals. One analyst blames this failure on 'caution . . . their economic and professional prospects [being] still questionable', and 'weak leadership' overmuch under the spell of President Roosevelt.[6]

In the aftermath of the end of hostilities in Europe and Japan, the Jewish interest in the USA gained momentum in line with the increasing role of the state in world affairs and the advent of the United Nations with its headquarters located on American soil and its proceedings heavily responsive to American leadership, finance and political power. Meanwhile, an exhausted

British Mandatory left the Palestinian impasse in its lap, having succeeded in the Western Desert in preserving Zion and Zionism from the Nazi threat and an extension of Holocaust tragedy to 'the holy land'.

In 1946–47 a United Nations Commission (UNSCOP), going over the old familiar ground of the Peel Commission in 1937, reached – as it had done – the conclusion that partition was inevitable, an attempt to give expression on the ground to the reality, stemming back to Balfour and the Declaration, of incompatible ambitions. Now, however, given the grim retrospect of the 1940s and the abandonment of old notions about 'absorptive capacity', the sanction of urgency had multiplied enormously. In relative marking time while the larger war lasted, the parties in Palestine squared up for a decisive issue. The scenario has been reviewed elsewhere.

The present concern is with the timely emergence of American Jewry's Zionism at the crucial hour in Washington and New York. Historians are in debate about its complex impulses. There was the will somehow to deny to Hitler the last word, to retrieve Judaically whatever might be still retrievable in Jewish hope and pride. There was a growing sense of a dramatic possibility – a Jewish nationalism on biblical soil, in which American Jewry might take profound satisfaction, to the deepening of their own psychic security, while absolving them of more than vicarious participation from afar, except in the case of the few emigrant enthusiasts.

There would seem to have been an inner case made for the legitimacy of a Jewish 'nationalism' of which American Jews could safely – and proudly – be 'godfathers'. Perhaps Pinsker and Moses Hess had been right, back in nineteenth-century Europe, about emulating Mazzini and Italian 'auto-emancipation'. Jews in the USA need not concede that their *patria* there was *Golah*, or 'exile'. Finding it a transatlantic 'Zion' did not preclude their full participation, by proxy, in an exciting recovery of Jewish 'independence'. Perhaps old reservations about politicizing could be forgone. There was the immediate American precedent to hand. J. L. Talmon wrote:

All of mankind's history has been a history of invasion, conquest of nation by nation, deportation of populations or their absorption by others, not to speak of extermination.[7]

It would not be that way with Zion. There need be no Palestinian version of 'Bury my heart at Wounded Knee'. Zion in statehood form would be at once successful and innocent. Did anticipation of what might transpire on the ancestral ground of Abraham and the covenant meet a deep spiritual need in American unease about its jeopardy amid assimilation, intermarriage and the secular mood by inviting it into vicarious satisfaction where 'holiness' abode on earth, haunts being recovered after long centuries of 'hope deferred' or denied?

A supporting ingredient in the effective unison of Jewish will among growing numbers in the USA and activists in the *aliyahs* at war's end was the increasing impact of 'Christian Zionism' among churches and groups in the States who read biblical psalm and prophet in imperceptive terms and saw a divine fatedness about the aims of Zionism. The grimness of Holocaust revelations deepened this sense of an arguable authenticity about Zionist aims which Christian conscience should unreservedly uphold in indifference to non-Jewish tribulation. There was much irony in this situation when such Christians were welcomed, in due course, in the new state by the Ben Gurions or Begins who inwardly scorned their logic. A recent Jewish writer captures the ambivalence:

> No sooner does a visiting American, European, African politician land at Ben Gurion airport than he is issued a *kipa* and whisked off to offer penance at Yad Vashem, the Holocaust Memorial Museum [*sic*] where he will pose looking soulful.[8]

Irony, however, does not annul realities. All in all, by 1946 in the evolving situation American Jewry – and the US government – were in far different fettle and mind from Woodrow Wilson's neglected Commissioners of 1919. The desperate enmities they could only report in vain arrived, enormously aggravated, in the same Oval Office where Wilson had languished in physical collapse.

IV

The open American bias toward Zionism in the crucial UN Partition vote of November 1947 and in the prompt recognition of the new State of Israel in May 1948 is all the more striking in the light of the misgivings that attended it. Wearied and frustrated by the contradictions of the Mandate, the Attlee Government in Britain decided to remit the issue between Zionist demands and Palestinian resistance to the new international forum as successor to the old League of Nations. The USA played a decisive part in the politics of the ensuing struggle for the votes of the fifty-six eligible members. Even Jewish observers now concede that partition would never have been approved by the larger UN of subsequent years. Washington had leverage over South American representatives and others were responsive to the astute manoeuvrings of Jewish advocates. The story has often been rehearsed. The Jewish factors that would become so marked a feature of Washington lobbying were already effectively deployed.

British withdrawal was to be followed by the creation of two independent states, a Jewish one (not yet named 'Israel') comprising some 52 per cent of the territory of mandated Palestine and a Palestinian one enclosing 48 per cent. Thirty-three nations approved the Resolution, thirteen, including India, opposed it and there were ten abstentions, including the waning Mandatory power. It is often forgotten that the Resolution required an international regime for Jerusalem, a customs union of the two states, joint currency and economic development, equal access to water and power, and common operation of ports and airports.[9]

Those items of wishfulness were soon forgotten, though the provision about Jerusalem deserves to be in present view. The boundaries, based on a Commission Report, were arbitrary and artificial and would soon be proved – in conflict – eminently revisable. Yet it is important to remember that, insofar as Israel has juridical validity in international law, they remain its basis and its definition in respect of Palestinian identity, all else being the progeny of strife monitored, thus far, only by truces. The point is the more significant, seeing that what may indeed be internationally juridical under the UN is effectively determined pragmatically by the USA. Lawyers' wigs have never yet been seen to sit comfortably on heavy armaments.

The experience of nearly four decades has proved that when the UN thinks it may be opining about Israel *de jure* the USA is deciding about it *de facto*, whether by the fact or threat of veto, or by curiously allowing its own strictures about arms use or loan conditions to go freely by default. It is this phenomenon that impresses external observers as being, perhaps in Alice's words, 'curiouser and curiouser', in the relations of two states so contrasted in the ties between them.

Yet, as if to underline the point, there was a strange hesitancy in the spring of 1948. Anxious about the ominous clouds of coming conflict, the issue of the Negev region, and economic factors around the oil of Arab states, America called in March for the setting up of a 'temporary trustee-ship' for Palestine, suspending the implementation of partition 'without prejudice to the character of the eventual political settlement'. Zionists were aghast. The US had just failed to get the Security Council to endorse the General Assembly's partition resolution. 'Trusteeship' had been a fall-back position. Ambassador Austin at the UN now seemed to make it first-line policy. The influential Mrs Roosevelt threatened to resign from the US delegation. There is confusion about Truman's own role. The question of US arms for coming to be embattled 'Israelis' as on no count forthcoming was also in the picture.

The soon to be named 'Israelis' were already making 'trustee' notions academic. Arabs, after the massacre of Dair Yasin, were leaving Jewish assigned areas. Truman's ultimate policy, whatever these waverings, was not in doubt. He immediately recognized the new State of Israel at its birth and thereby set a prime US seal upon its destiny. That spring episode, ephemeral in retrospect and undeserving of attention here for any other reason, may be seen as a wry symbol of how scruples about undue pro-Zionism in Washington could arise – and could repeatedly be overridden.

Such, broadly, has been the theme of the story. Palestinian sources were never able to mount, still less to match, the Jewish roles of influence. They had no Weizmann with presidential, no Abba Eban with media, access to the organs of policy-making and decision. Indeed, a vital feature of Zionism has been its renewed ability to have the right man in the right place. Weizmann's cultivating of the Balfour circle back in 1917 was model for his influence with Truman thirty years on. Ben Gurion might see him, *post facto*, as an expendable figure-head but without him there would have been no state. Similarly in the crisis of 1967, the suave, reassuring tones of Ambassador Abba Eban, commanding prime radio time, ensured maximum US favour for his case-making.

The story has one significant exception in 1956, when Eisenhower compelled Ben Gurion to abandon the ill-conceived Israeli share in the Anglo-French collusion in the Suez Canal crisis in the autumn of that year. Seen in Israel as a pre-emptive strike, as opportunistic bravado in America, it could be decisively annulled by a vigorous president determined not to be gainsaid. The aggression being flagrant and the calculations faulted, the retribution could be magisterial. Israel's only profit, apart from some ignominy, was the temporary elimination of some Egyptian weaponry. These were poor exchange for the forfeiture of the 'innocent' image. US authority had for once been hostile to Israel. The writ of the great power to be seen as an 'honest broker' that Eisenhower exemplified was often to be called into practical question in subsequent decades.

As noted in Chapter 4, UN Resolution 242 concerning the Six-Day War and its rewriting of the territorial map was a study in the deliberate art of loopholes. Perhaps only so could 'resolution' have been 'agreed'. In successive inconclusive debates about its meaning and implementation as successive crises arose, its ambivalence has given frequent occasion to US veto or obstruction in enforcing any Palestinian reading of its intentions. Proceeding from Resolution 181 as valid, it called for the evacuation of 'territories occupied' but did not say whether or not it meant *all* of them.[10] Withdrawal to 'mutually agreed borders' further allowed of endless prevarication.

The American factor was also significant in the issue of racism in the UN debates of 1975. It was one that sober counsels might well have left dormant or quiescent. For it had always been a taxing matter successfully to disentangle legitimate critique of Zionism from suspicions of anti-Semitism. For many in Israel and American Jewry they were equally branded as one vicious prejudice. Yet there was no doubt of discriminatory practices against native Arab-Israeli and Palestinian *de jure* owners of land and property to which they were denied access. Concerned Israelis themselves acknowledged the growth of an inferior class, economically marginal whether in 'legal' or 'occupied' Israeli territory. A (Palestinian) identity that was being steadily nullified by Israeli insistence that it dealt only with 'Arab powers' inevitably harboured psychic resentments that demanded some vital airing and the General Assembly was the evident forum.

That the issue deserved more than crude dismissal was clear, for it went to the heart of Jewish self-understanding, where indeed its solution belongs, rather than in some 'Gentile' forum for ever suspect as such.[11] Nevertheless it bore sharply on the whole *raison d'être* of Israeli nationalism as the yearned-for fulfilment and securing of a covenantal identity based on divine election guaranteed in 'holy seed'. It deserved better of US representation at the UN than to be execrated as a crude wickedness.

It would seem that when, in 1977, Anwar Sadat accepted Menahem Begin's invitation to visit Jerusalem and addressed the Knesset, his brave gesture took US policy-makers by surprise. They were always aware of the need to offset suspicion that they, or the US Jewish lobby, were conspiring to influence Israeli diplomacy. When the visit issued into further contacts, US good offices were bound to be required. 'Good offices' in truth they proved to be under the alert and persistent care of President Jimmy Carter. 'Broker' would be too brash and brazen a term for the Camp David marathon of 1978 – American peace concern at its finest.

President Carter, however, could not be blamed for the *double-entendre* implicit in the accord, nor for the enigma of Begin's psyche and policy. Israel, of course, was not then dealing with the Palestinians and would not be for another whole decade and more, and so Americans were not either. Sadat's main purpose was to retrieve Sinai and repair his own refugee problem of some half million from the Canal zone.[12] Israel was pursuing its policy of dealing only with 'Arab states' and doing so one by one. But Sadat could not isolate Egyptian objectives from 'linkage' with a Palestinian solution. It was this that he and Carter thought they had ensured – but not by Begin's lights. Post-Camp David negotiations, prolonged and tedious, did secure Israeli withdrawal from Sinai – never 'promised land' – with only a few settlements forcibly evacuated. It was a fair deal as between Israel and Egypt. Thanks to scattered Jewish settlements in Sinai close to Eilat, which had to be dislodged, it was a less punctilious evacuation than the one Eisenhower had secured in 1956. There was much misgiving in Israel about the 'linkage' Sadat had secured between the Egyptian points of Camp David and the 'solution of the Palestinian question in all its aspects'. In this case, it was a symptom, not of the bias but the very frustration of American policy, that President Carter had to acquiesce in Begin's warning that the Hebrew text of this ambiguous reference to any notion of Palestinian autonomy referred to 'the Arabs in Eretz Israel'.[13] He (Carter) could only respond that the official version would be the English text.

It is painful to ponder that Sadat paid with his life for this verbal subtlety. For 'linkage' – his only defence against accusations of 'betrayal' from other members of the Arab League – was ill-fated from the start. Egypt was, indeed, excluded from the League for a whole decade, yet Sadat, via Camp David, had availed to attain for the first time a significantly powerful recognition of the idea of Palestinians as a 'nation' with right to their territory. Carter, for his part, discovered the limited reach of good offices and good intentions in Washington when they sought to be even-handed. Promptly after Camp David Begin annexed the Golan Heights, which had only been 'occupied' since their seizure in 1967. Clearly the demilitarization of Egypt's restored Sinai, and the agreement which clinched it, secured Israel's southern flank, to the discomfort of the states to east and north, Syria in particular.[14] Perhaps there was some rough justice in the Golan, seeing that Syrian posturing and rumouring had been the main cause of 'Abd al-Nasir's devastating miscalculation in 1967. US peace-making, for its part, learned yet again how thankless a role it proved in the arena that Zion and Zionism had so charged with cross-currents of passion.

It could be said that the implications of Camp David in and after 1978 – if we substitute Jordan for Egypt – had been present in the William Rogers 'Plan' of 1970. For it envisaged a 'linkage' of a Palestinian 'solution' with an Israeli 'peace' with the State of Jordan. In that setting, however, the sheer space of Sinai and the total absence there of any Palestinianism made the entire equation, or nexus, different.

The Rogers Plan sought to be even-handed by securing for Israel an agreement with Jordan and, at the same time, proposing Israeli withdrawal from the West Bank so that it could be integrated into the Kingdom of Jordan. This, like Camp David later, would ensure another Israeli border. It could also promise a conditional self-realization for the Palestinians.

Some in the United Nations were impressed as an arguable implementation of Resolution 242 and – by some Palestinian lights – it could have been seen as a sane option.

However, it contravened the growing Palestinian identity and ignored the deep problematics in Jordanian–Palestinian relationships. Thus it miscarried and, thanks to those problematics, had grievous consequences which would embroil US policy for all Rogers' many successors into the 1990s.

To be sure, half the population of Jordan were by then citizens of Palestinian origin. But there were deep tensions, tribal perhaps in the desert kingdom, political and economic. Before and after the 1967 catastrophe, Jordanian dignity had been impugned, when not flouted, by Palestinian guerrilla action against Israel – action which provoked retaliatory tribulation and raised the sharp issue of Jordanian sovereignty. The Palestine Liberation Organization had emerged during the 1960s and its hopes and fears were at odds with a degree of Jordanian suppression of Palestinian identity.[15] Back in 1951 King Abdullah had been assassinated on emerging from the Aqsa Mosque by a fanatic invoking anti-Hashimite extremism.[16]

Such virulence apart, the Palestinian perception, finding its tortured way from the image of hapless refugees to that of national peoplehood, was increasingly minded to refuse Rogers' 'Jordanian option'. Arguably the decision could be seen as rereading old Ottoman-style Arabism, redrawing the map of destiny, and it was certainly a costlier decision than a pragmatic one could have meant; the fates in the psyche were moving towards a 'nationality' conceived in and by 'a people believing themselves to be such'.[17] Israel, moreover, was resistant to any idea of Jordanian sovereignty enclosing the West Bank area as the price of 'securing' peace eastward. Peace that-ward would be surer with the West Bank retained. The US had done its best for the UN but the parties, despite the labours of Gunnar Jarring, its envoy, would not approve.

US policy-makers would have been less than human not to have wearied of a sequence of frustrations thus complicated by intractable claims and counter-claims and harassed by the steady partisan attentions of the Israeli lobbying in the American capital. Moreover, there were constraints from those sources that impeded – or queried – the kind of full amenability to United Nations decisions and the *de jure* international authority they were assumed to possess.[18]

V

From these more even-handed ventures in peace diplomacy and in response to perceived Palestinian obduracy, American policy assumed a prolonged posture of negating the growing Palestinian insistence on separate nation-style identity. It accepted the Israeli stance of non-negotiation with other than Arab states, excluding Palestinian elements from the equation pending a total renunciation of violence. With US diplomats in London and Khartoum and nationals elsewhere in the travelling world at risk of their lives from Palestinian violence, the stance was intelligible. However, it effectively terminated any significant handling of the basics, leaving Israel, under Likud, to pursue its settlements unhindered with the perfect alibi of the claim that there was no negotiable party in the frame.

A more foresighted policy would have seen that it was a prescript for impasse and played into the hands of the Palestinian argument for desperation, if not despair. When in 1984 the USA made formal alliance with Israel, agreeing on strategic co-operation, it called into radical question its capacity to be an honest broker between the parties in the Middle East. America was concerned, before the demise of Soviet super-power status, to have a firm ally in the region able to test out its weaponry. The stance undermined American will to genuine disavowal of the disaster into which Israel blundered by invading Lebanon in 1982.

The degree of unmitigated pro-Israeli support in the sequel not only stimulated the Intifadah inside the occupied territory but denied to Palestinian counsels any credible incentive to repudiate armed resistance – though this may at times have been the ostensible purpose. It failed to reckon with how far its partners, Begin, Yitzhak Shamir and others in their day, had long sustained terrorism as a policy, or to recognize that 'accepting Israel's right to exist', and doing so unconditionally, ignored the ever-crucial question of 'which Israel?', territorially expressed. For both acceptance and Israel were inchoate notions without negotiation and negotiation was made *verboten* without submission to the prior demand. 'Inadmissible' was inscribed on the door the Palestinians were exhorted to enter – a situation made the more partial to impasse by the isolation of Palestinians in exile in Tunis and elsewhere from those within the territory.

When in December 1988 the PLO did finally record its readiness for a policy of co-existence, the Likud government dismissed it as not genuine and the USA continued to maintain an Israeli right to determine which, if any, Palestinian 'negotiators' it would countenance, to the point of deciding the delegations themselves. Fictions about Jerusalem residence or PLO connection had to be maintained and even persisted into the Madrid

Conference of 1992. American policy found itself involved in secret or transparent feats of 'connivance' which a more even-handed and robust approach would have scorned as uncongenial to a super-power. It was all a long way, in the post-Ottoman Middle East, from where America had begun in the vision of its Woodrow Wilson. Was his bespectacled ghost somewhere brooding round the Oslo snows in 1993?

It might be said that the congenial image of Hanan Ashrawi went far to help reconcile Americans in the early 1990s to the reality of credible Palestinians, the contrary image of a *kuffiyah*-draped, khaki-clad Yassir Arafat having too often repelled them. But in 'the land of the free', should it have taken a Western-educated articulacy to engage them with a people seeking freedom? Admittedly Palestinians themselves had passed through an evolution from futility to pragmatism. The data have been traced in earlier chapters. Could a more generous US policy have achieved this evolution earlier and at greatly less human cost? It is harder to be prudential realists, pragmatists reading odds sanely, if you are consistently villainized and perceive your destinies subdued to criteria you have no peaceable opportunity to disqualify or change.

There was, of course, always the issue of who spoke for Palestinians. Before and after the final realization, in Israel and the USA, that the clear answer was 'the PLO', ambivalence on all sides had every opportunity to cavil or demur. The problem of differing wings and sides in the equation had been evident enough in the counsels of Zionism, 'doves' and 'hawks' being present – relatively – in every cause. It had been possible for Israelis both to admire and disown the perceived excesses of diehards or for these, in due time, to metamorphose into ministers. Given the added factor of dispersal, Palestinians had less occasion to rein in or discipline their rasher, wilder elements, though not escaping the consequences – as when in May 1988 a Libyan ship attacked the coast at Tel Aviv and the US suspended the dialogue which had hardly begun. Terrorism outside the control of the main PLO all too readily delayed or denied its own momentum towards understanding.

It is strange to outside observers how forbearing, if not manipulable, the super-power repeatedly proved *vis-à-vis* its protégé. This was notably so during the period of Secretary James Baker. At one point when he (or his President) suspended the promised cancellation of loans, or grant of them, because Israel had continued its settlement-building policy in contravention of the loans' condition, Israel reacted angrily to 'blackmail', the allegedly improper use of charity for political ends, or – worst of all – an American attempt to control Israeli sovereignty and freedom of action. The motive was the Likud aim of creating 'facts' that would later prove 'irreversible'. But further settlements violated not only USA understandings but several Resolutions of the United Nations which forbade pre-empting not-yet-resolved issues at stake.[19] The great USA was to be cast in the role of financier and provider of *carte blanche*. Could it not have been more consistently robust in ensuring it was not so? Cliency is seldom a school of gratitude but it is an ironic measure of the USA–Israel relation that a reasonable, if gentle, *caveat* from the one should have been seen as near insult by the other.

VI

Part of the answer to that anomaly betakes us to the role in America at large and Washington in particular of the Jewish lobby. AIPAC (the American/ Israeli Public Affairs Committee) must rank among the most skilful and effective of pressure-activists in the annals of the corridors of power. It commands a nationwide network of personal media vigilantes, alert to monitor the slightest hint of pro-Palestinian opinion on the part of US Congress members and pursue the offenders with rebuttal, to be sure, but also with skilful threats to their re-electability. It can muster its influential ranks to drain away the sources of electoral financing or divert them massively towards an opponent next time round.

The career, notably, of Senator Charles Percy of Illinois was brutally terminated in this way, in response to a mildly expressed reflection on the imbalance of US policy.[20] Since senators are hardly elected before they have to calculate for the next encounter with the suffrage system, they are unlikely to be inattentive to the lesson in Charles Percy's eclipse. For the timorous, however, the sort of protest that might begin to wonder about how viable genuine democracy remained in the US in areas where AIPAC was concerned, would likely be discreetly muted. It seems odd that non-citizens from without enjoy a greater liberty of comment and perhaps even of perception. Thanks to this intimidatory element in the lobby system, thus optimally ruthless, objective assessments in reasonable debate go darkly by default.

One sinister feature of the pro-Israeli lobby in the USA is its cynical distortion of the meaning of 'anti-Semitism'. It might have been assumed that an -ism about defamation and gross calumny, for Jewry's own sake as its age-long victims, ought only to be charged where it truly existed. Sound anti-defamation as the urgent prerogative of Jewish dignity deserves better than to be prostituted and purloined by propagandists 'anti-Semitizing' sober, benignly-meant and carefully reasoned criticisms of Israel, sympathy with non-Israelis or anxiety about the use of vilification in the stead of debate.

Examples abound in recent American public affairs of baseless and malignant charges or insinuations about anti-Semitism. Wild, unproven and shamefully routine, their frequency threatens to bring back – at least in this context – a McCarthy-style intimidation by innuendo, liable, if unresisted, to stifle all sane debate and honest scrutiny of public policy.

Not only so, but powerful financial and economic sanctions are available to sway the attitudes of candidates for office. There are ways, by multiplying the nominal sources, of evading congressional rules limiting what a lobby may officially expend on any one candidate. The media, if not directly mortgaged, can be manipulated by advertisement placing, while academic institutions and organs of political and moral debate are susceptible in numerous subtle ways to the appropriate pressures.

The whole scenario of Israeli 'interests' in the United States, in policy-making, finance and the economy, makes a wry commentary on the notion of 'host nation' that Zionism heartily disowned and vowed to anathematize for ever as the illusion offering only assimilation or persecution from an incorrigibly 'Gentile' world. For the United States is the perfect 'host-nation' of Zion, the ever-dependable ensurer of Israel's viability by finance, arms, diplomacy and generosity. The crucial cliency is rarely acknowledged as such by Israel. For independence is the true mythology and any sensitive critic can understand why. Nevertheless the USA is, and has been, the pliable host-nation ever since Harry Truman recognized the new state, Eisenhower's realism in 1956 notwithstanding.

An episode in President George Bush's tenure gave a touch of irony to this 'way things are'. Making the waiving of certain loan repayments, or loan-grantings, conditional on Israelis indicating their acceptance of a veto on more settlements, he told them, in response to their pained demur: 'Ring the White House as soon as you are ready: we will delay no longer.' Such modest pressure was unusual but the pleasantry is plain. For Jerusalem had been long in the constant habit of 'ringing the White House', or sources adjacent, whenever something critical needed the President's usually compliant attention. Outsiders have long wondered anxiously, in these realms, about how policy squares itself with its own historical referent concerning 'dispassionate attachment' and 'the cultivation of peace and harmony with all'.[21]

Such outsiders, being such, may wonder too about how logistics work to override the precept of George Washington. Some have thought it advantageous to have an armed reservoir of indebtedness at the heart of the

Middle East and on the flank of vital oil resources; others that there is point in proxy testing of new technology at war, when occasion offers. Lobbies apart, there is a deep well-spring of sentiment and admiration, on Judaic and/or biblical grounds, for the feats of Zion and, since 1967, an American fellow-feeling for the remarkable prowess of Israelis, their Masada spirit in the 1967 victory and later at Entebbe, or when 'taking out' nuclear power in Baghdad. Also, AIPAC and its co-publicists apart, there has long been a distaste for, and enmity to, the image of Islam which some Muslims have done little to disqualify and others much to vindicate. For some there is what might be called 'a visceral fear' of Muslims, underwritten by the head-line mind in and through the general media.

This aspect of the American mood deepened after the real, or apparent, collapse of the Soviet Empire. If the old confrontation had ended, maybe the strategic interest of the USA diminished somewhat, while Arab powers were less able to play one power off against another as minnows in the stream must do. More importantly, if there were some psychic need for some new 'hate', some necessary 'the Philistines be upon thee, Samson' in the world scene, Islam was well suited to afford it.

Despite the number of Palestinians in the Americas, they have not been able to muster the collective means of swaying US policy or opinion, or their organs, with the finesse, the thoroughness or the impact of the Jewish lobby. For they start from a much smaller base of popular appeal, a much poorer range of assets social, monetary and academic. It has sometimes been said that the best hope of the Palestinians has been the potential in perception and in heart of American Jewry as a whole. Some aspects of Jewish heart-response to the Palestinian nexus of Israel we must remit to Chapter 11. The Madrid Conference delegation from the PLO was right to seek 'an act of will that would make a just peace a reality'. A large factor in Israel achieving such 'an act of will' must lie with the will and wisdom of American Jewry, identifying with the generous tradition of a whole nation (Lincoln's 'malice toward none') as being American in their Jewishness and Jewish by the righteousness of their finest prophets. Or, if only reckoning on the lower category of peace-brokering as the role-presumptive of the USA, an 'attach-ment' to 'dispassion' would seem to be imperative as between the parties urgent for the peace.

VII

There remains only to note that the Jewish factor in the USA has been phenomenally lavish in its unfailing benevolence to Israel, both from government grants, loans, investments and pledges and via the personal, organizational munificence of Israel Bonds and donations and funds tirelessly remitted to, first, the Jewish Agency and then its successor in the state itself. It is trite to depreciate so-called 'cheque-book Zionists', for without them and without the USA the State of Israel could not subsist or would subsist only in the direst terms of out-Sparta-ing Sparta in impossibly drawn-out privation. Remarkable feats of endurance have been recorded in the absorption of destitute immigrants, the draining of swamps, the fructifying of the land and the nurture of the arts. But all these had their *élan* from the confidence of diaspora pride and provision in the entire enterprise which no merely local determination could have achieved in dire self-reliance.

The American monetary and financial participation in the founding, survival and sustaining of Israel has been staggering in its generosity and staggeringly exceptional, far outweighing that to any other cause or country and at times exceeding the sum total of all others. It remains the most astonishing measure of the patronage of one state by another, the more remarkable in that some of the citizens of the patron were unaware at times of how massive it was. Their nation, to be sure, behaved generously to other states in the Middle East region, notably Egypt and Jordan, but never in comparable terms of 'passionate attachment'. The exceptionality of the Israeli connection was never in question spiritually. Thanks to the relevant lobby, it was rarely sufficiently interrogated within the democratic process.

There is an intriguing footnote to this dimension of Israel's love-affair with the USA. As Leah Rabin learned to her embarrassment, no Israeli may hold a bank account in America.[22] The only place for the golden eggs was inside the economy and exchequer of the beneficiary state. The US wealth potential might stay in no private corners, no personal coffers.

The most striking symbol of this unique inter-state US–Israeli nexus, and its deeply impressive sacrament, is the Washington Museum of the Holocaust. Such commemorations of one nation's experience in the capital of another are rare. The impact of the Holocaust Memorial is evidence enough of its utter legitimacy in its American context. Yet it holds within itself an unresolved dilemma well phrased by a writer in *The New York Times* on the day of its opening:

The surest engagement with memory lies in its perpetual irresolution. In fact, the best memorial to the Fascist era and its victims may not be a single memorial at all, but simply the never-to-be resolved debate over which kind of memory to preserve, how to do it, in whose name and to what end.[23]

It was perceptive comment, in no way disqualifying the forms of stone and art and artifact in having the past not die, yet pointing to the ever open issue these leave to silence.

Notes

1 B. A. Rosenblatt, *Social Zionism: Selected Essays* (New York, 1919), pp. 131–2.

2 See S. B. L. Penrose Jr, *That They May Have Life: The Story of the American University of Beirut* (New York, 1941). A personal reflection is in my *The Arab Christian* (London, 1992), pp. 218–22.

3 Cited from George E. Kirk, *A Short History of the Middle East* (1948), pp. 152–3.

4 David Phillipson, *The Reform Movement* (New York, 1907), p. 493: Point 5 of the Platform.

5 Ben Gurion insisted that every Jew everywhere was duty bound to come to Israel. The irony was that many in the USA made Israel viable precisely by staying away and donating from diaspora wealth.

6 See Norman Cantor, *The Sacred Chain: A History of the Jews* (London, 1994), pp. 394–5.

7 J. L. Talmon, *Israel Among the Nations* (London, 1970), p. 142.

8 Mordecai Richler, *This Year in Jerusalem* (London, 1994), p. 116.

9 It has been an issue ever since as to whether these visionary elements simply became obsolete when militancy on both sides drowned them out of all perspective. Israel could see them as 'out-of-date and pointless'. Yet as long as only truces persist, at least that about Jerusalem remains *de jure* right – as explicit in the post-1993 'accords' which 'defer' but do not 'exclude' Jerusalem. A sharing of the city remains on the legal agenda.

10 The French 'territoires' allows a restrictive interpretation; the English, lacking the definite article, might do so also.

11 The very fervour by which some Jewish writers deny ethnicism (e.g., Jacob Agus, *Jewish Identity in an Age of Ideologues* (New York, 1976), pp. 280f.) is eloquent of how fervidly other Jewish exponents assert it. One can hardly banish it from the biblical stress perpetually on 'seed', 'generation to generation', on 'circumcision' as a sign of masculine virility, the laws of purity, anathemas on intermarriage, and dietary practice as segregating from Gentiles – a term, inclusive of *all* other mortals, that is hardly eloquent of inter-racialism. Moreover, the Jewish sense of divinely ordered differential has been borrowed elsewhere with dire racial consequences.

12 It is often forgotten that this figure of Egyptians refugees in their own land was no less than two-thirds of the original number of Palestinians displaced in 1948. Egypt paid a heavy price for its involvement with the Palestinian cause.

13 When Begin's 'acceptance' of Camp David was challenged in the Knesset by his own party and other right-wing elements, he vowed that he would never surrender 'one inch' of the land of Israel. Hence, as noted in Chapter 4 above, his letter to Carter 'clarifying' his understanding of what had been 'agreed' and avoiding all mention of 'Palestine' or Palestinians and insisting on 'Eretz Israel'.

14 As Benjamin Netanyahu notes in *A Place Among the Nations: Israel and the World* (London, 1993), p. 254: 'The demilitarized Sinai is sufficiently vast that if Egypt were to violate peace with Israel, Israel would have time to mobilize its defences and counter-attack.'

15 In the early days of Imam Hussaini's bid for the leadership of the Palestinian cause against the Jewish Agency, the Hashimites forbade Palestinians to describe themselves with

the word. There were hard issues at stake, then and later, about the emerging struggle for immediate identity within the wider Arabism. Post-1967 developments only made them more acute.

16 His grandson, the future King Husain, was at his side, fated to inherit all the tensions and perils the event symbolized.

17 Definitions of 'nationality' and 'nationalism' are various and elusive. This seems as workmanlike as any. One might compare the 'definition' of music as 'what moves within you when you are reminded by the instruments'.

18 In its postures within the UN the USA in the General Assembly and/or Security Council often proved, by its sheer status, a significant factor in the virtual 'dead-lettering' of findings or resolutions intending constraints on Israeli unilateral actions, just as it was acquiescent about infractions of bilateral understandings.

19 Camp David, for example, had incorporated Resolution 242 and undertook to ensure the conclusion of the Palestine case 'in all its aspects'. Begin's 'acceptance' of this, challenged in the Knesset on his return, was 'hedged' around by his later 'letter' re the Hebrew text. The liberty to multiply settlements and so forestall ultimate negotiations was certainly excluded. Likewise tampering with the juridical status of Jerusalem. Israel could be oblivious of UN Resolutions, despite owing its *legal* being to that of November 1947.

20 Senator Percy, Chairman of the Foreign Relations Committee and a widely respected senior figure in Congress, visited Israel in 1975. On his return he urged that his country should 'deal with the PLO' (almost twenty years ahead of when it finally did), and warned that 'Israel and its leadership, for whom I have a high regard, cannot count on the US in the future just to write a blank check'. He also offended AIPAC by supporting sale of AWAC planes to Saudi Arabia, though he had voted 87 times in support of Israel in Congress. His re-election campaign in 1984 was effectively torpedoed by malign accusations and concerted vilification. He was depicted as deluded about Arafat as 'moderate'. The head of AIPAC boasted that 'All the Jews in America from coast to coast gathered to oust Percy to the tune of four million dollars'. There have been sundry other 'victims' in Congress of such anti-Palestinian chicanery. It was remarkable that so few US citizenry were appalled by the Percy story.

21 See the full analysis in George W. Ball and D. B. Ball (eds), *The Passionate Attachment: America's Involvement with Israel, 1947 to the Present* (New York, 1992).

22 The wife of Yitzhak Rabin, who caused a minor political crisis when discovered as having broken the law.

23 The date was Friday, 23 April 1993, the writer James E. Young.

10

The iron in the soul

I

In a novel about his hero Samson, Vladimir Jabotinsky, among the most
ardent of Zionist militants, called upon his readers to 'gather iron'. He may
have meant a veiled allusion to the Hebrew lack of it, noted in Chapter 1,
in Samson's day. Jabotinsky himself was certainly tireless in that task. The
armament-running vessel, with Begin on board, sunk by Ben Gurion's
Haganah off 'Philistia's' shore-line in 1948, was named *Altalena* in his
honour, borrowing the pen-name under which he wrote.[1] Could the 'iron'
allusion, however, have had Psalm 105:18 in mind, where – recalling the
trauma of Joseph – the writer has 'the iron entering into his soul'?

The phrase has a double sense. There was a halter of iron around the
'neck' of the prisoner, so that in physical fact Joseph 'entered into it'. But
the other meaning at once belongs. The experience, as we would now say,
'steeled his soul' to patient fortitude. In his vibrant Zionism, Jabotinsky
exemplified in different terms how a combative energy in a belligerent
cause could engender a corresponding toughness of will. 'Arms and the
man' could well have been his theme. He embodied what he demanded,
namely the tenacity of the old Maccabees whose very name comprises the
Hebrew initials of 'Who is like You, O Lord, among the mighty?' There
was no ambivalence about his politics. Stressing the sharp ethnicity of
Jewry, he insisted that there could be 'no alien minorities' within the state,
for 'they would weaken national unity'. He saw 'the transformation of
Palestine into a Jewish state a postulate of the highest justice, to which all
opposition is unjust'.[2] There was a certain avenging in his creed:

Anyone who has himself suffered for a long time under the yoke of a stronger one will oppress those weaker than he.[3]

The character and temper of Jabotinsky's Zionism, therefore, is well suited to serve this chapter's task, which is to explore, in Palestinian experience, both elements of 'the iron in the soul', the physical traumas and the inner travail of spirit. For his own forthright nationalism left him innocent of the obfuscation about motives and ends to which so many were prone in their measure of necessary tactics. The Bible sufficed him as a more thrusting mandate than Herzl's *Der Judenstaat*. He did not want Zionism to behave as some silent conspiracy. He thought his case for ruthless Jewish domi-nance in both power and numbers greatly hardened by the severing – as he saw it – of Trans-Jordan from the mandating intentions of the League of Nations, a point frequently made in Zionist emphasis on the territorial 'minuteness', and therefore vulnerability, of the smaller land area.

Thus, on every count and with his admiration of old Samson, Jabotinsky's 'iron in the soul' makes an apt parable for the tale and toll of Palestinian experience. With his strong pursuit of Hebrew as a man of letters cherishing a national speech, he might even serve as *provocateur* of the Palestinian Arabic writing in which resistance found its voice and agony its cry. Voice and cry are not a literature of despair only because they give it such eloquent expression. There is 'the iron' but there is also 'the soul'.

II

It is a literature about dispersion, about the 800,000 Palestinians uprooted from what, by 1949, became truce-demarcated Israel, many of them to be further displaced in 1967. The incidence of human tragedy is not mitigated by the arguments of propaganda, though for the propagandists it may seem to be. The pain of Palestinian dispersal from lands and villages is not undone – indeed only intensified – by dint of old controversies about its occasion. Nor is it solaced by repeated reminders that an Israeli-style resourcefulness from Arab neighbours could have quickly brought it to an end.

These have been the two exonerating perceptions to quieten Israeli consciences willing to deduce them. They had a desperately hollow ring beneath the tents round Jericho and Gaza. The immediate history after the hasty British withdrawal, its circumstances satisfying nobody, could never have escaped controversial reading. Passions were too high and consequences catastrophic or propitious. Did Arab command instigate civilian flight to have the peasantry out of victory's assured climax? Or was it massacres like that at Dair Yasin that used terror to create a tide of exit? Either way, the sequel was a massive exodus of refugees whose vacated homes and fields have never been substantially regained and availed all too readily for Jewish immigration. The cost in Israeli life and limb, the urgent evocation of courage and the defiance of odds – these could inwardly atone for what they gained. Otherwise, the long Jewish diaspora might have educated its newly national escapees into the truth that anguish is not mitigated in its incidence by debate about its antecedents. However evacuation was contrived, whether by mistaken Arab bravado or by Jewish brutality against the unarmed, the sequel was the same in the suffering undergone – a suffering sharpened by the steady realization that, land-wise, it would prove conveniently irreversible.

Or was it? The other bitterness in Palestinian refugeedom was the charge that it was made a cruel pawn in Arab politics. Chapter 7 has reviewed the hard misusing of the Palestinians by the Arab powers. These, with their vast resources of oil wealth, if matched by vigorous measures of re-patriation, could soon have accommodated the exiled Palestinians anywhere in the vast Arab hinterland. That they failed to do so is an indictment that, by the same token, arguably exonerates the Jewish state that had afforded them a superb example. No blame could attach to it if the model was not emulated.

By these lights, Palestinian refugeedom became no longer a tragedy but merely a 'problem'. 'Do not allow finality to that which befalls you' had always been a principle of Zionism. You are only defeated when you acquiesce. Never capitulate to that which you are summoned to change. Yet to have organized resettlement would have conceded the permanence of exile. By anything like a 'nationalist' doctrine of 'the land', that conclusion meant betrayal. Events, of course, were in flux and politics move only in a present. 'Pawns' in a conflict the refugees might seem to be and, for some cynics, it may have been so in fact. But were not early settlers on the soil in the Zionist venture 'pawns' in a future yet to be resolved? Jeopardy has not seldom to be sustained in waiting terms.

Any patriation elsewhere implied that the former *patria* was no longer cherished as such, no longer existent in the mind or on the ground. Fidelity could not accept that implication nor conspire to give it form. Refugees did not want, for the most part, to go elsewhere. Dair-al-Zur is not Kafr Yassif, nor Amarah Qilqiliyah. The methods of Palestinian villagers may have been primitive. Indeed they were no kibbutzniks, but their land-love was genuine, their soil sacred in their eyes. There could even be a certain nobility in 'pawns' who opted for a wind-swept tent in which they might still await their stony Bethels as their own. They were not then to know that Arab – and international – politics would prolong their agonies through three generations. There is only cynicism in the view that sees their sufferings as a mere device to maintain pressure on Israel, forlorn as that notion would have been, or to perpetuate a claim on international charity.

Could resettlement have been energetically, and so forcibly, implemented in at least ostensibly temporary terms? A case in that sense could well be made. In some ways, in point of fact, it happened by the absorption of many Palestinians into Jordanian citizenship and/or the labour market in Gulf oil. But these were the more urban skilled people. Temporary arrangements are liable to prove permanent and Israeli attitudes gave no indication to the contrary. The sort of fidelity to place and soil which Zionism had demonstrated had also to hold for a Palestinian diaspora. That fact may not absolve the Arab powers of their all too easy acquiescence but nor should that reproach be turned to a glib disowning of the exiles' tribulation as if they were wilfully deserving sufferers.

III

Moreover, by having repudiated partition and succumbed in battle, Palestinian fortunes were subject to a subtle change deriving from the Israeli acquisition both of sovereignty and territory. Abba Eban made the point sharply:

> For the first time [1948] we were able to explore some of the effects of sovereignty on the style and atmosphere of the Jewish dialogue with the outside world [sic]. The phrase 'none of your business' could not rationally have been uttered by a Jewish spokesman in all the previous centuries.[4]

Now the words were all too readily feasible. *Raisons d'état* would be available, if not to exonerate, at least to discount the impact they had on others. The applications of laws about land ownership, their suspension on pretext, the power of the army to designate military areas, the rigorous control of Palestinian wells, water resources, planting operations and economic activity in 'the territories' after 1967, as well as confiscations – all these went far to disable Palestinian enterprise or consign it to precariousness. 'None of your business' was a crippling retort to such Palestinian grievances and even when the courts found pro-Palestinian pleas sustainable, governmental legislation usually availed to counter them and close the loopholes.

However, it is grief rather than merely grievances with which this chapter is concerned, the grief of deepening frustration and utter helplessness in the face of mounting distress. It was little comfort to reflect that the very Knesset itself, where Israel's policies were sharply debated and laws decided, stood on confiscated Arab land. There, in symbol, was the whole drama of a power which – apart from such suffrage influence as Palestinian minority voters in Israel proper[5] could exercise – took its entire counsel only with its own perceptions of security, Jewish ideology and economic superiority. The lot of displaced Palestinians was impotently to watch the steady 'ratchet effect'[6] of Israeli measures, each building on the last in the name of the irreversible. Some of these aspects we have traced under the theme of ambivalence. When the early 1970s gave way, in 1977, to a Likud government and assigned the Palestinian provisions of Camp David to oblivious neglect, the locals could only watch the subtle, if also blatant, enterprise of Jewish settlements in the territory still, ostensibly, subject to negotiation by international resolutions. Whereas Labour in power placed settlements in the Jordan valley, peopling a strategic frontier and keeping open an option of territorial compromise, those of Likud were purposely dispersed between Arab towns and villages, allowing for a network of highways linking Jewish populations and virtually confining Palestinians to the resulting enclaves of dubious economic viability or access only on the sufferance of Israel.

Whatever the evolving outcome of land issues left as events then stood in Chapter 4, the prospects of Palestinian prosperity are bleak. When Begin came to power in 1977 there were only 23 settlements on the West Bank, plus one in Gaza. At his resignation in 1983 there were 112 and five respectively, including virtual towns near Jerusalem. Settlements have been heavily subsidized to admit of easy commuting to Jerusalem or Tel Aviv. Deliberate policy, not urgent need for *Lebensraum*, dictates these developments. They have an irrevocable intent. Only in 'non-holy' Sinai have Jewish settlements ever been dismantled.

The pain of mind for Palestinians is not only in their inability to halt a stealth of deprivation. It is also in the bitter reversal of categories: 'Who is now the stranger?' In Hebraic tradition there runs an admonition about 'the stranger who is within thy gates'. He, too, must have Sabbath rest. What, though, when it is 'the strangers' gates' themselves? How does the command about 'loving him'[7] obtain when he is in fact being usurped? Or do we abandon altogether the idea of 'gates' at all – a notion the very command seems to require in validating the Jewish ones? We are back to the truth that 'occupying' or 'administering' is not 'owning', 'annexing' or 'possessing'. Logically, the very concept of 'aliens' and the practice of 'love' to them are cancelled if lands called after their peoples' name are not inviolate.

The tribulations we are exploring, however, are beyond mere logic.

'Gates' that may be physically infiltrated or commandeered are not emotionally surrendered. Yet resistance is made forlorn by the heavy odds against it. To be sure, Israeli Defence Forces are provoked by stone-throwing children, by demonstrations and strikes, by the ardour of the Intifadah. There are, happily, those Israelis who pause to query the state that has even children defying it with stones, and women with bare fists. Others drown conscience in holy violence and justify oppression as the only terms in which to read the challenge.

Then the confiscations follow, the demolition of dwellings, the de-homing of activists, the proscription of well-digging, vine-planting and crop-growing, and the depopulation of villages. Military exigencies can be claimed to enforce dispossession and arbitrary measures taken from which there is no redress or – if the courts allow it – new orders may overrule them. The warrant is doubtless set to rely on necessities of state and public peace when these would be more truly served by honest reconciliation.

It is not simply that the settlement policy spells dispossession and disaster for adjacent peasantry. It is also that violence is engendered by creating mutual insecurity. Evicted or imperilled farmers are provoked, however hopelessly, to retaliation or at least to angry dismay. In response the settlers develop their own vigilantes. The army often leaves them to their own good auspices, failing to protect their victims so that these, in turn, find little ground to expect any state exercise of neutrality as between its favoured and its unfavoured subjects. Annexation of 'the territories' may be demographically impossible – a fact which does not mitigate the injustice of the occupancy. Nor is there any Palestinian comfort in the inability or unwillingness of the United States to use its financial largesse for Israel to ensure a stricter righteousness.

IV

Another grim feature of 'iron in the soul' belongs with mutual embitter-ments among Palestinians themselves. The rise of Hamas owed much, from 1987–88, to a perception of PLO political futility. There are suspicions in some quarters that Israel may even have encouraged Hamas in order to embarrass the PLO, which in any event was an amalgam of sundry groups whose alliance was often precarious. When Israel at length moved fitfully towards the idea that selected PLO elements[8] might be held negotiable, Hamas became the main adversary. The parties in all prolonged conflicts are permeable to intrigue, shifts of loyalty and disputed passions among themselves. They are also highly susceptible to infiltration.

Secret agents, spies, informers, dissemblers become the stock-in-trade of confrontation. It was so in the birth throes of Islam as a religious power-structure in Medina. Would-be neutrals were caught in the cross-fire between the powers in the twin cities of nascent Islam. How sure was their neutrality? Might there be some *nifaq*, 'hypocrisy',[9] untrustworthy because not avowedly committed, or useful – as spies are – for the same reason. Some of the bitterness latent in the New Testament between Jews and Christians in Asia Minor stemmed from the same surmise about 'crypto' people dubiously 'in-between'.[10]

Palestinianism has been tragically afflicted this way. So many of its lives have been lost not only to Jewish action but to Palestinian, brother against brother. The reasons are not far to seek. Always, therefore, at stake in peace possibilities was what Israel would do with detainees, what the PLO would do with 'informers'. Of the latter there were those recruited to infiltrate PLO cells for the better efficiency of the Beth Shin or the IDF. An oppressed people, a people at war, will never achieve a unanimous cause free of conspiracy and betrayal. Factors of poverty, despair, human frailty, suborned character, or the cunning of recruiters, will always yield the necessary material. Palestinianism has been no exception.

Hence the heavy toll of suffering and death, the dire cost in life and limb between fellow-nationals in Palestine. The length of the encounter and its urgency only intensified the resentment at actual or suspected treachery. Where the rewards are high, the stakes are heavy. At least until the murder of an Israeli Prime Minister by an Israeli fanatic, Israel had always prided itself on the superb efficiency of its intelligence arrangements. Palestinian patriotism could not match it in expertise. By the same token it paid the price in treasons. Or should we say that these stemmed from its own political misreadings in the 1940s? Either way, the cost has been paid. Bereavement is bereavement whatever its incidence in the fair and the foul.

The pain for Palestinians of the incidence of Zionism was not confined to Palestinian territory. It served also to set Arab against Arab. Israel might insist that this was due to inherent Arab strains, yet there is no doubt that the ventures of Zionism greatly accentuated them. The tragic events in Jordan in 1970 are one example, the traumas of Lebanon another. It was no coincidence that the massacres at Sabra and Chatila took place in the very month (September 1982) of the Israeli expulsion of the armed PLO forces from Beirut. Their departure left unarmed refugees at the mercy of the Maronites, whose anti-Palestinian enmities stemmed directly from a perception of them as injurious exiles from the south. The anguish of the departing PLO militants over their defenceless civilians was no small element in their stiffened defiance in Tunis, any fruits of which the victims of Sabra and Chatila would never enjoy.

In the graffiti on the West Bank during the Intifadah 'the iron in the soul' drew with a pen – or a daub – on the stones. It suggested a grim humour and a high bravado not lost on authority, which took harsh and wary notice of the scribes with punitive retaliation. Israeli *amour propre* was touched to the quick by slogans like 'prison is for relaxation', 'our people outmatch all repression', 'stone-throwing is for exercise', '*Fatah* passed by here'. Even the black smudges of erasure witnessed to a populace alive with its soul, liberating its consciousness in the very throes of adversity. The state which had made such splendid success of its proud Hebrew as the language of recovered identity could neither misread, nor brook, the significance of Arabic scrawl crudely advertised on walls.[11]

Before coming to the writers in the literature of grievances and grief, there is one final point about the graffiti. Much of it from Muslim graffiteers extolled the 'martyrs'. Suicide bombers might think they had a Jewish precedent in the warriors who destroyed themselves on Masada as a last gesture of futile defiance. A gentler faith would have to insist that 'martyrdom' is never truly found – nor heaven by it – except in a *love* that suffers and undergoes what others do in taking life, never from a risk taken in carrying death to others. Heroes perhaps the latter may be held – depending on the view one takes of heroism. Aspects of the question 'What do we do with tragedy?' will come in Chapter 12. However, even with a perverse theology, Palestinian graffiti across the West Bank through long years of corporate pain did witness to a people in the making with a soul.

For some there was a living martyrdom in long imprisonment accompanied by the several devices of a torturing authority urgent to extract information. That Zionism has always been at odds with itself about applying or avoiding the engines of a police state is no surprise, given a Palestinian dimension in the way. A 'holy land' admits no exemption from the familiar *équipage* of power when needing to ride roughshod over a resistant population. It sadly follows that Israeli prisons have long been arraigned by inquests concerned for human rights. They are listed alongside conspicuous offenders across the globe.[12] Long incarceration without charge, the use of torture and intimidation may be – and have been – alleged warranted by the perils the state faces in its perceptions of security. It is also pleaded that, while Palestinians resist, Zion is 'only on the way' and therefore not to be judged until, being at peace with its setting, it can be at peace with itself. To be sure, exceptional standards should not be demanded if Jewish exceptionality is not supposed to admit them. Either way, the tragedies of incarcerated heroes are yet more 'iron in the soul'.

V

It has long been clear that Zionism, insistently requiring statehood, represents a sharp politicization of Judaism. Responsively, Palestinianism is adamant for statehood. This reciprocal priority of the political dominates the long story. Yet it cannot wholly occupy the heart. The emotions with which it is charged cannot find or fulfil themselves only in policies, strategies, wars and physical heroics. They release themselves in poetry, in prose and verse.

> The tempest in the mind
> Doth from the senses take all feeling else,
> Save what beats there.[13]

Or, if not in all and sundry, then in those whose spirits are proxy for the whole. This Palestinian literature accompanies, but in its own idiom transcends, the shifting tale of politics. It is the soul interpreting the iron.

It is a literature that mirrors the Palestinian experience, musing on the several measures of the world of fact and wistful for what is forfeit. F. W. H. Myers' lines on 'The Scapegoat' might serve to carry its pathos:

> . . . out into the wilderness . . . through Edom
> By Horeb and the heaps of Abarim . . .
> and sought in vain old pastures.
> Is there grass in Hazeroth
> Or sweet fresh water in the salt dead sea?[14]

The sense of exile broods over it, an irony more striking in that Zionist visionaries of gentle heart had thought of *their* return as figuring the end of all human exile. Palestinian poetry takes up the converse and at times reads its own displacement as symbol of a whole humanity adrift from moorings and bereft. The physical traumas of dispossession find voice in songs of land celebration. Abandoned terraces and vineyards become the more endeared by the sharp wound of absence. The sense of a loved genealogy – always a marked feature of Arab culture – compels a celebration of the aged generation still lingering or departed. For this literature is now half a century old and has to console itself against the ravages of hope deferred.

One might illuminate this quality by citing, for parallel, the art of the Israeli artist Marc Chagall. For the sheer human passions and perplexities that inspired his portraiture of ghetto and pogrom inhabit the poetry of Tawfiq Sayigh and his fellows, the stories of Ghassan Kanafani and the

Palestinian novel. The symbols of pain and desolation move with the themes of sacred story as in the Jewish art of Marc Chagall, where the prayer-shawl drapes from the Cross. There is the same appeal to the great referents of religion, the clues enshrined (if clues they be) in the traditions of the holy. An angry agnosticism clings to the vestiges of patient hope.

The religious relationships of this literature call for fuller study in the final chapter. It remains remarkable how far it has been taken with the imagery of Jesus' crucifixion, so that Muslims have incurred the rebuke and aroused the consternation of Azharite authority for their involvement with this 'un-Islamic' trend. The Palestinian sense of a country also 'crucified' may be dangerously close to potential ambiguity by seeming to draw in anti-Semitic terms from the death of Jesus.[15] That lurking peril, however, given vigilance, may not preclude the mystery of the victimized and the immolated abidingly signified in Jesus' crucifixion wherever its relevance is urgently discerned.

Returning to secular dimensions, the reader finds a close kinship in Palestinian verse with the tensions in Western poesy this century. Ezra Pound, T. S. Eliot, A. E. Housman, Dylan Thomas and their kindred in varied aspects of 'alienation', whether from place or piety, excited Arab spirits to comparable unease. *The Waste Land* of T. S. Eliot prefigured the sense of 'life having undone so many' that described the cutting off of student careers, the blight of prospects, the bereavement of property and the surrender of significance that accompanied Palestinian displacement. Adversity in its harsh external shape of landlessness and statelessness sought out the vocabulary of Oriental myth and sceptical pity to describe and deplore its world. The very form of 'free verse', shedding old conventions and relying on subtle imagery, was calculated to delineate a shattered personhood forsaken by canons of normality.[16]

This sense of things is allied for many writers with perceptions of the overall futility and irrationality of the political theatre, the vagaries and treacheries of Arab power wielders, the cross-purposes of Palestinian factions, and the sundry arenas we have surveyed in foregoing chapters, of guile and subterfuge practised and received. For sensitive pens the world is too Kafkaesque for comprehension or personal address.[17]

One random example of this futility belongs with the fate of one of their own literati, the eminent Egyptian writer Yusuf al-Siba'i. A splinter gang of Palestinians, based in Iraq, vowed to assassinate any Arabs who had gone to Jerusalem at the time of President Sadat's historic visit there in November 1977. Al-Siba'i, a close personal friend, was among them.[18] He was duly shot in Nicosia, Cyprus, by gunmen who then took hostage nineteen others who were attending a meeting of the Afro-Asian People's Solidarity Organization. Eleven of these were flown out on a hijacked plane which, refused permission to land in Libya, returned to Larnaca, where fifteen Egyptian commandos, attempting to storm the plane, were killed by Cypriot soldiers. The Palestinians surrendered and the hostages were then freed. Al-Siba'i had written stories exploring the débâcle of 1948, in an effort to join creative writing with the world of political failure. If the juncture did little for the quality of his art, at least it demonstrated where the writer's anguish lay. His violent death might be read as a symbol of the political fatedness of literary inspiration in a context far-removed from the conventionalities and literary self-admiration of the Arabic of an earlier generation which had not known the existentialists.

If Palestinianism and its Arab allies elsewhere found their history a baptism into European-style loss of bearings, personal, religious and societal, with literature its existential mirror, a comparable play with irony was their strongest card. Irony can indulge defiance of the fates even while it concedes disasters. It is the surest weapon in the armoury of the daunted. Thus Samih al-Qasim, an Israeli-Arab journalist in Haifa, writes lines heavy with satire for 'those who started thinking after June 5th, 1967'. 'A little citizen', he resigns from 'the death insurance company', repudiating 'the ambassadors of death' in the futile 'Ministry of Information'. He lists himself with 'the angry people who cease dancing on graves'.[19]

Ahmad Husain, Haifa-born poet–teacher, writes of 'A Vendor of Souvenirs in Nazareth' (the baneful irony of 'tourists'):

At the peak of your involvement selling
an olive-wood camel
or a Bible sheathed in solid metal . . .
Then what can anything mean?
Suddenly you want to go deep into remote times,
To become an inscription on the walls
of an Assyrian temple,
To die accepting your death
Or begging for crucifixion . . .
Overwhelmed by a sudden feeling that you are an imposter,
Perhaps deceived yourself,
Or at least you are Barabbas.[20]

Or there is the anthologist of Palestinian poetry, Dr Salma Jayyusi, in 'Songs for an Arab City', anticipating unknowingly the irony of the Oslo theme of 'Jericho first':

Among your palms I find my familiar mist,
Painful division I discover walking beside your river
Fighting memories, but your waters are deceptive
greeting me playfully, yet when I reply
They hold their mirror up to my face.[21]

In a poem entitled 'Refugee', Salim Jubran, a journalist and member of the
Israeli Communist Party, cherishes the fidelities of nature amid the strife of
arms.

The sun crosses borders
without any soldier shooting at it.
The nightingale sings in Tulkarm of an evening
Eats and roosts peacefully with kibbutzim birds.
A stray donkey grazes across the firing line in peace
and no one aims.
But I, your son made refugee – O my native land –
Between me and your horizon the frontier walls stand.[22]

Elsewhere, in lines born in Nazareth, Tawfiq Zayyad addresses his
adversaries in proud defiance.

In their chains my pride is fiercer
than all arrogant delirium.
In my blood a million suns defy a multitude of cruelties.
My love for you, you people of boundless tragedy
Lets me storm the seven heavens.
For I am your son . . . your offspring,
In heart, in conscience and tongue![23]

The imagery may seem indulgent to the sober critic but the passion is
sustained by reality itself. These Arabic verses belong with a daunting
day-to-day world. Personal guns abound in Israel. Some 160,000 Israelis
hold licences for private arms. All able-bodied males have been through
army service and do reserve duty every year, often keeping their weapons at
home. Gun shops during the Intifadah did a lively trade in 9mm and other
guns; 100 rounds of ammunition are permissible for every Israeli owner.
Travelling into 'occupied territory' contributes to an armed mentality
among Israelis, while a Palestinian 'resistance' – terrorists apart – has only
recourse to stones and slogans.

Known widely now for her TV presentation of an articulate Palestinian
brief, Hanan Ashrawi visualizes what an Israeli soldier is thinking on patrol
in the West Bank. She writes:

It's not the sudden hail of stones,
Nor the mocking of their jeers
But this deliberate quiet in their eyes that
Threatens to wrap itself around my well-armed
Uniformed presence and drag me into depths of confrontation
I never dared to probe . . .
I am forced to listen to the echo of my own gunfire
And hear gas grenades in the midst of
A deafening silence . . .
I refuse to be made into a figment of my own imagination.
I catch myself at times, glimpsing
The child I was in one of them.[24]

In 'Death Sentence', Sulafa Hijjawi lyricizes ironically over the erasure from the map of a beloved village named Zeita. The very trees and tulips cling to her for shelter as, in a few moments of destruction, she becomes mere rubble, no 'bread oven remaining'. But,

Now in the evenings in the song of our wind,
Zeita arises, igniting its scarlet spark upon the plains,
And by morning Zeita returns to the fields as tulips do.[25]

Notable among these singers of the soil is Jabra Ibrahim Jabra, who is also a painter and novelist and Bethlehem born. In 'Zero Hour' he broods on a martyr's sacrifice.

My pain returns in your absence
Words do not penetrate the shield you've made of death . . .
Is this why we saw visions
And accepted the agony of belief?
And why we shouldered the cross across the world
Certain that after crucifixion
Comes the resurrection?[26]

Most familiar among Palestinian poets to Westerners through translation is Mahmud Darwish, born in 1942 near Acre, who finally moved out of Israel in 1971 after periods of harassment and imprisonment. His poetry is a

mixture of agony and ecstasy, of pride and despair, of resistance and recognition of the dominating evil that foils heroism. . . . This sensitive recognition . . . sustains his inspirational power . . . the riches of his imagery . . . and the depth of his ennobling vision.[27]

Palestinians have celebrated 'the Day of the Land' on 30 March since 1976. Darwish elegizes it in a long poem, the soil 'the extension of his soul'. 'What song is right for this dew and this incense?' 'I am the land in a body.'[28]

At times Darwish's poetry holds allusions that are lost in translation from the native tongue, for Arabic excels in exotic imagery and, for the prosaic, remote analogy. There are times when one might think him angry with God for not existing, the pleas being so ardent and the hopes so desperate. Sexual love consoles what political realism and bitter conflict unforgivingly oppress. One poem, however, is grimly direct. 'Register me, I am an Arab', it insists. Details follow, minus any name, identified by stone-cutting, or throwing, with roots running deeper than the very olive trees. Ancestors? Centuries of peasants. Address is a forgotten village. Now register further:

> I hate nobody, neither do I steal,
> But when I am made hungry
> Then I will eat the flesh of my oppressor.
> Beware of my hunger and my anger.[29]

For some readers, the poetry of Tawfiq Sayigh is the most evocative of all. He is a Jeremiah stuck fast in the mire, pleading for more than a rope which might extricate him, yearning for hands themselves in a closer gesture of compassion.[30] Or he is passportless,

> Approaching but no entry,
> Travelling but no arrival:
> Without it there is no entry,
> And you don't carry it, therefore, no entry . . .
> You approach salvation
> But salvation slips between your fingers . . .
> What is my charge so that I may defend myself?
> But there are no embassies on the sea.[31]

The echo of T. S. Eliot is clear in

> My land is a wasteland, its cities are silent:
> Even the vultures have abandoned it.
> Its trees have been uprooted,
> Its earth is mud and excrement . . .
> That to which I returned yesterday
> Is a handful of earth which I lost.[32]

VI

'The soul in the iron' comes not only in poetic strain. Drama, the short story and the novel are its vehicles too. One dramatist, Mu'in Basisu, returns to the theme of Chapter 1. In his *Shamshun wa Dalilah*, he presents a Palestinian family who have suffered acutely under Israeli occupation and exile. The father clings desperately to a key and title deeds that show his ownership of a well in Jaffa, despite the futility of the idea that he could ever return to repossess it. His two sons are exasperated by this passive attitude, mere gesture. The only daughter loses her tiny child in an Israeli raid and succumbs to madness, which drives her brother to take up armed struggle, the other having fled the land. After 1967, as the play has it, a Samson appears, his long hair dangling like bullet tape. He tries to recruit the girl to become an informer but, failing to do so, falls for another woman who cuts his hair and, for the time being, neutralizes his oppressive ventures.

Basisu's plot is clumsy but the passion of his writing is impressive. He is in the school of Jabotinsky on the other side and similarly fascinated by the legendary hero. In another play he draws on the fate of the Amerindians as a warning that extermination waits for those who do not rally to repel imperial intrusion.[33]

Among short stories, few are so pointedly grim, in the context of our Chapter 7, as Ghassan Kanafani's *Rijal fi-l-Shams* ('Men in the Sun'), written in 1963.[34] Kanafani was the victim of a terrorist car-bomb in Beirut in 1972, where he was a Palestinian representative. The story has three generations of a Palestinian family planning to get to Kuwait where employment may enable them to support their people. Subterfuge has to be their procedure via a water-tank driver who agrees to transport them across the desert, with middlemen involved in the risky process. By these they are brazenly cheated. The truck-driver, who is impotent from a war-wound – the detail is significant – and also forgetful, is delayed at a frontier by an altercation about his girl-friend. Making up lost time he drives furiously to the next border where, opening the tank, he finds his three cargoes dead. Finding a garbage dump to bestow the bodies, first stripping them of what might be useful, he muses why they did not bang on the side of the tank.

The story has a vivid impact, conveying a powerful image of callous futility and a despairing irony of dependence and victimization, the pitilessness of the sun and an agony of 'death in the desert', a bungled 'liberation' compelled by its conditions to conspire with horrid tragedy. Nowhere has the Palestinian tribulation been more tersely, more eloquently told. Ghassan Kanafani was still in his twenties when he wrote the story. His was a mature and telling voice for enemies to silence.

Notes

1 The Haganah wished to honour a truce agreement relating to acquiring arms which the Irgun under Begin wanted to defy. The *Altalena* was shelled by shore batteries when Begin refused to comply. At stake was the issue of leadership in the transition to statehood from armed conflict with the British in which the factions had competed.

2 See Zeev (ed.), *Ktavim* (Works of Jabotinsky), vol. 9, p. 128. A voluminous writer, Jabotinsky (1880–1940) was the major inspiration and mentor of radical Zionism, with a wellnigh Fascist attitude to Jewish nationalism. He had a near contempt for any Arab counterpart but saw clearly that Palestinians were 'in the way'. For the Jewish race, any notion of a 'federal' relation with them was 'disgusting and detestable'. Giving evidence to the Peel Commission in 1936 he proposed to the British that they should ally with his Betar militia and develop a powerful Jewish force within the British Army.

3 Ibid., vol. 9, p. 261.

4 Abba Eban, *An Autobiography* (London, 1977), p. 119.

5 The phrase 'Israel proper' indicates the 'Israel' delimited, designated and decided by the UN vote of 1947, confirmed after 1967 in Resolution 242 by the latter's reference to 'evacuation of territories occupied' *on the way* to agreement on 'secure borders'. It is the UN vote which alone gives juridical being to the State of Israel. Other 'Israels' are *de facto* but their status pragmatic only. This has always been the problem in the plea about 'making peace with Israel', or 'acknowledging Israel's existence, or right to exist', i.e., which Israel?

6 A phrase often used to denote the steady series of *faits accomplis* by which successive stages of the story were achieved and achieved irreversibly.

7 Deuteronomy 10:19 enjoins 'love of the stranger' on the Jews in the land (cf. Exodus 23:9), reminding them that they had been strangers in Egypt. Egypt had at first been hospitable but turned to 'oppressing' when the 'guests' proved too numerous. The citations could have an ironic meaning, seeing that it was the sheer numbers of the Palestinians that argued their 'oppression' by Israel. 'Strangers' are tolerable, if few and not 'in charge'.

8 The PLO were totally *non grata*, possibly 'West Bankers' (if not resident in annexed Jerusalem). There was a variety of slowly adjusted categories of 'inacceptability' as parties to negotiation or merely 'contact'.

9 *Nifaq* and the *Munafiqun* (practitioners of *nifaq*) are very prominent in the Medina Surahs of the Qur'an, people who feigned allegiance but meant no good. Prudence rather than conviction motivated them, or deliberate guile and malice. Surah 49.14–19 tells of 'Arabs' professing 'faith' which Muhammad was told to repudiate as being only 'submission', made to 'do him a favour' or themselves insurance. The distinction is clear in this passage between two ways of 'islamizing', i.e., prudent accession or authentic belief.

10 Especially in the Fourth Gospel. When Judaism was protected as a *religio licita* and Christianity not, the latter was vulnerable to informers. Congregations might be infiltrated by spies, or uneasy about 'crypto-recruits' still (maybe genuinely) dubious, e.g., about 'table-fellowship' with 'Gentiles'. It is this aura of disquiet which underlies the Gospel of John, not anti-Semitism.

11 See J. M. Peteet, 'The graffiti of the Intifada', *The Muslim World Quarterly*, vol. LXXXIV, nos 1–2 (January 1994), pp. 155–65.

12 Amnesty International is the major monitor of prisoners' rights across the world. Its most recent Report, issued on 22 May 1996, lists Israel with Kenya, China, Turkey and Mexico among violators of human rights, including deaths of prisoners under torture by Shin Bet interrogators. The Israeli human rights organization B'Tselem estimates that since

1987 5,000 Palestinians every year were subjected to such types of torture as hooding, beating, sleep deprivation, and long shackling in comfortless postures. The legal limits, described as 'moderate physical pressure', are interpreted in generous terms, pleading the exigencies of suicide bombing and other outrages.

13 Shakespeare, *King Lear*, III.iv, lines 13–14, changing Lear's personal pronouns to inclusives.

14 Frederick W. H. Myers, *Collected Poems* (London, 1921), pp. 99–100. When borrowed, the allusions are uncannily apt. 'Abarim' were the fords, passages and ridges across the Jordan opposite Jericho, stretching from Gilead to the river Arnon. 'Hazeroth' means the villages hard by Gaza (cf. Deuteronomy 2:23). They were named after the Avims who dwelt there. Myers, of course, was concerned only for the dereliction into which 'the scapegoat' was driven. How strange it is that the Jewish people with whom 'scapegoating' was original in ritual have themselves so long been made to accept the role as their own fate.

15 The association *might* be made to mean 'The same people still doing the same things'. It has often been wildly alleged that 'Good Friday is the source of anti-Semitism', 'a direct line stretching from the crucifixion to the Holocaust'. This utter travesty – when credited – makes it vital to repudiate any 'Cross imagery' concerning the Palestinian tragedy as carrying any anti-Jewish connotation.

16 The journal *Hiwar*, founded in Beirut by Tawfiq Sayigh, led the advocacy of 'free verse', invoking, among others, the style of T. S. Eliot in a concern to shed the patterns of traditional rhetoric and language-worship. This brought a new *angst* into writing, a passion for meaning instead of an indulgence of form. See, more broadly, Salma Khadra al-Jayyusi, 'Modernist poetry in Arabic' in M. M. Badawi (ed.), *Modern Arabic Literature* (Cambridge, 1992), pp. 132–79.

17 The *Qasidahs* of Tawfiq Sayigh are designated with the letter 'K', making plain the association with Franz Kafka and his world of enigma and anxiety.

18 Yusuf al-Siba'i (1917–78) was a novelist whose works combine the conflict of love and social obstacles and also the personal strains around political crises. He might be held a significant representative of an Egyptian 'Palestinian-ism'.

19 Samih al-Qasim (born 1939), playwright as well as poet, is cited here in the translation of Issa Boullatta, *Modern Arab Poets, 1950–1975* (Washington, 1976), pp. 117–18.

20 Quoted from Salma Khadra Jayyusi (ed.), *Anthology of Modern Palestinian Literature* (New York, 1992), p. 171; trans. Lena Jayyusi and N. S. Nye.

21 Ibid., p. 185; trans. author and Salma Khadra Jayyusi.

22 Ibid., p. 190; by Salim Jubran, trans. Lena Jayyusi and N. S. Nye.

23 Ibid., p. 329; by Tawfiq Zayyad, trans. Sharif Elmusa and J. Collom.

24 Ibid., p. 337; author writing in English.

25 Ibid., pp. 168–9; trans. May Jayyusi and N. S. Nye.

26 Ibid., pp. 178–9; trans. Sharif Elmusa and Jeremy Reed.

27 Salma Khadra Jayyusi, 'Modernist poetry in Arabic', pp. 176–7.

28 *Anthology*, pp. 147 and 151; trans. Lena Jayyusi and C. Middleton.

29 Mahmud Darwish, *Awraq al-Zaitun*, 'The Leaves of the Olive' (Beirut, 1960), (Dar al-Tali'ah), p. 197.

30 Tawfiq Sayigh, quoted from *Modern Arab Poets*, pp. 141–2, from *Al-Qasidah K* (Beirut, 1960). Jeremiah's experience in the pit and his painful rescue (by ropes under his emaciated armpits) by a compassionate negro named Ebed-Melech is told in Jeremiah 38:6–13.

31 *Modern Arab Poets*, pp. 146–7.

32 Tawfiq Sayigh, *Aydan wa Aydan* ('Also and Also, Again and Again'). Through his translations from Eliot and his lively literary criticism, Tawfiq Sayigh contributed greatly to the influence of Eliot in Arabic poetry. The Egyptian Salah 'Abd al-Sabur was another noteworthy admirer of Eliot's poetry and verse drama.

The 'handful of dust' reference is to Tawfiq's taking into exile with him a fistful of Palestinian earth which, on return, he scattered in a gesture of despair.

33 Mu'in Basisu linked Palestinian liberation with other movements across the world. The Amerindian allusion is ironical, in that Golda Meir, Israel's only woman Prime Minister, often retorted to US critics of Israel's 'take-over' of Palestine with the reminder that they too had 'possessed' themselves of 'colonies' inferior enough to be virtually emptied of 'natives', whereas Israel was a 'mother country' being reconstructed and no colony. Nor were Arab peoples as easily subduable as the Iroquois or the Dakotas.

34 Ghassan Kanafani (1936–72), *Rijal fi-l-Shams* (Beirut, 1963; ET London, 1978).

Permission to quote is acknowledged:

for passages to which notes 20, 21, 22, 23, 24 and 26 above refer: Salma Khadra Jayyusi (ed.), *Anthology of Modern Palestinian Literature*. Copyright © 1992 by Columbia University Press. Reprinted by permission of the publisher;

for passages to which notes 31 and 32 above refer, drawn respectively from Issa Boullata (ed.), *Modern Arab Poets, 1950–1975* and Issa Boullata, 'The beleaguered unicorn: a study of Tawfiq Sayigh', *The Journal of Arabic Literature*, vol. IV (1973), pp. 63–93: Dr Issa Boullata, McGill University, Montreal.

11

'The searchings of Reuben'

I

The 'Song of Deborah' in Judges 5 is the earliest Hebrew classic of biblical literature, a splendid celebration of military triumph immortalizing in Jewish saga the cunning audacity of Jael with her lethal tent-peg and hammer and the forlorn mother of Sisera waiting in vain for the homecoming of her stricken son. What could be 'the searchings of Reuben', Jacob's firstborn, in that moment of superb climax?

The Reubenites had not been present when sudden rainfall after the battle had been joined swelled the river Kishon and trapped the heavy chariots of the enemy, first in its mud-flats and then in its torrent. Far from 'these waters of Megiddo' were 'the waters of Gilead' on the other side of Jordan. There the sons of Reuben had held aloof from the encounter with the forces of Sisera. The Hebrew of the Song, which is puzzling in places, leaves us to conjecture the reasons why: sloth, prevarication, quarrels, or a will to pastoral security?

Eager to engage all the tribes in the strains of the music if not in the honours of the fight, the singers can only have implied reproach for the absentees, either disdaining their ignomity or deploring their cowardice. Warriors throughout history have been keen to see non-combatants as 'holding their manhoods cheap' by withholding from the fray. We must assume that 'the searchings of Reuben' had to do with the arousal of a sense of shame attending on news of Deborah's overwhelming success with its signal tokens of Yahweh's presence and favour. Or is it 'factions' that we should read in the Hebrew text, people left debating and quarrelling while the heroes knew no qualms and spared no pains?

Either way, there is something apposite about the Bible's earliest victory-paean, and 'searchings of heart', in the theme to which we now turn in this chapter, namely Zionist self-celebration and scrutiny in prospect of the jubilee of statehood in 1998 and in retrospect on the long century since Herzl's dream. For, as with Deborah and her cohorts, so with Ben Gurion and his inaugural state-making; there have been signal triumphs and divided minds. The parallel is apt in telling ways. There has never been unanimity about the ends and aims of Zionism, its warrant and its wisdom. As then, so now, there have been wellnigh incredible feats of opportunism vindicated by arguably divine facilities of circumstance and event. There have been notable peaks of leadership that coincided personalities, the Deborahs and Jaels, with the ripe occasions for their interplay. There have been the Reubenites, still debating while decisive energies were bringing things to pass and the actuality of success either way was not in doubt. 'The governors or the marshals of Israel', as Judges 5 dubs them, 'commemorate the victories of the Lord, his triumph as the champion of Israel' (5:11, 14).

Deborah's Song celebrates somewhat in the manner of imperial Rome inscribing 'Judea capta' on the coinage when Jerusalem had fallen. The temper differs but the sense of finality is one. The theme we have explored of 'Palestina capta' is different again but no less firmly engraved upon the territory. No one doubts the irreversibility of the Zionist achievement. Short of worldwide disintegration or nuclear holocaust, international politics is hardly likely to see, or permit, any replication of the feat of Salah al-Din in the elimination of the Latin Kingdom of Jerusalem. The Jewish state is fully entrenched on the world's stage and lyrical celebration belongs with its solid actuality. What Deborah and Barak compressed into the drama of a single day was painfully, tediously, stubbornly contrived through the toils of a long century from the 1890s to the 1990s.

The several salient features of the history we have reviewed. The purpose of this chapter is to ask what might be the self-scrutiny of retrospect and prospect, 'the searchings of Zionist heart' that no satisfaction can exclude. There was mention of Reuben in the very exuberance of Deborah. So it is still. Maybe the elusive Hebrew of Judges 5:12 yields us a clue. 'Lead thy captivity captive, thou son of Abinoam.' 'Capture your captives', 'take prisoners in plenty' are possible renderings.[1] That physical literalism surely leads further. 'Captivity captive' has a haunting ring elsewhere in psalm and New Testament.[2] 'Your very capacity to be victorious has to be taken in hand.' Master your own mastery. Beware of the prison of your own liberation.

Respond to the responsibility of your own spoil. Israeli statehood is only the more entailed with Palestinianism by the very reality of its success.

II

The testing of the faiths that inform Palestinian response to experience as 'captivity' will concern Chapter 12. Here we have to do with how Judaism duly masters Zionist success, how 'the sons of Abinoam, "father of pleasantness"', take in hand their contemporary dream-fulfilment grounded in the dream-frustration that is Palestinianism.

That the two are reciprocal is evident enough. The relation of Judaism as a spirituality to Zionism as its politicization has been throughout ambiguous. If Jewry is a 'nation' rightly enshrined in political statehood with its concomitants of force, power, chicanery and coercion, can these be duly sacralized as the spiritual legitimacy of a divine covenant? Can Yahweh in covenant be feasibly 'Caesarized' in statehood?

If Jewry is essentially an ethnic identity it ought to enjoy, as most humankind does, a territorial locale reasonably associated with its history, its culture and its heritage of kin and family. That enjoyment will be subject to the vagaries of time and the risks of conflict, exile and displacement. When the risks supervene, there will be the same Judaic, as there is 'Gentile', pro-priety in striving to reverse them. However, can some sacral distinctiveness attend on such tenure, disruption and recovery? Can ethnicity exceptionalize its relation with the transcendent in special terms that override or disavow the morally authentic which alone is proper to transcend?

Aspects of these issues we have studied in Chapter 5. The anomaly of the unethical 'holy' need not detain us further here, except as a dimension of this larger predicament of a Judaism taken hostage by a Zionist form. That predicament, it would prove (and prove to be of a desperate order), was clear to some from the beginning. The question was always urgent: Could the transcendent relevance of 'election' and 'covenant' be entrusted to what could only be their compromise, once the necessity of power, tending to violent injustice, was not only conceded but strenuously embraced? The corollary, plainly, was to see diaspora as vocation, not from timidity or the apathy of the ghetto mind, but as the destiny of any ambition to be 'people of God' in the world. Some 'nation-state of God' could have no such mandate and deserve no such destiny.

By implication, the Zionists thought otherwise; or were they by some conspiracy of neglect willing the issue out of sight? For a time, as we have seen, the contradiction could remain dormant, shrouded in illusions of viable 'federalism' or joint rule – illusions which had never been consistent with Zionist intent, pragmatically useful as they might be on the way to purposes dispelling them. Once the actualities – post 1948, 1956, 1967, 1982, the 1990s – became legible enough there was no pretending that the Judaism of Jews accepting to be Zionist with no 'searchings of Reuben' was not putting its whole integrity at risk. Ought they not, in the words of Eleazar on Masada, 'to have conjectured the purpose of God much sooner'?[3] As Aldous Huxley elsewhere observed:

> The end cannot justify the means for the simple and obvious reason that the means employed determine the nature of the ends produced.[4]

We are bound to ask what Judaism was doing with, and to, itself in the marriage with political Zionism.

That its inception was greeted with enormous reluctance is well known. Its origins were with a very small minority, visionaries enamoured of European romantic nationalisms or realists convinced of the irredeemably hostile untrustworthiness of 'Gentiles' everywhere. 'Enlightenment' had proved, would increasingly prove, that Jewry would never be securely 'acceptable' in non-Jewish society. Anti-Semitism was incorrigible. Nazism by the 1930s would make this logic absolute but, earlier, despite a long retrospect of persecution, there remained a huge majority of European Jews either vocationally citizens of 'Gentile' states or confident of a viable compatibility. Indeed, as we have seen, Zionism provoked assertion of these themes precisely by jeopardizing the sincerity of would-be 'good European' Jews. In counteraction, Zionists did not scruple to employ anti-Semitic epithets to disown such pusillanimous brethren.

Hitler would grimly prove where wisdom lay for the communities his conquests swallowed. Zionism became a desperate imperative, an implacable logic. Even so, elsewhere in the world a secure and flourishing diaspora has been a *sine qua non* of the very feasibility and continuity of the Zionist state. The realism of Ben Gurion was able to accept the annoyance of the paradox since it was also his life-line.

Conceding all the 'pros' of Zionism, the formidable 'cons' remain. They remain not only through the paradox of a Zionism that stays in chequebooks; they remain because of the deepest measures of Judaic faith.

III

It might be said, in brief, that the problem of Zionism is the dilemma of apartheid and compatibility, and that the statehood proposed as resolving it only reproduces it. The twin terms are used with positive intent. Boswell reported Samuel Johnson saying that

> The great business of his life was to escape from himself: this disposition he considered as the disease of his mind, which nothing cured but company.[5]

That sentiment is sharply relevant to what Jewry has in hand with itself. Its instincts are enormously self-preoccupied. Every awareness of identity is moved to idiosyncrasy. Corporate peoplehoods all have their interior perceptions of themselves and wed these to land and kin and soil and scene and speech and ancestors and progeny. All, in some measure, by rite and ritual, ceremony and sacrament, enshrine themselves in transcendent reference. The Judaic version of this human quality finds itself *sui generis*, more articulate, more intense, more insistent than any other – or, at least, labours and lives under that assumption.

That fact has only sharpened the need to 'escape from themselves', to need the vital differentia and yet to register their burden. Believing the differentia reciprocated in transcendent Lordship makes such escape impossible. Identity and divine destiny are inseparable. Moreover, this self-perception requires to be perceived. It cannot be a hidden 'secret', a mystery only inwardly known and cherished, for its public acknowledgement is material to the discharge of its meaning. Hence the sharpened yearning of the 'covenanted ones' to be – and yet equally not to be – what identity has made them. Have not Jews, from time to time, read their anguish in the world as a strange form of self-hatred?

The whole dark, tragic story of anti-Semitism confirms that situation. Jewry needs the 'Gentiles' to authenticate distinctiveness and finds the need tending to a painful apartheid in the world that can neither be transcended nor endured – given that all humankind was made and meant, in Johnson's word, for 'company'. Did not Zionism argue that 'assimilation' and by it, on these terms, eventual extinction was all that society offered as a Jewish option, unless it fell to outright persecution? Political Zionism thus became a passionate register of the fundamental contradiction in diaspora. Diaspora left no option of necessarily secure apartheid within itself and no secure occasion of feasible compatibility. The equation would have to be resolved in the appeal to territorial statehood politically established and militarily preserved.

Such was the very core of the case for statehood. Jews should strive to resume the political form they had enjoyed in brief and chequered centuries under David and Solomon and their successors and again, ambivalently, under the Maccabees. The urge was reinforced by fond ancestral memories of that sweet autonomy and of the endearing hills and valleys of its terrain between the sea and the desert, at the junction of continents and neighbour to great river-based powers in history. If Jewry, as defined by Judaism yet now distinct from it, was indeed a 'nation' then it was entitled to recover and enjoy its political, territorial expression where, like any other people, its presence would belong. It might, like other nations, have remnants here and there and anywhere outside that habitat, but unless these were incidental and peripheral, they would violate the whole logic and sharply jeopardize the meaning of its vital land and state expression. Indeed, they would undo the whole venture into physical concentration and the political ideology by which it was legitimized.

Such surviving remnants, by these sights, would simply be perpetuating the contradictions and futilities of diaspora. They would be denying the principle of national identity, continuing to practise in 'Gentile' waters, markets, academies and councils where Zionism held they had no Jewish case to be, since the religiousness by which they might have so remained was no longer the definition of their being. Had not Herzl argued that if the 'Gentiles' had what they called their 'Jewish problem', he would concede it to be indeed such and resolve it for them by 'abstraction'? They would remove themselves. The apartheid of Jewry which, by these tokens, *all* parties found agreeable would be autonomously achieved, mutual incompatibility having been amply and painfully demonstrated over bitter centuries.

In the event, diaspora, it proved, would emphatically remain. No statehood could have been viable without it. Forgoing the consistency of its logic, Zionism proved to be wiser than it knew. The state and the diaspora could be mutually beneficial, the one inspiration and comfort to the other, sustenance in one direction and romance in the other. Paradox never did disqualify an idea or an ideal but it did mean in this context that Zionism, in some parts of the world, cancelled the logic of its own necessity and that its perception of all things Judaic as essentially political queried the entire rationale for a Judaism otherwise understood.

It is here that the deepest reaches of any 'searchings of Reuben' belong. Everywhere in the world the search for a viable negotiation between due apartheid and compatibility, between the self that cannot be 'escaped' and the 'company' that must be kept, continues and, in places, readily succeeds, though the stresses abide. What of the quest for a fulfilled separateness *and* a human compatibility in the territorial terms in which Zionism was determined to locate it and conceived to find it?

What is clear at once is that recovered territory can in no way deliver and must inevitably confound it. 'The fate of location' in Chapter 2 has seen why. Historical memory does not depopulate. Partition, conflict, expulsion, contrivance of circumstance, inducement and the rest may partly avail to do so. The process has gone very far in some areas but the vigorous policy of 'settlements' can never resolve the basic facts of Palestinian–Arab demography. In some form and shape, physical human compatibility is mandatory for the viability of any sustainable apartheid.

It was realized by alert minds in 1967 that the facts of demography, *pace* the Revisionists with ambitions over Jordan, made that river the definitive limit of a Jewish state. It was clear in 1982 that the physical occupation of Damascus would have lured Israel into frustration, for all its military possibility. It is yet to be revealed, after the Oslo Accords, what shape any Palestinian entity may take on the West Bank. No full, authentic statehood is emerging in which Jewish settlers would consent to reside but, rather, enclaves of Palestinian population skirted by a network of Jewish roads ensuring that enclaves only they remain. How the spiritual 'counsels' in Palestinianism may respond belongs with Chapter 12. On other counts, the prospects seem forlorn, precarious, restless, volatile and wearisome, a subtle, or less than subtle, denial of co-existence.

The question, therefore, lurks all the time: How will this solution – if such it be – bear on the quality of that Jewish homogeneity that Israel so evidently yearns to enjoy? 'Racialist' is a description Zionists have been at pains to scout and deny, but that Israel is an ethnic expression is not in doubt. It seeks to be distinctively, undilutedly Jewish in the several forms that Jewishness contrives. Hence, of course, the act of refraining from 'annexation' of the West Bank in 1967 and the brief glimpse of a trading of gains for the prospect of peace. Small, containable minorities of non-Jews do not threaten – and may even enhance – the state and its image in the world, in the confines of pre-1967. A large non-Jewish population, however, legitimately disaffected and resistant, not only stains the image but threatens the quality of the state by the repression it is held to need, so that the idea of homogeneity is at war with the reality.

So the positive apartheid, territorially grounded and politically contrived, that Zionism intended and intends, remains permanently elusive unless and until a compatibility can be attained. Is there any chance that the jealous identity can evolve the crucial tolerance of inescapable 'company', or is this, as for Samuel Johnson, a 'disease of the mind'?

'Disease' of the years it certainly spells, the years of Israel's half century in being but also the years of Zionism's long gestation. Could it be that the impasse around the Zionist prescript for Jewry, politicized and militant, proves it to be a tragic aberration? It needs time, the apologists said, when such fears found voice in anxious quarters. But time of itself will only hold the sequences set for it. Israeli politics is an affair of Byzantine complexity. No doubt, in pragmatic ways, uneasy contrivances may obtain, hiding or deferring the essential inconclusiveness, or perhaps Zionism will prove only to have changed the shape of the puzzle as to what Jewry really and truly is, its own lights as to the answer being perennially at stake.

IV

The vexed question of the city of Jerusalem brings the whole into a single focus. It may be conveniently delayed to the end of the agenda but it continues to symbolize all else. The city represents the apartheid ambition at its most passionate. It is the indivisible, single, inalienable capital of the State of Israel. The long, medieval Ottoman Arabness of its old suqs, its confessional quarters within walls quarried from its ancient past, might also be thought inalienable, better sewered and lighted no doubt under an Israeli mayor but still a durable 'sign' of 'company' to an 'undiseased mind'. Not so; the spreading modernity to the west and the bastion-style suburbs burgeoning outwards into its post-1967 territorial enlargement must comprise the old nucleus from the Jebusites to the Turks in one Jewish capital. It is conveniently forgotten that the only juridical basis (as distinct from facts of conquest) of the state claiming this inalienable capital is a United Nations vote providing for its international administration. That time has doubtless overtaken that provision has not thereby cancelled its significance. Israel in 1967 refrained for sound reasons from annexing the West Bank. The same reasons, had they not been merely prudential, would have no less argued the non-annexation of the capital. The Jerusalem that ought, on every sane count, to be the shrine and abode of a willed compatibility is made instead the inflexible pride of a Jewish otherness, the reassuring evidence of a Jewish political exclusivism, yet loaded with religious implications for others that monopoly can only alienate and embitter.

Temple Mount becomes here the ultimate irony. A sacred Islamic shrine, 'the further sanctuary' noted in the Qur'an, occupies the site of Abraham's testing and of Solomon's 'house of the Lord'. Muhammad's strange 'rapture' into transcendent revelation, as Muslims perceive, cohabits with the most hallowed liturgies of Jewish sacrifice. The centuries of Moriah, David, Jesus and Muhammad overlay each other in one charged locale, one mythic site.

Legitimacies quarrel here, deplore their forfeiture and supersession, or celebrate their warrant and their prestige. The surcharged holiness, electrified by passion and history, examines and explores the sanity of religions and constitutes surely the most telling plea for a mutuality riding out the passions of envious diversity. Where Zionism is most adamant its own quest is most at risk.

V

It could be that the 'searchings' we are pondering around the Zionist story are leading, via fallacies, to discoveries that were never intended or foreseen. It could be that the very will to ensure apartheid in the terms outlined has tended to a paradoxical experience of the contrary, and that a sort of integration transpired which was never intended. The exigencies of statehood have made Israel a very 'Gentile' entity. The very terms of the search for a decisive Jewishness contrived a novel version of what Jewishness might be. A will to be 'normal' was latent in the will to be 'different'. If it was the ghetto which perpetuated how Jewry saw itself – and saw falsely – then it has been the state that constrained the new image into disconcerting forms. 'Compatibility', after all, has to do with what is being mutually undergone. If it is not undergone deliberately between the parties, it happens inexorably around them. Statehood has in no way undone diaspora, inasmuch as Palestinians are no less neighbours than 'Gentiles' in Brooklyn or Golders Green. They are there, however, in the difference that statehood makes, as neighbours, not simply as part of the streetscape, the markets and the scenery as in diaspora. They are there as refugees, hindrances, whose *ger* or *goy* status is sharpened by Judaic statehood at their expense into enmity, antipathy and an alien quality altogether different from the one seen by Jews of old when looking out from the ghetto.

The 'Enlightenment' drew Jews out from the ghetto. When Zionists saw that as a false dawn, there was no returning to the ghetto which through long centuries had preserved the rites, customs and practices which spelled their privacy with God and so neutralized the menace in diaspora. Nationalism in statehood form became the Zionist prescript for a new Judaic authenticity, redeemed both from the ghetto condition and from the frustrations of diaspora. The irony is that while Israeli statehood emphatically de-ghettoizes Jewry, it in no way escapes the problematics of diaspora. Its very autonomy engages it inexorably with peculiarly vexatious forms of diaspora encounter, forms all the more exacting by being interior to the conscience and the peace of the independence itself.

There follows a tangle of reversed experiences, superbly de-victimized yet untoward enough to put into question the entire strategy of Zionism as an authentically Jewish existence – unless, that is, Jewry is to renounce the privilege of divine 'election'. Some of the experiences we have noted in Chapter 6. Not only do they put Israelis at odds with themselves,[6] they immerse them all in a commonality with the rest of humanity in Palestinian shape. A recent Jewish reporter of the mind in Israel writes of visiting a slum-like Palestinian village, Dheisheh, and adds

> Even as I luxuriated [*sic*] in guilt, I had to acknowledge a deeper feeling, one that I had not plucked out of my liberal convenience-store. I was grateful that for once in our history we were the ones with the guns and they were the ones with the stones. But . . . I also found myself hoping that if I (and my Toronto friends) had been born and bred in the squalor of Dheisheh . . . we would have had the courage to be among the stone-throwers.[7]

Consciences are alert enough in Israel for such sentiments to be frequently expressed. There comes a sense of common humanity kindled by the aware-ness of suffering and injustice, but the sentiment is promptly neutralized by memory of past injuries received elsewhere and by the instinctive alibi of state-necessity. Will there ever be a politics of humankind?

The question weighs on any and every statehood. There is nothing unique to Israel in the exonerating warrant of state order. What is unique is that this nationalism is still married to actual, or alleged, divine mandation so that, logically, it becomes legitimate not merely in defiance of human compassion but by permission of divine aegis and covenant. It must follow that the question presses: Ought not Judaism to be 'just a religion', holding divine vocation in the only terms (those of the spirit) in which it can be rightly had? Or, conversely, if the destiny of Jewry is to be a nation-state with all the concomitants thereof, must it not renounce the claim to divine 'election' except in the terms in which such awareness might obtain in the conscience of any human polity in never private form?

This inescapable moral 'involvement with mankind', in which all histories are at once special and universal, may be grasped in the reverse direction from that in the above example. Consider what happens when foreign dignitaries, as earlier noted, make visits to Israel and are taken to the Yad Vashem Holocaust Memorial, duly clad in black and wearing the head-cover that briefly incorporates them into Jewry, and perhaps a shawl.

Emotions are inevitably tense and inexpressible – at the barest, a will to participate, perhaps to atone, to abnegate what is there in grimmest evidence. Yet a mutuality is also undergone. Love, mourning, sorrow, integrity have to make of it what they will, as the generations pass. It is a highly fraught encounter either way. What it never fails to be is an appeal for inter-human community. Contrition cannot be had if power can be exonerated. If humanity was betrayed in the victims, it was defiled and betrayed in the perpetrators. At the Yad Vashem Israel poignantly insists that it belongs with mankind. The experience of statehood, which alone can ceremonialize the truth of the Shoah, gives it no immunity from 'Gentiles'. Rather, it cries out for their participation in the deepest trauma of its Jewishness.

Why, a reader may be wondering, does the obvious have to be laboured in this way? Zionism never proposed to itself some exemption from humankind. On the contrary, it sought the normalcy every state experiences. It never intended to ghettoize itself in nationhood. Indeed; but may normalcy subsist with 'chosenness' if the latter is assumed to hold alibis, or grant licences, or transcend the guilts and obligations where normalcy commonly arrives?

It is in this context that the observer must understand the sharp antagonisms that exist within Israeli society and politics. The point might be cryptically made in the remark of a Jewish speaker concerning the 'settlers'. 'They are', he said, 'the Jewish State's Jews.'[8] His meaning was that the Gush Emunim, 'the block of the faithful' who passionately create and demand the settlements, are indeed 'the faithful' who understand what state-building means, namely the invocation of divine right, the claim not merely for *Lebensraum* but for establishments that banish, forbid and preclude tenancy by those to whom 'the land' was never given and whose removal is a divinely ordered task. They are 'Jews indeed', in contrast to 'the Jewish state's' other nationals who read their Jewishness in lazier, vaguer or irenic terms.

Or did the comment mean that they, the 'settlers', are the 'Jews' of the state in that they properly incur the opprobrium and scorn of public opinion and are 'rejected' like their forebears in Europe for being 'different' and despicable? Liberal Jews would then be so 'Gentilized' as not to recognize what Jewish destiny demands and to treat the 'right ones' as once did the anti-Semites.

Either way, the point is clear – that 'the Jewish State' is in dispute about its 'Jews', who they are and why and wherein. There are those who regard the tomb of Dr Baruch Goldstein, murderer of Palestinians at their dawn prayer in a hallowed place, as a national shrine, a focal point of truly Jewish reverence and awe. Or there are the half million *yordim*, 'those who go down', who have left the state since 1948, moved – if not wholly – by despair about its ideology and its viable unity of will.[9]

All in all, it is evident that the option for Zionism and the actuality of the state have in no way resolved the nature of identity. They have merely given it a sharper focus and a more urgent crisis, precisely because the state form of the supposed 'resolution' has deepened and radicalized the issue between holiness and ethics, between what can be understood as claimed by God and what must be understood as claimed by neighbour. The radical depth of that issue lies simply in the fact that another people have been tragically invaded and distressed. It has often been observed that how people relate to Jews is a test-case of what humanity they are. The dictum might be reversed, so that the Jewishness of Jewry is tested by their relation to humanity. The test itself might suggest many different criteria. The urgent point is that Zionism inevitably makes Palestinian humanity the crux of the decision.

VI

'Searchings of Reuben' in the old themes of Deborah's Song had to do with those who were by 'the waters of Gilead' not 'the waters of Megiddo', the remoter and the nearer parties to the action. As then, we might say, so now. There have always been degrees of conviction and of ardour in the ranks of Zionism and divided counsels about its fulfilment. These have variously ebbed and flowed in the sequences of its long and anxious history. All the foregoing in no way detracts from the achievements, nor argues some disputing of their actuality. Zion has resoundingly attained its political fulfilment. The story is a foremost saga of the twentieth century. No one has the right to recommend for Jewry a perpetual ghetto nor to castigate their distrust of the Enlightenment – least of all those whose prejudice contributed so criminally to arousing the distrust. The reality of Israel liberates the Jewish spirit and provides a heartening symbol for the Jews it will never make its own citizens. It makes for (if only partial) mitigation of enormous wrongs. It vindicates nationalism as no less a right of Jewry than of any other people. And its relation to the Shoah can perhaps best be captured by the words of Nietzsche in another context: 'When you gaze long into an abyss, the abyss also gazes into you.'[10]

It is precisely these great positives of Zionism that make for the 'searchings', which become the more insistent by the very fact of attainment. That, too, admits of different counsels. 'Recognize the whip hand you enjoy; hold the noose tighter; carry the impetus further; spare not', or

– possibly – 'Now is the time to risk magnanimity; concede a viable Palestinianism; beware of arousing a final despair; let a compatibility in territory and polity be the ultimate security of your realized apartheid.'

Earlier chapters in backward review and present analysis do not suggest hope of the latter. There is no need here to rehearse the portents. Yet it remains true that the alternative is stark. The Jewish necessity to be 'separate', 'a people dwelling alone', is perpetually at issue with the inexorable human necessity to be in some sense participatory with all humankind. To face the two necessities and somehow coincide them is in no way enabled by romantic recourse to state nationalism. On the contrary, all that Israel has been constrained to be, to do and to become in the pursuit of the Zionist goal has intensified the strains. There is much about Zionism that sharply embarrasses Judaism, much in Judaism to be dismayed by Zionists. Yet they mysteriously and uneasily belong together and it is only by the lights that unite them that they can hope to validate each other.

The ultimate 'searchings' in the tension we are trying to comprehend here must go right back into the doctrine of 'God', of Yahweh, as the 'God of the covenant' bestowed on his 'chosen people'. It is common in Jewish thinking to read the 'peoplehood' as the very crux of 'monotheism'. Ezekiel Kaufman, for example, in the eight volumes of his *Toldot Ha-Emunah Ha-Yisraelit*,[11] understands 'monotheism' as inherently 'political' in the sense that the 'oneness of God' is entrusted as faith and truth to the particularity of Jewry. Hence the coinciding of the 'paganism' which had to be ousted from the land, with the peoples dwelling there. Their 'idols' and their occupancy were one and the same inauthenticity. The habitat, actually theirs, had to be taken from them in the context of a disavowal of their idol worships, Yahweh, the One only Lord, being committed, territorially and electively, to his Judaic 'people'.

It is thus in the name of the Oneness of God that Jewish self-image is of separation from the nations and their ways. Monotheism is, so to speak, the necessary politics of Jewish immunity from idolatry and mythology, such as the 'nations' cherish. Jews may not assimilate because their 'national' character is stamped indelibly with vocation to an unyielding idea, namely 'the Lord our God is the only Lord'. It is true that mentors of Rome like Cicero and Tacitus saw Jews as the people who refused the universal Roman tolerance of pagan worship. In that sense it was their monotheism which exempted them from Roman idolatries and, by so doing, strongly accentuated their unique identity.[12] It might be right, in this sense, for Rabbi Abraham Kook to claim that

> For a whole people to proclaim the Name of God as an expression of its
> being – this is found only among the Jewish people . . . The Jewish
> people is the base on which God's throne rests.[13]

In these terms he saw their 'divine vocation' as the direct custodianship of
the unity of God. Only the Jew is the monotheist.

This reading of an essential equation between monotheism and Judaism
as the meaning of 'I will be their God and they will be my people' falls foul
of vital considerations in both parts of the equation. Those that arise in
sharpened form by the expression of this Yahweh–Israel bond in terms of
political statehood have been evident enough in all the foregoing. The
'searchings' that concern us here are theological alone. They surely turn on
two counts. The one is the query whether this 'monotheism' was not, in its
historical origins, in fact a 'monolatry'. The other is whether the vocation
and destiny, which any perceptive mind outside Jewry could gladly
acknowledge as indeed for 'the blessing of the nations', must – in the name
of divine unity – preclude distinctive vocations, perceptible and authentic
in a divine economy, that are in no way confined to Jewish norms nor
requiring ethnic 'national' agencies as such.

It seems clear from the biblical text itself that the Hebrew sense of
peoplehood under 'divine calling' began in purely tribal terms. People-
memory has certainly done much with the patriarchs that the sort of strict
criteria that historiography would now employ has no possibility of
'correcting', even if that were desirable. They are figures from the mists of
time, in nomadic quest of meaning and destiny. Abraham may have
believed in a 'travelling Protector' not rooted to a locale, so that he could
journey with him. Yet in that 'company' Abraham was 'seeking a country',
tribal being married with 'land by promise' under the pledge of 'the God
of our fathers'.

It took centuries for this worship of a patron-God to come to the
splendid monotheism of Isaiah 40 and comparable passages. For the
psalmist in Psalm 95, Yahweh is 'a great king above all gods'. He may have
victories over them but to do so, they must exist. There is in many psalms
a trust and worship that are still essentially monolatrous not monotheistic.
The memory of Exodus gave enormous fillip to the gathering sense of a
divine destiny electing a unique people, but Chemosh could still be understood as bestowing Moab on the Moabites (Judges 11:24). The *Baalim*, the
gods of place, of fertility and of family, were long co-existent with the
emerging universalizing of the status of Yahweh and a slow realization that
'having no other Gods but me' was a tribal command superseded in the

truth of one inclusive 'Lord of all the earth'. Pseudo-deities would still need anathemas, for idolatries are endemic. The veto, however, could no longer have a tribal enmity about it, for 'the only Lord' was 'the God of *all* the kindreds of the world'.

What, it would be right to ask, ought to have happened to the sense of peoplehood, Hebrew and Judaic, which had been the matrix of this great discovering of unity, this passage from the monolatrous to the monotheist? Should the detribalizing of the divine nature not have engendered a detribalizing of the divine economy? It was around this time, thinking in centuries, that Jewry experienced that strange phenomenon of the abeyance of prophethood, so hard to explain. Jewry via exile and subjection to the nations began to draw heavily on sources of 'Eastern wisdom', witness Jesus Ben Sirach and Ecclesiasticus. It also oscillated considerably between acceptance of proselytes and lack of interest in recruiting them.

The preservation of identity through all the vicissitudes around the turn of the calendars in the Roman years became the primary responsibility. The truth of monotheism still needed its urgent custodians. Yet need the custody remain unshareable? Might the truth of divine unity not be perceived to ride with a plurality of 'people election' into its witness and care? Particularities necessarily persist, but does not the summons to worship a unitary Lord incorporate into its copyright a community, not now a singularity, of those who bear the Name? Is there a people-privacy about a public sovereignty? Was the nascent Christian church misguided in believing that 'the light enlightening the nations' could be genuinely entrusted to them, in no way diminishing the 'glory of his people Israel'? Further, might not such entrustment de-ethnicize altogether, so that persons of any and every race might be recruited into a different sort of 'peoplehood' precisely in responding to a common witness that had made them a unison of faith and love? In a word, did realized monotheism not require another look at the whole concept of 'the Gentiles'?

The historical answer of Jewry over the centuries to these questions, an answer in the negative, is familiar enough. The destiny that Yahweh had originally particularized in the first tribal terms had, perforce, to remain even when faith had learned his all-inclusive Lordship. The burden of the questions in the present context is that Zionism restores to Jewish exceptionality on God's behalf a sharply political, 'national' proprietorship that is in stark contrast with diaspora forms. It is, moreover, a proprietorship that has within it tensions that renounce the trust altogether yet continue to invoke or exploit aspects of the traditional divine destiny, in respect of land and promise, in the interests of secular statehood.

The Jewish conviction that an inclusive monotheism made no difference to unchanged and unshared Jewish particularity, in the sense and the care of such faith, could claim to be vindicated in the diaspora condition in a way that is not possible in the necessary devices and belligerence of statehood. For these so heavily accentuate the factors that, via injustice or enmity, violate the human meanings of monotheism. The nationalism, unless pursued on a desert island, compromises, if it does not supersede, the quest for holiness as the vocation of a 'priestly people'. For, expressed in national statehood with all its exigencies of power and force, the appeal to the divine reverts back to a sort of monolatry, an idolatrous invocation, insofar as it aligns God with state interest, contravening the inclusive ethicism of an authentic monotheism. Yahweh becomes the legitimation of the state's ultimate sovereignty.

The most conspicuous tokens of this situation are the instincts of quite secular interpretations of the meaning of Israel to utilize, if not to invoke, the practical advantages of 'covenant' and 'election' under God, and readily to profit from Western religious perceptions that release for it much needed political, financial and material support via tourism, sympathy and 'lobbies'. The authentic monotheism which the Hebrew prophets at their finest taught Jewry and humankind means an all-embracing ethical Lordship under which no particular destinies or ministries or chosennesses can properly violate the common equal humanity so affirmed. If they do they become a new monolatry, 'taking the Name in vain'.[14]

'Thou shalt have no other gods but me' in monolatrous times simply meant 'Leave other gods to their other peoples'. There is a sublime sense that when we understand that 'God is One', the other precept about 'having gods' becomes unnecessary. It can never remain what it once could have been, namely, 'I will have no other people but you'.

The ultimate 'searchings of Reuben', therefore, are here. To see the heart of the issue of statehood this way is in no way to decry the strenuous efforts after honesty, justice and political wisdom in the Israeli conscience. The ethicism of the great prophets is not moribund. Deeply human values are treasured and pursued. Proof might be drawn symbolically from a recent appreciation of Jerusalem:

> Jerusalem today grows daily more beautiful, as flowers, trees and fine buildings proliferate. Jews cherish and adorn Jerusalem, like a long-lost bride . . . [15]

Beyond such a discernible symbol are the insistent aims of various 'peace movements' and the urgent debate within politics as to the state's conscience about land, water, soil, people and its own inner as well as outer well-being. It is not the absence of such soul vigilance which is at issue; it is rather the basic irresolution in which the state aegis leaves it and, *qua* statehood, must perpetually leave it. In diaspora there was no inherent conflict with a vocation to be priestly people sanctifying the divine Name; in statehood there inherently is such compromise. The pursuit of 'normalcy' by Zionism leaves no 'Zion' in the non-normal terms coveted by *sui generis* 'covenant'.

Is this to say, then, that Zionism has misread its Judaism, that Israel should never be a political people, that diaspora was their only proper destiny, that the risks and traumas of diaspora were their only valid calling? Must not 'Yes!' to these questions be a harsh verdict – one which no 'Gentile' thinking could presume to reach? Certainly, any verdict must be from Jewish minds. Surely the issue, however, is not un-Judaically expressed. Can religion provide a legal right to territory except (as in the demand for Pakistan) on the basis of actual population majorities? Will 'existing populations' be there in contravention of divine law? Does religious Zionism, in some sense, imply a criminalization of Palestinians? If so, will it be Judaism that approves or forbids it?

Claude Montefiore saw the issue clearly as early as 1918:

> If Jewish nationalism attempts to free itself from religion, i.e. from Judaism entirely – that is Scylla. If it connects itself with religion – that is Charybdis.[16]

Ought not the state, he went on, to grant to *all* citizens what Jews themselves had needed in their diaspora, i.e., no religious 'tests' for full citizenship? Yet would not such openness throw open also the very Judaism supposedly desired by the state's creation? Perhaps then Judaism itself would no longer be either definable or achievable in the state auspices avowedly designed to fulfil it. It has sometimes been recalled by puzzled Zionists that the original pious tradition that took returnees to the sacred soil had the devout intention to die there. There are few things in modern history more vital than the state and people of Israel. It was a returning into resolute finality, into security and authentic being to symbolize a universal redemption. Yet, if diaspora was no place to die, is Zionism where Zion truly lives?

Notes

1 The Revised English Bible and the Jerusalem Bible respectively.

2 Notably Psalm 68:18, which Paul (or a 'Pauline' writer) in Ephesians 4:8 turns around from the imagery of a procession displaying captives to one celebrating the liberated.

'Captivity', for familiar reasons, is a salient theme in the Hebrew Bible. Zionism turned on the case against diaspora as a prison, to decry perceptions of it as a destiny.

3 The famous words of the Zealot leader prior to the final suicide, as reported by Josephus; cited from *The Jewish War*, in Yigael Yadin, *Masada: Herod's Fortress and the Zealots' Last Stand* (London, 1966), p. 232.

4 Aldous Huxley, *Ends and Means* (London, 1937), p. 9.

5 James Boswell, *Life of Johnson* (Oxford, 1953), p. 106.

6 Over, for example, the legitimacy, the increase and the rationale of 'settlements' on Palestinian land. Their deliberate, financially subsidized creation was the Likud policy of the *fait accompli*, something wellnigh irreversible, to be inherited by any possible government with a will to curb – or reverse – it in the interests of human well-being shared by all inhabitants. There is a long ideological distance between the streets of Mea Shearim and the beaches of Tel Aviv.

7 Mordecai Richler, *This Year in Jerusalem* (London, 1994), p. 222.

8 The speaker, Eliayakim Ha'etzni, was referring to Kiryat Arba, close to Hebron.

9 See Matti Golan, *With Friends Like You: What Israelis Really Think about American Jews* (New York, 1962), pp. 8–11.

10 Friedrich Nietzsche, *Beyond Good and Evil*, trans. Helen Zimmern (Edinburgh, 1909), no. 146, p. 97.

11 Ezekiel Kaufman, *Toldot Ha-Emunah Ha-Yisraelit* (Jerusalem, 1956).

12 Christianity, in its different idiom, made the same rejection of Roman idolatry but did not enjoy the status of a *religio licita* in which to do so. Thus its rejection of emperor 'worship' in the name of monotheistic faith entailed the long periods of desperate persecution.

13 Abraham Kook (1865–1935) as reported by Ben Zion Bokser (New York, 1978), p. 11. One might compare the observation of Rabbi Abraham Heschel that in Israel 'God has an address on earth': *Israel: An Echo of Eternity* (New York, 1968), p. 223.

14 Cf. the words of Jesus according to Matthew 5:48 about 'being perfect as your heavenly Father is perfect'. The 'perfection' here – evidenced by 'rain and sun indiscriminately on the just and the unjust' – means 'inclusiveness', non-partiality. In this way, to know the unity of God is to acknowledge the unity of humankind.

15 Margaret Brearley in P. W. L. Walker (ed.), *Jerusalem Past and Present in the Purposes of God* (2nd edn, Carlisle, 1994), p. 124.

16 Claude Montefiore, *Outlines of Liberal Judaism* (London, 1918), p. 309.

12

The tests of faiths

I

'When you're desirous to be blessed I'll blessing beg of you.'[1] In the most insistent of antagonisms there is what binds the parties. The most rigorous of apartheids cannot escape the rejected. In acts of alienation we engage our identities the more. The self-determination which may be a political objective remains an existential illusion. Your neighbour is as you are not simply in sharing the human condition,[2] but also – if so it be – in the very cohabitation of contention. Palestinianism has been the pre-eminent fact of Zionist experience in chosen land; Zionism has been the pre-eminent experience in Palestinian fact.

This situation has to be acknowledged as setting the supreme test of the religions. The previous chapter has tried to probe 'the searchings of Reuben', the liability of Judaism in the Zionism it has equivocally activated in Israeli form since late in the last century. The purpose of this chapter is to weigh the role of Islam and Christianity in the mind and processes of Palestinianism in the same period. The 'tests of faiths' have to do with mosque and church in the several areas of trial and temptation, of tribulation and tension, in which history has involved them these hundred years. How have their resources of doctrine been interrogated, their springs of action and reaction proved, through all that previous chapters have reviewed?

The 'tests' of faiths in the encounters of history belong with their 'temptations'. The two words have a common lineage and are akin to the Qur'an's Arabic cognate *fitnah* – a term with fascinating connotations from 'persecution' to 'sedition'.[3] The first concerned the tests the first Muslims underwent from a hostile paganism, the second those a more established faith-people had to endure from traitors or renegades within. *Fitnah*/test/ temptation attend the path of believers and their believing through the strains and hazards of 'the time being', as poets might call it. These, through the long and bitter phases of Palestine–Israel, from Herzl to Hamas, have sifted action and reaction, outer resilience and inner self-reckoning. 'What does the Lord require of you?' was the prophet Micah's question long ago (Micah 6:8); 'To do justly, to love mercy, to walk humbly with your God' the entire answer.

What, though, when 'your God' might imply a partisanship in the Lord, in Allah, in Yahweh, himself? And how should the justice, mercy and humility bear on the disparity, perhaps even the enmity, the possessive pronoun might entail? Clearly, religions in the context of the tortured politics we have reviewed are vulnerable to the most radical risks and liable for the most searching answers. *Allahu akbar* could be the most eloquent subduer of strife with its insistence on transcendent sovereignty worthy of exclusive and universal obedience stilling all national pretensions, all notional belligerence. Yet the same cry can be recruited, with clenched fists, for precisely those pseudo-lordlings in league with human passion. Faiths need a certain critical distance from themselves if they are ever to serve the politics of peace and fulfil the fidelity they confess in the *fitnahs* of their world.

These being so subtle and so stern, it will be well, before enquiring of Islam and Christianity in the Middle Eastern scene, to consider what, in elemental terms, the encounter of Zion with Palestine and of Palestine with Zion deserves of them and, in deserving, demands.

II

Perhaps some devotees, in all religious camps, would want to say that they do not have to relate their given faith to the flux of time or to the immediacies of human experience, to political history and its sources of perplexity. All they need to do is to continue doggedly asserting what has always been believed as being unchangeably absolute. If so, they are only seemingly 'faithful', while being, in truth, complacent and disloyal. For what claims to relate to 'all times and seasons' cannot escape the here and now we call 'today',[4] with all its antecedents.

What then, religiously, does it most plead to have interpreted and mastered? How are wounds stanched and the sting of enmities drawn? How is evil retrieved and tragedy transmuted? These are the ultimately religious questions. The tests of faiths lie first in their capacity to recognize them for what they truly are; then to bring their meanings to bear upon them in love and truth, meanings that are housed in their perceptions of God and their practice of compassion.

The case made here is that the long *agonistes* situation we have reviewed presses upon Muslim and Christian alike four interacting dimensions of religious reckoning. Other summaries might be suggested by other minds but could scarcely dispense with these, namely, the incompleteness of the concept of 'justice', the capacity to read tragedy, the recognition of vicarious experience, and thus the will to move through suffering into forgiveness. Underlying all four must be the awareness of a common humanity in spite of, or in defiance of, the bitterness of its having been forsaken by the other party. Before coming to reflect on the perceptions and resources of mosque and church in these four claims on their religious mind and will, it may be well to explore briefly how they are paramount and why.

The Palestinian case for 'justice, only justice' has been powerfully argued by Na'im Ateek in a brave book of that title,[5] the phrase drawn from the Book of Deuteronomy as often urged by Jews and Judaism. Israelis are often heard protesting that their nationalism is subjected to prejudiced norms, as if probity was a standard to which they were uniquely liable.[6] Injustice, in fact, assumption or criticism, is seen to be the other party's 'order of the day' on all hands. If the very Knesset of Israel stands on Arab land, how should its former owners feel, now exiled – or, more likely, the successor generations still uselessly holding on to the old keys, symbol of the access, the tenure, they will never regain?

Restitution, reparation, recovery of rights – these are legitimate demands on any civil or political order. *Fiat justitia*: 'Let justice be done'. No perceptions must be allowed to distort, deny or mitigate that moral necessity as a binding liability under God. Yet, when the utmost has been done about 'damages', apology, restoration, retribution and all other aspects of interhuman justice, there remain situations on every hand of irreversible wrong, irrecoverable right, and incorrigible evil. The wronged parties are dead, the wounds beyond cure, the victims betrayed, the issues overtaken, the facts suppressed and 'what is done cannot be undone'. The evil cannot be, as it were, un-enacted, nor the consequences reversed. That it should be so is part of the human tragedy. Say *Fiat justitia* as loudly as you will, intend it resolutely with all the energies and means of your society; there will still be wide and bitter areas of things unrequited and people abidingly wronged.

This is manifestly so in the tract of Arab–Jewish history we have been exploring. Had we righteous peace tomorrow, would that undo three generations of refugee misery, decades of patient, or impatient, pain? Nor is there even palliative – though there is often thought to be excuse – in the fact that one evil has been antecedent to another and the second was thought to represent some kind of repair of the first. The tragedies of Palestinians are not reversed by being sequel to the dire tragedies of Jews. The Holocaust, in all its enormity, does not comfort refugee camps, still less empty them either of tenants or of their anger. Satan does not cast out Satan; rather, he contrives ways to reproduce himself.

The incompleteness of the justice plea is evident immediately we recognize the futility of the notion of 'getting our own back'. We may think to, but the reality is not 'back', it is 'forward', not 'our own' as our old right in innocence, but 'the other's' as their wrongedness in our guilt. Retaliations, or situations that might be passively read as such, never avail as justice though they may seem to satisfy emotion. 'An eye for an eye' is the deed of the blind.

III

It must follow that a capacity to read tragedy is crucial to any religion's claim to interpret society to itself. Plainly history is not set to prosper good causes or blandly facilitate good wishes. It is full of what Paul called *ainigmata*, 'puzzling reflections in a mirror'. It requires of us 'a tragic sense of life', and does so, not to make us 'pessimists', or even 'pess-optimists', but realists ready to think beyond those alternatives of gay and gloom. For they have, in Blake's words, no 'arrows of desire', no 'mental fight', no 'building of Jerusalem'. The one may rise high, the other sink far, but both falsely.

The tragic sense of life understands the legitimacy, already argued, of the rule of law and the 'ought' in the fabric of the world. It also comprehends that suffering belongs inexorably with the human condition. It registers this, of course, in the hazards of our mortality, 'the ills that flesh is heir to'. The plagues and disasters in nature, the cancers and infections in the body, the atrophy of the brain – all these contribute their grim quota to our tragedy in life. But the more ultimate register is that of inhumanity in the interhuman, the guilt of structures and the wrongs of society, all stemming from the dominion/*khilafah* by which our creaturehood is dignified by the entrusting – and therefore trusting – 'Lord of all being'.

We have the measure of this dimension, which it falls to religion to interpret, if we reflect with some misanthropists that the whole human enterprise was a flawed design, a divine folly, from the start, that God ought never to have devised, as crux of his creation, the *imperium* we humans enjoy. Yet such thinking, that 'nothingness would have been better', is not only to conjecture impossibly, it is also to go out of this world. What is, is not faced by wishing it not so, only by responding to it and in it as it is.

And 'as it is' is beset with these tragic dimensions of crucified truth, blighted troth, contentious discord, open wrongs and unrequited evils, all of them requiring to be arraigned by 'justice' but not thereby cancelled or reversed. The *Palestina Agonistes* we have been studying, in part because too often unperceived, is one with the *Judea Agonistes* visible in both the trials and successes of Zionism. Like all human encounters, they counter-partner one another. In ethical terms they accuse each other because either concentrates on what the other did. In ultimate terms there is a tragedy that accusation leaves untouched or only serves to deepen.

Accusation, from the one side, only connives with the myth of innocence and so pretends a false exoneration. Israel is self-justified because Palestinians practised violence against the Jews. Palestinians, legitimately in no doubt of themselves as the grossly wronged and injured party, too long nursed thoughts of just reversal until at length conceding something irretrievable about their situation. Can that be matured into a positive acceptance (*pace justitia*)?

To think 'Yes' would spell authentic peace but, by the same token, would acquiesce in wrong unless it were reciprocal to a genuine Zionist repentance, which – given how Zionism sees itself – would be far to seek. Is it not, then, the task of the religious mind in Palestinianism to let the irretrievable become the accepted? Doing so would be to respond to 'the tragic sense of life'. For the question has to be asked: What kind of people would you be if you attained to driving Israel into the sea, as was so often said to be your goal? That may never have been remotely practicable either in local terms or by American leave. 'The sea' in this context meant the termination of Judaic statehood, not the Mediterranean.

The kind of people you would be is 'guilty' and 'inhuman', not because there was nothing to avenge – there was much – but because the avenging would, by its own logic, deserve retaliation. The entail of conflict would be perpetuated more bitterly still. Success would incriminate to the point of destroying the very justice on which its violence sought to rest. The vindication of rights would spell the perpetuation of crimes. The victors become violators. Victimization is not reversed in the making of victims.

This truth – at once moral and religious – is simply the form of human tragedy, of tragedy as a vocation to compassion. It leads us to the third of the dimensions earlier proposed, namely the deep vicariousness of human experience, and the fourth, the call to embrace forgiveness.

IV

Vicarious is a word rare enough in currency but constant in experience. Society is a collision of the bruisers and the bruised, a collusion, we might almost say, between circumstance and circumstance whereby X causes and Y undergoes adversity. There is no human immunity from humanity and the cost is invariably grievous, more grievous than the contagions of illness by which we infect each other, because the social inflictions are wilful and devious. 'Bound in the bundle of life', we cannot escape each other and what is 'advantage' to one is loss to the other. Triumph here is akin to defeat there: *patior ergo sum.*

Where we are oblivious or malicious about wrongs inflicted they are the more compounded. The US team at the UN wanted the Cana massacre of April 1996 'buried and forgotten as soon as possible'.[7] Tragedy is intensified by obscene neglect. Examples are endless of the human capacity to be inhuman. Violence characteristically discounts its own perversity. It exonerates itself by repudiating the interhumanity it has betrayed. Guilt-ridden in fact, it wills to be rid of guilt in self-perception. It disowns the nexus that binds the parties.

What of those who undergo the wrong? The nexus is grimly real in the suffering they incur. It cannot be shed by act of will, for it is now in the fabric – or the ruin – of their lives. Perhaps, though, an act of will can transmute it by acceptance of a certain kind. This is the meaning of 'vicarious'. It suspends the enmity, remits the offence and intends reconciliation, where there is any will to penitence. There comes about then a certain kind of 'bearing' which 'bears away' – not the evil as if it had not been evil, but the evil as now bereaved of the momentum it would otherwise have gathered. This alone is the way in which forgiveness comes – a forgiven-ness turning on a forgiving-ness that has made it possible. Such is the ultimate peacemaking.

This may seem far from the brazen realm of politics but it remains what religion has to realize in any broken, tortured situation – realize, that is, as a perception of what such situations take, and realize in the actuality of relationships. The will to move through suffering and tragedy by such practice of redemption will always be the crux of how the sovereignty of God is fulfilled in the turmoil of the human scene, he being, as the Qur'an says, 'ever mighty, ever wise'.[8] It was suggested that enquiry might first discover what would be required of religion by the dynamics of the situation in its deepest claim on mind to read it and spirit to resolve it. It remains to study the faiths in place to read and resolve it.

V

Islam has obvious priority, being the dominant majority faith and being bound, as no other faith is so deeply, into the very being of Arabism, via the text of the Qur'an and the supreme figure in the Arab story. Yet the role of Islam in Palestinianism is a very complex theme. One has first to decide which 'Islam', among the several understandings of what its role and nature truly are. It has to be remembered that, via the Arab Revolt, the Arab nationalisms, Syrian, Jordanian and Palestinian, were achieved against the basic political structure of Islam, namely the Caliphate, then in Ottoman hands. That in no way meant, or intended, an abeyance, still less a repudiation, of Islam as a religion. But 'as a religion' is a very Western, non-Islamic, form of words, something Islam never was after the Prophet's *Hijrah* from Meccan preaching to Medinan rule. For it saw itself as necessarily consisting of *dawlah* (state) as well as *din* (religion).

Indeed, the new national expressions took strongly state form, with Islam, in varying senses, their state religion. Yet subtle shifts have happened in its temper and self-perception, around which many tensions gathered. 'Secularity' is a term that begs many questions. As a complete repudiation of belief, worship and the sense of God, it affects only a minority of Muslims and a minority that will be only tacit, rather than aggressive or avowed, in their unbelief. However, as an infusion of influences not original to, or exclusively from, Islam in spheres of law, society, commerce, education, the media and the arts, secularity might be said to have gone far in Muslim societies. Hence, no doubt, the vehemence of those who resent and defy these instigators of change.[9]

It will, therefore, be fair to pursue our central concern for Islam's *religious* role in the Palestine–Israel encounter in those inherent moral and spiritual meanings of Islam which persist through and beyond the sundry legal and political shifts of Islamic self-definition. This will not be to ignore those shifts, since they bear hard on the capacity of religious meanings to affirm and apply themselves, but we can be absolved from exploring them in detail. The significance of what the secular denotes is no small part of authentic religion.

These preliminaries are necessary to an understanding of Islam and the PLO or of the PLO and Islam. The PLO has avoided, by and large, undue identification with Islamic motifs. It has Christians in its highest ranks and aims to enshrine a nationality, not a creed. More importantly, its counsels have studied to counter the kind of dismissive contempt from world opinion that attaches to some images of *jihad*.[10] There has been more than enough dismissiveness of its credentials without that lethal one. To be sure, for some within its ranks there has been a sense of divine mission and divine legitimation, but the National Charter was moved by one important criterion.

It envisaged its future statehood as ready to comprise Jews present by 1947 in its citizenship. Anti-Zionism, anyway, was all too easily identified with anti-Semitism and it was vital to insist on the distinction and to exclude any potential hostility to Jews as such from the state and the society that the PLO desired. No real situation has ever put this intention to the test,[11] but ideal and image are mutually important, not least for an entity so beleaguered and maligned as the PLO.

Other organs of Palestinianism have been less circumspect, and though Hizballah relates to Iran and Lebanon, something of its aura attaches to Palestinian sympathizers. It is significant that militancy for Palestine only became sharply Islamic in tone and temper with the emergence of the Hamas movement late in the 1980s.[12] That emergence owed much to despair about the 'peace process' and its many ambiguities and pitfalls. Hamas believed in enlisting the Islamic dimension to give vehemence and drive to a cause it perceived as compromised or stymied by its secular ambience. That the Hamas mind was so long in arriving at articulacy seems evidence enough of the steady secularity of the mainline PLO policy.

That raises the intriguing question whether an observer could wonder if that secular stance was not − so to speak − a Muslim phenomenon. Was Nasserism in Egypt 'Islamic'? How far was the Syrian Ba'th in its origins 'Islamic'? The questions have point. Yassir Arafat's PLO was inspired, operated and sustained by Muslims. He himself is a *hajji*, having performed the pilgrimage to Mecca. It could be thought that his early links, as a protégé, with the Mufti Amin al-Hussaini, an ill-fated figure in the Palestine–Islam equation, would have augured badly. However, his beginnings in leadership of a students' union in Cairo were not in mufti-style terms. It will be fair to conclude that the major Islamic role in the politics of the PLO has been moderate and, though violent until it unviolenced itself, unbigoted.[13]

VI

What, however, of the spiritual potential of Islam in those reckonings with tragic experience that go below the calculations of organization and the strategies of liberation? Do the Qur'an and Islam enable the vision and practice we have earlier seen as the crucial – and costly – factor in peace?

Answer had better begin with contrary evidences. Though, as we have seen, the *jihad* concept has at times been muted, belligerence has mandate from the very structures of Islam. After thirteen years of steadfast *risalah*, message-giving, Muhammad migrated, both physically and mentally, into the quest for power. Medina became an Islamic city-state. The first signal victory of his forces against the pagan Meccans was *Yaum al-Furqan*, 'the day of the criterion', which stands, rather like the Jewish exodus, as the 'arrival point' of consciously political, encounter-vindicated Islam.[14]

By that symbol and its further phases of physical triumph, Islam became the most politicized of religions. It did not, in Constantine's way, take over a faith for the convenience of empire; it contrived empire for the further-ance of faith. Its historic readiness to marry truth and power has remained broadly uninhibited until the coming of modern secular misgivings about the physical empowerment of spiritual belief. Though the PLO and some others have availed to dissociate their cause from secondment by religious dogma, there remains the hard question about Islam's resources of will to take the old prophet's wisdom: 'Not by might, nor by power, but by my Spirit' (Zechariah 4:6).[15] It is on record, for example, that on the catastrophic Friday of the Six-Day War in June 1967, the preacher in the Great Mosque in Mecca used the text: 'Do not weaken and sue for peace: you will be [or are] the upper ones.'[16]

That sentiment is admirable as long as encounter stays the shape of things. 'Suing for peace' may be cowardly, weak and contemptible. What of 'making' it as a positive heroism? He would be a fool who tried to derive pacificism from the Qur'an and folly is not intended here. But the firmer Muslim instincts and precepts are in the legitimation of religious force, the more urgent – in the present actualities – become the arguments whereby these might be tempered and queried.

Perhaps what we are feeling for is 'largeness of heart', a fine generosity of spirit, the will to let compassion override enmity. What then of *sharh al-sadr*, 'a widening of the heart', in the Qur'an – reproving the opposite *daiq al-sadr*, 'the constriction of the heart'?[17] Surah 39.22 reads: 'He whose heart God has enlarged into *islam*, he enjoys light from his Lord.' Or should we read Islam, the established structure? For the Arabic *islam* is both common and proper noun, a sense yielded to Allah and/or allegiance under 'the Five

Pillars'.[18] If the former, then there is a case for the divine mind working with the human mind towards the will to peace. All will turn on the theology we have; Allah must decide where Allah's heart-opening goes.

Frequent in Quranic experience runs the quality of *sabr*; it is a significant dimension of the Muslim ethos. How should the 'patience' of 'the patient' be read? Is it a stout endurance which will not flinch? There are passages which say as much. Or may it sometimes be what bears redemptively?[19] At least it should counter the kind of impetuosity that thinks 'Force is all they understand'. It could be a firm antidote to being 'swift to anger'. Again, since *sabr* is that with which Allah allies, all will turn on our perception of theology. 'God is with the patient', says Surah 2.153 among many other passages.

'Forgiver', in three grammatical forms, stands clearly among the divine Names in Quranic usage, both simple and intensive, while *maghfirah*, 'forgiveness', occurs some thirty times, often relating to the lot of the faithful in eternity, and akin to the idea of a wage received (*ajr*). The command to 'seek forgiveness' of God (*istaghfir Allah*) at least implies that a will to be forgiven is crucial to receiving it. The command can relate to occasions of the utmost success attained, as in 110.3: 'When God's help comes about . . . then seek His forgiveness.' Palestinians have had no such occasions of 'manifest triumph', so maybe 'God's help' and 'victory' have to be known by other criteria.[20] But that forgiveness is always needed may, even in unrelieved adversity, inspire the will to grant it.

Blood price as 'better' than the exacting of blood revenge, legitimate as the latter may be, is commended in Islam.[21] Could it sustain a case-making for peacemaking rather than a perpetuated war posture? At the barest level there is *Dar al-sulh*, 'the realm of conciliation', in between the old alternatives of *Dar al-Islam* and *Dar al-Harb*, 'the abodes of Islam and of war'. According to 16.126, 'exercising patience' is better than retaliation, while 42.43, where the context is about retaliation, declares: 'Whoever exercises patience and practises forgiveness – that is the staying power that masters things.'[22]

However, through all these passages runs the theme that desisting from resistance is when *fitnah*, 'active hostility', capitulates and ceases. Islam was ready for peace only when it had prevailed. Waiting for the only issue that leaves you in undoubted mastery has been the characteristic attitude of Islam. Right loyalty excludes compromise.

That dictum, however, though instinctive and traditional, fails to probe deeply enough into what might be loyalty and what compromise. Still more precious loyalties can be compromised by imperceptive adherence to lesser ones. Apply to 'armed struggle' and the hard heart of violence the Qur'an's own question: 'Do you consider the fire you kindle?'[23] Fire excites but destroys. It flares like the anger that kindles it but feasts like a savage on the human prey. It burns for justice and consumes a creaturehood that is common. 'Consider the fire you kindle', lest inexorably it is avenged on those who give it fuel.[24] All passionate causes become potential excuses, absolving what should only be condemned.[25] Maybe in all such vehemence, though sponsored by justice, there is, as Napoleon reputedly said of Muhammad, 'Quelque chose que nous ignorons', something we have overlooked or grimly fail to know.[26] Abating anger and curbing enmity may be the truest shape of compromise, the surest loyalty to the greatness of Allah, 'exalted be He above all that ye associate'.

VII

Dissociating faith from power may seem dubious to the Muslim heritage of robust, even at times implacable, religion. Yet it has become a necessary feature of the present in Islam. Palestinians are distinctive in their travail; but they are not alone in their condition as, in measure, hostage to those more powerful than they or to political factors they cannot regulate but only undergo. They share with many in Islam the necessity of risk and impairment in the equations of the world. The old dream that Islam always ruled while other faiths might be permitted as innocuous *dhimmis*, or minorities, is ended for many contemporary Muslims. Minority status is new in its permanence and in its demands on self-perception in new terms.

Yet it is not new if one notes the internal making of Muslim minorities within Islam as a whole, notably the Shi'ah. The triumphalism we associate with post-*Hijrah* Islam in Medina – hardly bought as it was – passed into the Sunni suzerainty of Damascus. The people on the losing side of those early fissures in Islam were the Shi'ah, the partisans of 'Ali, the ill-fated fourth Caliph, and Husain, the tragic martyr of Karbala'. The cardinal factor in their long experience, apart from times and areas of power, was vulnerability. If for different reasons, vulnerability is the experience today of very large and significant segments of Islam. They are vulnerable in the sense that they do not enjoy an Islamic statehood. Their well-being depends, in measure, on democratic opportunity where it avails, which they may share but cannot dominate. It also turns on the readiness, or ability, of other religions and societies to offer them tolerance and goodwill. These, Islamic power structures elsewhere would be expected to reciprocate to *their* minorities.[27]

This dual situation, when rightly perceived, gives a new perspective on power, the lack of it, and liability for a compassionate identity, unless confrontation is to be our only thought, our sorry fate. Vulnerability was always part of the human condition. Islam is learning, has to learn, that Muslims cannot hope to be immune from it in the vagaries of history or contrive to exceptionalize themselves as never tragic. It follows that all faiths need, in their deepest assets, a clue – in both doctrine and practice – to unremitting suffering. Palestine, within Islam, is prime territory for finding it.

There is an old tradition that 'Islam was born as a stranger'. It no doubt stems from the early Meccan sufferings. The Shi'ah developed in their tragedy a concept of *taqiyya*, by which they meant a piety that did three things. It is suggested here that these – with one radical revision – may be the clue to what a Palestinian Islam might borrow.

The three things were enshrined in an old tradition of the Prophet. 'Evil things', once seen for what they were in society, were to be 'changed with the hand' – action, deed, drain a swamp, dig a well, lend a hand, stanch a wound and so on. Where immediate action is possible, take it. When this is not possible, 'change them with the tongue' – protest, demonstrate, do not let the evil go unblamed, untrumpeted. Shame society into what is needed. If evils are not remedied by hand or mouth, the faithful should 'change them in the heart'.[28]

For Shi'ah thinking, the third meant that one still nursed a heart-resistance to what one could not alter. One did not concede its validity, even though all one could do was nourish an inner disavowal of it. At times this *taqiyya* almost meant a dissembled conformity under a regime one deplored or detested. Shi'ah Islam was often this way. One was outwardly supine but inwardly unreconciled. Vulnerable was wedded to passive, until occasion came to 'change the evil'.[29]

The tradition said that this third was 'the weakest of the three'. By some reckonings that might be so. Unlike 'hand' or 'tongue' it had nothing to show except what it could not reveal. As applied to the current question for peace in Palestine/Israel, must it not be said that 'changing it in the heart' is the strongest of the three? It is finally the heart that overcomes evil with good, by being not itself overcome by it. When 'the heart' finally concedes the necessity of co-existence, then 'hand' and 'mouth' can shape it in maps and treaties.

VIII

How might a partnership of Palestinian Christianity be seen *vis-à-vis* the foregoing concerning Islam and the four religious requisites with which we began? There is one immediate point to note and two broad quandaries attaching to Christian Palestinians and their role.

The point has to do with the steady diminution of the Christian population. The conflict brought drastic shifts in local societies. Bethlehem, which used to be an almost exclusively Christian locale, is now heavily Islamic.[30] There proceeds a steady 'museumization' of Christianity in the land of its birth, with Western pilgrims thinking largely of 'holy places' in neglect or ignorance of 'holy people'. Diaspora from Palestine is in no way confined to Christians, but proportionately Christians have departed more and further, mainly to the West in quest of education, employment and uniting of families. With readier connections and greater mobility they become more numerous in Toronto or Detroit than in Bethlehem. It is hard to see how anything less than a definitive, durable peace can reverse the trend.[31]

The first of the two quandaries has to do with the place of 'confessions' in Arab nationalism. Muslims, of course, continue to dominate but, in theory, 'nations' are one whole in statehood, whereas the old Caliphal order found Christians marginalized as *dhimmis*, protected but also inferiorized as non-participant in the *Dar* that Islam formed in believers. The new pattern of supposedly common citizenship meant both opportunity and greater danger. Minorities could now aspire to engage in public affairs but, by the same token, were under actual or implicit pressure to align with the Muslim formation of statehood and the broadly Islamic ethos of all Arab nationalism, by virtue of the central figure of the Prophet and the status, as Arabic, of the definitive Qur'an.

It was, therefore, difficult for Palestinian Christians to hold to their distinctive theology and spiritual norms in thorough identity with a nationalism controlled by distinctive Muslim criteria of religion, around which were radical issues of truth and meaning. Christians, moreover, were fragmented by divisions arising of old from language, locality and belief formulae.

There were some who advocated an almost total Christian 'islamizing' of the Christian mind, by observance of the Prophet's birthday, for example, and by 'interiorizing' almost to extinction the spirituality their Christianity informed.[32] The Ba'th Party, founded in Damascus by the Muslim Salah al-Din al-Bitar and the (Greek Orthodox) Christian Michel Aflaq, expounded a fervent religious nationalism in which the cross and the creeds were withdrawn into a privacy of subdued inwardness, which silenced any relevance they might have for the nationalism itself.[33]

Such reduction of 'Christian' to a nominal, hardly operative element could mean a very muted theological input from the churches to the sharp problematics of the living situation. Great patience and discernment were necessary for the Christian mind in national concert with a faith so confident of its finality as Islam. The Palestinian will for secular politics helped to ease this context but made a Christian frame of reference the more exacting.[34]

The second quandary of a Christian Palestinianism lay in the Hebraic antecedents of Christian faith, signalled in, and perpetuated by, the juncture of Old and New Testaments (as Christians describe them) within a single Bible. Islam has a much more forthright disjuncture from Jewish antecedents,[35] whereas the Christian Scriptures turn so crucially on their Hebraic heritage and Christian liturgies recite the perceived precedents of psalm and prophet.[36] Christianity thus had an organic tie with the biblical Israel that was experientially contradicted by the actual political Israel. The burden of this situation increased when the emergent state named itself 'Israel'.[37] Christians were used to Zachariah's Song: 'Blessed be the Lord God of Israel' alongside their bitter exile at the hand of the (to them less than 'blessed') Lord of Ben Gurion, Begin, Shamir and Rabin. The same song made double reference to 'the hands of our enemies' and 'them that hate us', i.e., the new Philistines.

The tension, so rarely appreciated by Western Christians,[38] was wellnigh intolerable. The *Benedictus* may have been a sharp focus but the issue ran through the entire relationship of Arab Christians with political Israel. It tended also to embarrass their nationalism in the eyes of Muslims. They were also suspect, in measure, by their close links with Western churches, Roman, Lutheran and Anglican, whose members may have come on tours as pilgrims but had scant awareness of the issue. From American Christian Zionists the painful irony was at times unbearable, with 'fellow'-Christians rapturous about the legitimacy of Israel by their lights on Scriptures to which Palestinian victims owed traditional loyalty.

It is little wonder if, amid this hard complex, Arab Christianity found it difficult to bring its faith to bear redemptively on the peace situation in either doctrinal relevance or active effort. Any quest for common spiritual dialogue with Israelis about the substructure at the heart of any solutions in fact tended to be checked or deferred on the ground that it would be exploited to show that all was well and that Israelis and Palestinians were fraternizing amicably enough. All was not well. Until there was political justice, theological talk was a snare and delusion. Israel, after all, had set the priority of the political at the very heart of Zionism and was only relating to others on its own terms of 'creating facts' and with such Palestinians as it chose to find suitable for converse. On that basis, authentic religious meaning in mutually positive terms was hard to seek, still harder to find. The dilemma was shared to a much lesser degree by Muslims, who were more comfortably dissociated from Hebraic antecedents.

Let not those circumstances, however, imply that there is no Christian undertaking on the four questions with which we began. On the contrary. It is time to take their Christian measure.

IX

Palestinian Christianity is uniquely experienced to meet the demands of its present vocation. For it belongs with the whole *mise-en-scène* of Christian faith as its native possession. At times there seems to be an Israeli will to relegate Christian origins to Asia Minor. Thus Teddy Kollek, former and long-time Mayor of Jerusalem, wrote:

> Christianity . . . sprang up and developed far from the scene of Jesus' ministry, notably in Antioch and other parts of the Middle East and the eastern Mediterranean, where his disciples recounted his parables, his teachings . . . Jerusalem itself remained comparatively untouched by the views expounded by the latest victim of Rome.[39]

Jerusalem and Galilee are not to be cheated this way out of the integrated meaning of Jesus of Nazareth, crucified in Jerusalem 'under Pontius Pilate'. One has only to ask how 'Nazarenes' should have reached as far as Antioch from their base in Jerusalem to know that local events had inspired their diaspora. The wide and rapid dispersion of Christianity was precisely the evidence of the meanings rooted in its first terrain.

It therefore has a distinctive sense of territory and Palestinians are its local residents. It differs from the Jewish title-deeds as Jewry finds them. It is not rooted in ethnic right and only indirectly in patriarchal heritage. It does not consist in covenant or election as these might turn on birth and soil. It is also distinctive *vis-à-vis* how Islam sees 'the holy land'[40] as, thanks to the first *Qiblah* and Muhammad's 'Night Journey', its third holiest shrine, a shrine to which pilgrimage has never been mandatory for Muslims as is the Meccan *hajj*.

The Christian distinctiveness of Palestine can best be described as sacramental. The point was partly made earlier, in Chapter 5. Event as history is crucial to Christian faith. It follows that the locale of event-history has a sacramental quality, enabling musing of the mind on that piece of earth, or pilgrim feet traversing it, to possess thereby the meanings it once enshrined.

Imagination is thus quickened to participate. Meanings 'come home' where their home was. Such is the way of sacraments, and sacred geography can be one of them, the physical bespeaking the spiritual at the rendezvous with history.

Distance does not preclude this transaction. For 'the road to Jerusalem is in the heart'. To be 'resident', however, as 'natives' are, is to be peculiarly in a privilege of grace. The Palestinian Christian is born into the very precincts of the faith, though the only Christian 'birthright' anywhere is that of faith. It will be the Christian answer from everywhere, local or distant, that we need to the same tests of faith we have related already to Islam, namely justice, tragedy, vicarious experience and the way through suffering to reconciliation.

Keeping in mind what has earlier been noted concerning the legitimacy of seeking justice and the qualified role of power in serving it, Christian origins in Jesus and the cross commit Christians to seeing redemptive love as the ultimate shape of human vocation. Redemptive love does not ignore or exclude the feasible tasks of justice and requital of wrong. However, it perceives reaches of evil in the human story that are beyond these necessary correctives. It perceives the real vulnerability inseparable from human society, the inhumanity of these to those, and the vocation through suffering to reconcile, to reinstate relationship on the other side of wrong and, so doing, to let 'grace more abound'.

These active perceptions do not discount power where power rightly obtains or law where law belongs, but finds these only partially positive and always incomplete by realistic measures of our humanness and – Christians would say – by adequate measures of divine sovereignty. We might formulate the issues by reflecting on the Islamic case as Fazlur Rahman has it:

> For Islam, there is no particular 'salvation': there is only 'success' (*falah*) or 'failure' (*khusran*) in the task of building the type of world-order we are describing . . . What was spread by the sword was not the religion of Islam, but the *political domain* of Islam, so that Islam could work to produce on earth the order that the Qur'an seeks.[41]

There is, then, a valid distinction between Islam 'as a religion' and Islam 'with political domain'. By Christian realism, that political 'success' will always be at best approximate, the 'failure' often endemic. Human well-being will always hinge on love 'bearing each other's burdens', even when state power has actualized the utmost it can attain. 'We are such stuff as sins are made on . . . ', 'such stuff as love is made by . . . ' in redemptive response to wrong.

For can 'ensuring the political domain' – Islam's or any other – ensure the occasion it seeks for 'due world order'? What if the enterprise proves self-defeating because other 'swords' are doing the same? Does not the whole tragedy in the Middle East stem from rival actual or would-be 'political domains' battling to establish their own 'world order', and in so doing entailing enormous tragedy, some upon others, all upon themselves? What then of 'success' or 'failure'? Can these ever be politically ensured, forcibly contrived without a sort of human 'failure' in the very success? Does not 'peace' between and beyond these 'swords' mean the pain of forgiveness, the bearing of wrongs and the release of something forever eluding the reach or the canons of power?

Christendom has frequently and shamefully betrayed such peace down the centuries by the 'swords' of power quests. Original Christianity is grounded in the ministry and self-giving of Jesus, perceived at the very birth of the church as the insignia of the divine nature. God's nature dramatized in Jesus a vindication of how bent it was towards us and at what cost, the cost being reciprocal to our entire need of what the divine nature undertook. There was, we might say, a *when* and a *where* in order that '*whom* we have in heaven' might be dependably known and known as the love that comes, and coming cares, and caring redeems. Then, by grace and faith, a sort of divine emulation becomes the ground of our ethics and the clue to our whole condition.

X

How, the cynic might ask, do you write forgiveness on maps, how accommodate it in the toils of politics? Is it an art of which states are capable, or only a feasibility as between persons? Machiavelli thought any ruler offering it or seeking it sick and deluded. Force, in the real world, is the ultimate determinant and forgiveness a fond illusion, a luxury for romantics, an indulgent irrelevance.

That policy tasks, frontier lines, territorial markers and economic decisions will need and demand their own practical agenda is true enough. But if religions have a role at all, then forgiveness, in the wake of all that has bedevilled precisely those issues, will be their vital enabler and their final arbiter. The goal of negotiation needs the way to forgiveness, given and received.

It is understandable that Jews should reply with irritation, even anger, to this conclusion. 'We should disown this disastrous urge to forgive', wrote Lord Jakobovits after a brutal killing.[42] Judaism has a long tradition of seeing itself and its people as the 'wronged' of this world so that forgiveness tends to be read as an evasion of guilt of which others should not be rid. The case for pardon seems almost an obscenity, wrong from aliens falling too heavily upon Jewry. Shakespeare's Shylock looks justified in his implacable urge to requite the hostile world. Were it not so there could be no tragic pathos in his own final desolation.[43]

Yet, when we reach contemporary Zionism and Israeli statehood, there is much less ground for this implicit Judaic sense of being 'more sinned against than sinning'. As we have seen, Palestinianism, beside being unhappily inept, has been darkly in the wrong *qua* violence and anger. Yet, in this encounter, there is a *nostra culpa* due on each side. From the horror of the King David Hotel bombing in 1947 to that of Cana in Lebanon in 1996, the wicked murder of the peace envoy Count Bernadotte and the savaging of Beirut in 1982, Israel's story has its crimes and foul deeds, reciprocal, it will be said, but not thereby exonerated. It is precisely because exoneration has to be denied to both that a mutual forgiveness alone satisfies the need of peace.

It falls then to religions informing these combatants to search their own resources of faith and Scriptures for all that may kindle and transact the will to be forgiven and to forgive. It is there strenuously in the Hebrew prophets and some psalms, where, however, it needs releasing from the exemptions it may presuppose around 'pagans', 'Gentiles', 'uncircumcised' and 'strangers'. It must also transcend the long tradition of the legitimate wars and conquests of Jewish kings and leaders, and be informed by its own long anguish.

Islam needs to maximize all the Qur'an and Tradition present concerning the divine mercy and compassion and human conforming to them. It will need to look beyond its innate instinct to see all things in terms of a conflict between Islam and non-Islam, perhaps by reviewing what those two descriptives might describe. Forgiveness for the other and forgivingness from within do not have to turn on prior submission. For, creeds apart, all humanity is in relation. It is precisely conflict that writes their ledgers of wrong, not identity that cancels them.

The Gospel with which Christianity was launched sets a brief but inclusive epic of forgivingness at the heart of its own story and, further, associates that epic squarely with the eternal nature of the divine mind and will. The epic comprised a drama of forgiveness concerning what happened at the climax of a ministry of word and deed, of teaching and compassion. It was a climax of rejection and wrongdoing. These were recognized as entirely elemental in our inclusive human story, our genius for guilt in our societies, our structures, our economies and our persons. Thus the crucifying of Jesus brought into one disclosure the things about us all that most cry out to be forgiven – what faith named as 'the sin of the world', that in us all because of which 'Christ died'.

In how he died it heard itself forgiven. Those were the words: 'Father, forgive them: they do not know what they do.' The words related – as faith came to recognize – to all that was explicit in the human deed they pardoned. If our penitent sense of things, of how we were there in the proxy for us of the doers, makes us all there in his forgiven audience, then we receive and 'believe in the forgiveness of sins'.

All, however, belongs with the heart of God. Otherwise all would be a construct of our imagination and, as such, a vain and hollow thing. If we have 'God in Christ crucified' by responsive faith, it is only because 'Christ crucified was in God', the evidence in history of the divine love – the sort of evidence we need if ever the enigmas of our history are to be read as compatible with a good and wise creation.

It is thus that, for Christians, the bringing of forgivingness and forgiveness to all human situations is, by the seal of divine mandate and example, the whole duty of man.

Notes

1 Shakespeare, *Hamlet*, III.iv, lines 155–6.

2 'As yourself' in the familiar translation surely cannot be read as making our love of ourselves the measure of love to another. By the very constitution of selfhood, housed in body, it can yield no valid analogy of relations outside the self. The meaning has to be: 'Love your neighbour; he is what you are – human, mortal, frail, needy, expectant and reciprocal to you in "neighbourhood".'

3 The word indicates whatever 'tries' the Muslim: taunts when believers were few, conspiracies when they came to power, even family affection when this dissuaded men from battle and possible martyrdom.

4 Muhammad is affirmed as 'a mercy to the worlds'. 'Worlds' are cultures, times, societies, as well as 'places'. Shabbir Akhtar's book *A Faith for All Seasons* (London, 1990) acknowledged that faith's duty to 'belong' in modernity, though arguing for a very unyielding kind of *tafsir* or exegesis.

5 Na'im Ateek, *Justice and Only Justice: A Palestinian Theology of Liberation* (New York, 1989). Moving from the Deuteronomic principle of 'righteousness', he links a sympathetic awareness of the European impulses to Zionism with a rigorous examination of the 'injustices' of Israel as Palestinians, within and without, have known them.

6 The protest is a fair one, since Zionism entails Jews – *qua* the necessities of statehood – in all the compromises, the subtleties and double-speak that go with politics and power everywhere. Israel is in that respect a very 'Gentile' entity. Yet, in measure, the unfair demand that things should somehow be 'different' with the 'chosen people' stems inevitably from the very claim to be such.

7 As reported in the British Press from New York correspondents, 10 May 1996.

8 Nearly the most frequent of consistently coupled divine Names in the Qur'an. The

unison of power and wisdom, the very juncture agnostics find most suspect (for whom not both are credible but only inept wisdom or crude power), was central to Paul's understanding of the God of the Gospel – in Christ.

9 One might cite the sharp reaction of Al-Azhar in the 1920s to the secular theory of Ziya Gökalp and 'Ali 'Abd al-Raziq, or the hostility of Abu-l-'Ala al-Mawdudi to the Islam of Muhammad 'Ali Jinnah in the birth-throes of Pakistan.

10 Usually connoting 'holy war' and associated in Western minds with violence and bigotry. However, even in its martial sense in the Qur'an *jihad* is held responsive to others' aggression, or is to be pursued until there is 'submission' and not, vindictively, beyond. However, some Muslims insist that all this is 'the lesser *jihad*', the greater one being the mastery of the self and its passions.

11 The PLO's readiness to co-exist with Jews resident prior to partition and within the indicated borders of the UN vote never had occasion to be made good. However, as and when any sort of Palestinian 'state' comes to be on the West Bank, how Israeli settlements there will respond and how they will subsist remains to be tested. Few if any will consent to live 'under' Palestine authority but will decamp, unless roads linking them contrive to coalesce them into autonomous areas and secure them from either threat or contagion.

12 Hamas has a more avowed Islamic character and appeals to *jihad*-style thinking and, in its suicide-bombers, invokes the idea of 'holy martyrdom' ensuring paradise. It also sees the Israeli antagonist in terms of old Quranic reproach and condemnation.

13 Palestinians are not unique among movements for 'liberation' in evolving through 'terrorism' to attainment of 'respectable' power, as circumstances were transformed, if not by the violence, then by supervening factors. It was so with Zionism itself, with Begin and Shamir, though (should we say happily?) not Jabotinsky, finding themselves Prime Ministers.

14 See Surah 8.41. Elsewhere the word is a title of the Qur'an, the Book which 'distinguishes' the true from the false. Badr was held to have done this materially for the Muslims, when the under ones roundly defeated the prestige people.

15 The words go to the heart of the issue in the antithesis of 'God's Spirit' to 'power and might', whereas a predominant view in the Qur'an would link all three in concord. Yet the very fact of entrenched Quraishi 'power' requiring to be defeated *en route* to a full Islam might be taken to argue legitimate power in overcoming it. How else would 'God's Spirit' defeat the pagans (a very Islamic question)? But, further, did 'force' in reality defeat them as pagans, or only subdue them as enemies?

16 See Surah 3.139 and 47.35: 'Do not weaken and grieve [3.139] and sue for peace [47.35], for you are the ones to prevail' [lit. 'the upper']. The call is to tenacity against odds, 'you are not defeated until you think you are'.

17 Surah 15.97 and 26.13. *Sharh*, when applied to a text, means 'expounding'; of persons, 'opening of the mind to take in'.

18 The distinction is very relevant, Arabic having no capital letters to distinguish between nouns 'common' and nouns 'proper'. There is an *islam* to God, e.g., that of Abraham and all early prophets, which did not comprise the Islam that did not then exist in respect of its five obligations and institutional structure.

19 One may 'bear' as warriors do in risking the wounds their militancy entails, or one may bear in taking injury and forbearing to fight. Too often, though not always, the 'fight' reaction justifies the initial assumption of the opponent, i.e., 'this man is against me'.

20 The verse speaks of people 'thronging into Islam'. It is inscribed on the Mausoleum of Jinnah in Karachi.

21 Surah 5.46 confirms the Mosaic law of limited retaliation, but forbearing is better. See also 2.178, 16.127 and 42.41.

22 The Arabic has been variously translated. 'The staying power that masters things' is a free rendering of (lit.) 'that is to whoever resolves or has purposefulness in the things'. Asad

has 'something to set one's heart on'; Arberry, 'Surely that is true constancy'. At least it is clear that a forgiving forbearance requires a firm set of soul.

23 Surah 56.71. It is one of four identical questions, also enquiring: 'Do you consider the semen you spill, the soil you till and the water you drink?', i.e., progeny, farming, watering and fire-kindling. The verb means both 'to see' (with the eye) but also 'to have a view about' or even 'visualize'. Clearly, the call is to a responsible perception of these four 'basics' of life and being.

24 In Jamal 'Abd al-Nasir's *The Philosophy of the Revolution*, trans. Public Affairs Press (New York, 1955), there is a graphic passage in which he describes a revulsion in the very act of participating in an assassination attempt. He visualized the grief of the victim's family and inwardly wished the non-success of the deed.

25 Muhammad Kamil Husain's *City of Wrong* (ET, Amsterdam, 1957; 2nd edn Oxford, 1994) argues from the crucifixion of Jesus the guilt of structures that plead political or other expediency in order to trample on justice. He insists in strongly Islamic terms on the duty of personal conscience to scrutinize and, usually, disallow the claims of corporate power and institutions. The English historian Arnold Toynbee, from his long experience of Near East politics, had the same deep suspicion of the wiles of human structures of power.

26 Comte de la Casas, *Le Mémorial de Sainte-Hélène*, ed. M. Dunan (Paris, 1951), vol. 1, p. 529. Napoleon felt that Voltaire had maligned Muhammad and that there was more than fanaticism and force in his story.

27 It is the justice of such reciprocal respect for human rights between cultures that moves some recent Muslim lawyers in international jurisprudence to appeal to the Meccan period of original Islam when it was only and essentially religious. See, e.g. 'Abdullahi Ahmad al Na'im, *Towards an Islamic Reformation* (Syracuse, 1990).

28 The tradition boasts many sources. Perhaps the foremost is *The Sunan* of Abu 'Isa Muhammad ibn Sawrah al-Tirmidhi (3rd edn, Beirut, 1978), vol. 3, p. 318.

29 Khomeini's Islamic Revolution was marked by an utter repudiation of *taqiyya* in respect of the Shah's régime.

30 The mosque and tall minaret facing Nativity Square are a post-1948-war construction.

31 See the appeal for return of Palestinians in diaspora in M. Prior and W. Taylor (eds), *Christians in the Holy Land* (London, 1994), pp. 225–6.

32 One notable example was Constantin Zuraqk, historian in Beirut and first Syrian Ambassador to Washington.

33 The story is more fully studied in my *The Arab Christian: A History in the Middle East* (London, 1992), chs 7 and 10.

34 Inasmuch as 'being secular' in politics argued a withdrawal of Christian meanings into the 'private sphere' immune from any bearing on political ends and means.

35 The common Abrahamic element was, as it were, de-Judaized in the claim that 'the father of faithful' was not a Jew, or Christian, but a *hanif*, a 'God-fearer' (Surah 3.67). After Muhammad's *Hijrah* to Medina, Islam developed a sharp contra-Jewish temper and its own idiosyncratic forms.

36 Scholars also think that the very shape of the Gospels and the narratives of the Passion of Jesus owe much to scriptural citation.

37 It was a much debated decision. 'The Jewish State' would not do, thanks to the question raised by statehood as to who 'a Jew' was. 'Zion' was too sacred and pretentious. Also 'The Rock of Israel' in the Constitution satisfied the secularists who did not wish a 'God' mention, and the Orthodox and religious who knew the meaning of the phrase in Deuteronomy 32:18, 'the Rock that formed thee'.

38 If Texas, for example, were to be held 'a promised land' by a migration to it, how would existing Texans feel if the incomers had a liturgy and made sacred a Scripture warranting the suffering the immigration brought to them?

39 Teddy Kollek and Moshe Perlman, *Pilgrims to the Holy Land* (New York, 1970), pp. 27–8.

40 Surah 5.21 is the only passage in which the Qur'an uses this phrase.

41 Fazlur Rahman, *Major Themes in the Qur'an* (Chicago, 1980), p. 63.

42 Lord Jakobovits, formerly Chief Rabbi in Great Britain, in a newspaper article (London, December 1995), following the brutal murder of a much-loved headmaster, Philip Lawrence, who was shepherding pupils outside the gate of his school. To be sure, talk of forgiveness can never rightly be glib or trite but the vehemence of the Rabbi's article was striking.

43 It is surely right to see deep pathos and genuine pity in Shakespeare's Shylock. The play is in no way anti-Semitic. The self-occupied 'Gentiles' – the courtly Bassanio and the vulgar Graziano – are in the dock.

Name index

Aaron 152
'Abd al-Hamid II 38
'Abdallah, King 92, 159
'Abd al-Nasir 59, 109–12, 158, 224
'Abd al-Sabur 184
'Abd al-Shafi, Haidar 128
Abinoam 187, 188
Abraham 19, 23, 67, 75, 76, 153, 193,
  199, 223
  in Islam 67
Achan 5
Acre 180
Aelia Capitolina 10
Aflaq, Michel 118, 216
agonistes, as applicable to Palestine 2, 8,
  14, 15, 19, 35, 53, 75, 82, 130, 147,
  206, 208
Ahad Ha-Am 27
Akhtar, Shabbir 222
Alcalay, Ammiel 31, 34, 49
Aleppo 113
Altalena 92, 106, 116, 168, 183
Amos 12, 82, 85
Anathoth 78, 84
Andrewes, Lancelot, prayers 9, 10, 16
Antioch 218
Aqabah 130
Arafat, Yassir 68, 74, 138, 139, 141, 161,
  211
  see also Palestine Liberation Organization
  in Subject index
Ashkenazi Jews 31, 49

Ashrawi, Hanan 145, 161, 179, 180
Asia Minor 218
Ateek, Na'im 205, 222
Al-Azhar 223

Babylon 24, 78
Baghdad 77, 164
Baker, James 141, 161
Bar Kokhba 10
Basisu, Mu'in 182, 185
Bathsheba 76, 82
Beersheba 18, 130
Begin, Menahem 37, 52, 59, 60–1, 65,
  69, 91, 93, 98, 100, 102, 123, 139,
  143, 154, 157, 160, 166, 168, 172,
  183, 217
  and Beirut 97ff.
Beilin, Yossi 130, 131, 145
Beilinson, Moshe 131
Beirut 18, 130
  invasion of 97ff., 100, 123
Benedictus 217
Ben Gurion, David 13, 20, 33, 36, 41,
  42, 49, 53, 63, 76, 92, 101, 106,
  141, 143, 146, 152, 156, 166, 187,
  189, 217
Ben Sirach, Jesus 200
Ben Yehuda 30
Ben Zvi, Isaac 36, 40
Bernadotte, Count, murder of 93, 144,
  146, 221
Bethlehem 180, 216, 224

al-Bitar, Salah al-Din 118, 216
Blake, William 86, 88, 207
Borochov, Ber 39, 40, 131
Brandeis, Justice 149, 152
Buber, Martin 144
Bush, President George 163

Cairo 111, 113, 138, 146, 211
Cana, massacre (1996) 209, 221
Canaan 10, 11, 12, 21, 71, 72, 75
Canal Zone 98, 125, 149, 157
Carter, President Jimmy 59–60, 157
Chagall, Marc 176, 177
Chatila camp 102, 122, 140, 174, 175
Chemosh (Moab) 19, 72, 87, 199
Constantine 212
Coupland, Reginald 135
Cresson, Warder 148
Cyprus 11, 177, 178
Cyrus 22, 79, 118

Dagon 1, 4, 7
Dair Yasin, massacre 91, 92, 93, 116,
    126, 156, 169
Damascus 55, 101, 119, 132, 192, 214
Damour 101, 122
Dan 2, 11, 15, 16
Dar al-Islam (and alternatives) 213,
    216
Darwish, Mahmud 45, 180, 184
David 2, 6, 11, 13, 28, 75, 82, 116, 152,
    190, 193
    'star of' 80, 88
Davies, W. D. 23, 33
dawlah 210
Dayan, Moshe 141, 143
Dead Sea 176
Deborah 187, 197
    Song of 186
Decalogue, the 83
Delilah 3, 6, 182
Derrida, Jacques 78
Deuteronomy, Book of 5, 6, 21, 40, 47,
    77, 97, 183, 184, 206, 222, 224
Dheisheh 195
din 210
Dostoevsky, Feodor 73
Druzes 99, 121

Eban, Abba 29, 30, 34, 58–9, 69–70,
    115, 156, 171, 183
Ecclesiasticus, Book of 200

Edom 77, 176
Egypt 11, 18, 20, 55, 83, 89, 110ff., 123,
    125, 158, 165, 183
    and Sadat 60, 157
    in the UAR 110
Eilat 110
Eisenhower, President Dwight 110, 126,
    156, 163
Eleazar 100, 189, 203
Eliot, T. S. 48, 50, 88, 177, 181, 184
    The Waste Land 171
Eretz Israel 24, 25, 55, 56, 60, 69, 101,
    158, 166
Esdraelon 11
Eshkol, Levi 111
Euphrates 77
Exodus, Book of 77, 83, 88, 172, 183
Ezekiel 12, 78, 79

Faisal, Emir 133, 144, 146
    and Weizmann 132
Fanon, Frantz 138
Frost, Robert 17
Fu'ad, King 113

Galilee 11, 84, 218
    'Peace in' (slogan) 97, 100, 102
Galut 152
    see also diaspora, Jewish in Subject index
Gaza 1–2, 11, 14, 18, 62, 64, 66, 68,
    111, 130, 146, 169, 172, 184
Genesis, Book of 12, 13, 75, 77
Germany 89, 96
    Third Reich 91
Gethsemane 84
Gezer 12
Gilboa, Mount 18
Gilead 72, 184, 186, 197
Gilgal 85
Golan Heights 112, 158
Goldstein, Baruch 196
Goliath 6, 11
Goller, Rabbi Izak 83
Goren, Chief Rabbi Schlomo 23
Graetz, H. 25
Gush Emunim 23, 33, 81, 196

Habibi, Emile 139, 146
Haddad, Major 99, 100, 146
Hadrian 10, 25, 123
Haganah 92, 93, 106, 116, 126, 133, 168,
    183

Haifa 107, 146, 178
Halakhah 48
al-Haram al-Sharif 65, 69
Hebron 22, 66, 67, 68, 85, 111
Herodotus 10, 25
Herzl, Theodor 20, 25–7, 31, 32, 36, 39,
   43, 85, 108, 131, 143, 169, 187,
   191, 205
   Altneuland 36
   Diaries 37, 49, 146
   early ideas 26
Heschel, Rabbi Abraham 21, 33, 47, 49,
   87, 203
Hess, Moses 25, 33, 38, 129, 145, 153
Hibbet Zion 30, 43
Hijjawi, Sulafa 180
Hijrah 210, 212, 214, 224
Hizballah 104, 211
Hopkins, Gerard Manley 10, 16
Hosea 33, 97
Husain, Ahmad 178
Husain, of Karbala' 214
Husain, King 98, 99, 112, 120, 167
Husain, Muhammad Kamil 224
al-Hussaini, Fawzi 144
al-Hussaini, Al-Hajj Amin 113, 132ff.,
   144, 145, 166, 211
Huxley, Aldous 189, 201

India 72, 149, 155
Iraq 113, 118, 129, 142, 177
Irgun Zvi Leumi 92, 93, 97, 106, 116,
   126, 133
   see also Begin, Menahem
Isaac 22, 51
Isaiah, Book of 12, 15, 78, 79, 199
   Deutero-Isaiah 78
Ishmael 22
Israel, people 2, 14, 37, 48, 76
   as 'European' 28, 29, 31, 43
   in land-love 10, 28, 71, 73
   as 'self-chosen' 76
   self perception 28, 196
Israel, State 14, 18, 40, 42, 48, 74, 81,
   87, 89, 156, 183
   deciding 'eligible' Palestinians 139f.
   democracy in 102
   a 'Gentile' entity 46, 196, 222
   intelligence 174
   Palestinian minority 32, 44f., 68, 139
   peace activists 67
   police state 175, 183
   private guns 103
   victim psyche in 103

Jabna 12
Jabotinsky, Vladimir 28, 30, 38, 40, 41,
   55, 59, 65, 70, 77, 101, 106, 117,
   134, 141, 168, 182, 183, 223
Jabra Ibrahim Jabra 180
Jacob 7, 51, 145
Jakobovits, Lord 220, 225
Jarring, Gunnar 159
Jayyusi, Salma 178, 184
Jeremiah, Book of 12, 24, 78, 79, 82, 84,
   181, 184
Jericho 5, 22, 40, 62, 64, 68, 84, 146,
   169, 178
Jerusalem 5, 11, 24, 45, 58, 62, 64, 66,
   68, 74, 80, 85, 91, 93, 104, 108,
   116, 137, 148, 152, 193, 201, 218
   East Jerusalem, status 62, 112
   Fall 12, 187
   internationalization 57, 154
   Latin Kingdom of 145, 187
   'next year in . . .' 85
   Sanjaq of 18, 130
Jesus 33, 83, 219, 220, 221, 222, 224
   see also Cross *and* God in Christ *in Subject*
   index
Jewry 2, 10, 46, 74, 78
   American 148ff., 163ff.
   Arabicized 30, 31, 44, 46
   and socialism 39
   victim experience 90ff.
Johnson, Samuel 190, 192, 203
Jordan, river 2, 10, 18, 20, 38, 62, 71, 77,
   184, 192
Jordan, State 98, 117, 119, 137, 139, 165,
   174
   see also Transjordan
Joseph 168
Josephus 10
Joshua, Book of 2, 11, 15, 17, 20, 32, 33,
   40, 47, 75, 84, 96, 97
Joshua, conquest under 5, 9
Jubran, Salim 179, 184
Judea 10, 11, 35, 60, 71, 72, 78, 104
   capta 187
Judges, Book of 1, 2, 4, 5, 6ff., 19, 87,
   96, 186, 187, 199

Kafka, Franz 177, 184
Kanafani, Ghassan 49, 176, 182–3, 185

Kaufman, Ezekiel 198, 203
Kenyatta, Jomo 74, 139
kibbutzim 43, 93, 106, 133, 170
King David Hotel bombing 221
King–Crane Commission 147, 150, 151
Kiryat Aba 203
Kiryat Shemona 104
Knesset 32, 166, 172, 206
  Sadat in 59, 157
Kollek, Mayor Teddy 218, 225
Kook, Rabbi Abraham 21, 33, 198, 203
Kook, Rabbi Zvi Yehudah 22
Kuwait 142, 182

Lawrence, D. H. 48, 50
Lazarus, Emma 74, 87
League for Jewish–Arab Rapprochement
  144
League of Nations 54, 114, 150, 154, 169
  Covenant 55, 134
  see also Mandate in Subject index
Lebanon 2, 11, 18, 65, 70, 71, 117, 118,
  174
  confessionalism in 99, 121, 139
  'Grapes of Wrath' 64, 65
  invasion by Israel 92, 97f., 106, 160, 221
  labyrinthine politics 98f., 120, 121,
    140, 145
  PLO in 60, 120f.
Levinas, Emmanuel 29, 34
Leviticus, Book of 21
Liberty Rock 74, 148
Lincoln, Abraham 73, 87, 143
Litani, river 97
Lodge, Henry Cabot 149

Maccabees 74, 168, 191
Maccabeus, Judas 28
Machiavelli 220
Magnes, Judah 41, 49, 144, 145
Maimonides 48
Manoah 2, 15
Masada 84, 85, 91, 164, 175, 189
  Eleazar on 100
Mazzini 25, 38, 145, 153
Mecca 210, 211, 218
Medina 210, 212, 214
Megiddo 13, 186, 197
Meir, Golda 33, 36, 49, 73, 74, 87, 139,
  143, 185
Melchizedek 78
Melville, Herman 150

Micah, Book of 15, 32, 205
Midrash 75
Milton, John 1, 3, 8, 14, 15
Moab 19, 72, 87, 199
Montefiore, Claude 202, 203
Montefiore, Moses 132
Moses 5, 23, 77, 80, 97
Moyne, Lord 146
Muhammad 211, 212, 214, 216, 218,
  222, 224
  risalah 212
  tradition of 215
Myers, F. W. H. 176, 184

Nablus 23, 108, 130
Naqqash, Samir 45
Nathan 82
Nazareth 84, 178, 179, 218
Negev 11, 40, 155
Netanyahu, Benyamin 63, 65, 166
New Testament 9, 10, 174, 187, 217
  cited 83, 87, 202, 203
Nietzsche, Friedrich 197, 203
Noah 46, 96
Nordau, Max 38, 40, 54, 77, 117
  see also Balfour Declaration in Subject
    index

Ottomans 18, 38, 49, 55, 108, 113, 114,
  132, 145, 149, 152, 193
  and Arab nationalism 38, 49, 129, 130
  Herzl and 26, 37
Oz, Amos 22, 23, 89, 90, 106

Pakistan 202, 223
Palmach 136
Palmyra 18
Paul 202, 223
Pentapolis, the 11, 12, 16
Percy, Senator Charles 162, 163, 167
Peres, Shimon 61, 62, 63, 70
Persia 22, 79
'Pilate's seat' 134, 135, 145
Pinsker, Leo 25, 38, 117, 129, 153
Pound, Ezra 177
Psalms, Book of 9, 96, 199, 221
  cited 11, 12, 16, 87, 202
  enmities in 9, 96

Al-Qasim, Samih 178, 184
qiblah 218
  see also Mecca

Rabin, Leah 165, 167
Rabin, Yitzhak 61, 66, 11, 142, 217
  murder of 63, 174
Rahman, Fazlur 219, 225
Ramallah 66, 130
Red Sea 77
Reuben, 'the searchings of' 186ff., 191,
  197, 204
Rogers, William, Plan (1970) 158ff.
Rome 145, 187, 203, 218
  Romans in Palestine 18, 84
Roosevelt, President Franklin 152
Rothschilds 40, 54, 132, 145
Russia 145
  as 'holy' 73
  Jews of 27

Sabra camp 102, 122, 140, 174, 175
sabras 30, 31, 43
Sacher, Harry 29, 30, 34, 36, 41, 49,
  69
Sadat, Anwar 59–60, 98, 123, 125, 157,
  158, 177
Safad 85
Saladin 137, 145, 187
Samaria 10, 12, 60, 72, 104
Samson 1ff., 164, 168, 182
  riddle of 3
Samuel 2, 3, 86
  Books of 13, 88
Samuel, Herbert 56, 132
Saul, King 13, 14, 18, 82, 86
Sayigh, Tawfiq 176, 181, 184
Scholem, Gershom 42, 49, 70
Second World War 136, 147, 151
Sephardi Jews 28, 31, 44, 49, 57
Septuagint, the 10
Shamir, Moshe 30, 34
Shamir, Yitzhak 61, 65, 70, 107, 139,
  150, 217
Sharm al-Shaikh 109, 111
Sharon, Ariel 60, 100, 141
Shem, tents of 14, 46
Shihab, General 122, 126
Shiloah, Yossi 45
Shiloh 13
Al-Siba'i, Yusuf 177, 178, 184
Sidon 101, 107, 145
Simon bin Gamaliel 13, 14
Sinai 2, 11, 18, 60, 71, 75, 76, 95,
  98, 110, 118, 125, 137, 157, 166,
  172

Solomon 23, 76, 97, 190, 193
  'Psalms' of 33
Spinoza 25, 82
Stern, Abraham 92
Stern Gang 92, 133
  murder of Bernadotte 93
Suez Canal 59
  crisis (1956) 59, 118, 125, 156
Syria 10, 18, 54, 98, 106, 110, 111, 117,
  129, 130, 145, 158
  stake in Lebanon 120ff.
Syrkin, Marie 41–2, 49

Talmon, J. L. 33, 49, 55, 56, 69, 153,
  166
Talmud, Jerusalem 24, 33, 78, 80, 130
Tekoa 85
Tell Zatar 122
Thomas, Dylan 177
Tiran, Straits of 110
Toynbee, Arnold 18, 32, 224
Transjordan 11, 101, 113,130, 169
Tripoli 101, 107, 145
Truman, President Harry S. 57, 69, 151,
  155, 156, 163
Tunis 102, 140, 160, 175
Tyre 101, 107, 145

Washington, George 147–8, 163
Weizmann, Chaim 27, 30, 31, 33, 36, 39,
  52, 57, 69, 132, 135, 137, 141, 143,
  149, 151, 156
  Diaries 34, 146
  relations with US Jewry 151–2
Western Desert 136
  salvation of 'Israel' in 153
White Paper (1922) 134
Wiesel, Elie 106
Wilson, President Woodrow 55, 114, 129,
  149, 154, 161
Wise, Rabbi Stephen 149, 152

Yad Vashem Memorial 154, 195
  mutuality at 196
Yahwist, the 75ff.
Yaum al-Furqan 212, 223
Yemen 110
Yom Kippur War 59
yordim 196–7
Young Turks 38

Zachariah 217

Zaghlul, Sa'd 113
Zayyad, Tawfiq 179
Zealots 84

Zechariah, Book of 79, 80, 212
Zeita 180
Zephaniah, Book of 12

Subject index

accusation, mutual 208
agnosticism 177, 223
agriculture, in Palestine 43
ainigmata 207
aliyah 30, 39, 154
Allah 205, 212, 213, 214
Allahu akbar 205
ambiguity 51, 54–5, 64, 149
ambivalence 17, 24, 51–2, 59, 62, 67, 68,
    95, 109, 112, 123, 144, 151, 172,
    177
  at Camp David 157
  in Balfour Declaration 54ff.
  in Oslo Accords 62, 66
  in Resolution 242 124, 156
American/Israeli Public Affairs Committee
    (AIPAC) 67, 152, 162ff., 167
  and vilification 167
American University of Beirut 150, 166
anomaly of 'the holy' 71ff.
antipathy 6, 8, 26, 45, 48, 75, 144, 195,
    204
anti-Semitism 26, 39, 40, 46, 82, 83, 105,
    106, 136, 157, 177, 184, 189, 190,
    211, 225
  and Nazism 89
  perverse usage in charge of 48, 162,
    163
apartheid
  Jewish 68, 189, 191ff.
  within relationship 6ff., 43

Arab League 98, 113, 158
  Egyptian expulsion from 123
  frailty 113ff., 122ff.
Arab Ottomanism 38, 39, 45
Arab Revolt 38, 129, 132, 145, 150, 210
Arabic literature 182ff.
Arabism 28, 38, 45, 99, 109ff., 122, 128,
    129, 142, 159, 167
  and Christianity 216ff.
  and Islam 210ff.
  tensions 120
armistices 30
autonomy, and Mandates 149

Balfour Declaration 27, 35, 48, 53, 54,
    55, 69, 88, 93, 114, 130, 132, 148ff.
  status 54f.
Ba'th Party 118, 211, 216
Beth Shin 81, 174, 183, 184
bias, usual in casualties 107
Bible
  enmity in 6f.
  ethos 2, 8, 47, 199, 203, 217
  tension of priest and prophet 82
Biltmore decision 52, 115, 144, 146
  see also partition
Bilu'im 132
Black September 98, 119f.
blood-price 213

Caliphate 113, 129, 210, 216

Camp David 59ff., 123, 146, 157, 158, 166, 172
Canaanites 9, 10, 33, 76, 87
  expulsion of 6
  influence 6
  shrines 4, 13
'chosen people', concept 9, 25, 47
  Americans as 73, 150
  'self-choosing' 76, 86
Christianity 19, 203ff.
  Arab 28, 215ff.
  conscience in 154
  land 'holiness' 84, 85, 217
  origins, in Jerusalem 218
  and peace 216ff.
  role 204ff.
  the sacramental in 84ff., 216ff.
Church, Christian
  inclusive peoplehood 200, 219
  Jewish enmity from 105, 106
    see also anti-Semitism
  Jewish view of 79
co-existence, Jew/Arab 63, 85, 144, 215
  denial of 192
    see also apartheid
compassion, practice of 206, 219f.
  see also Seventh Day, The
compatibility 9, 14, 21, 43, 46, 47, 104, 189, 191, 198
  in Abraham? 67
  forlorn hope 116
  vetoed by statehood 144, 196
confiscations 172f.
conscience
  and guilt 89, 195
  in Zion 78, 80, 83, 89, 188, 194
containment of Zionism, case for 115f., 126, 136
covenant 5, 9, 14, 20, 47, 67, 71, 85, 153, 188, 195, 218
  with Abraham 73, 199
  Ark of 13, 85, 88
  Davidic 73
  Noahid 73, 87
  prestige of 14
  and race 157
  Sinaitic 75
Cross, the 177, 184, 216, 221, 222, 224
  divine forgiveness and 221
  in Marc Chagall 176

de-construction, and prophecy 78

demographic factors 77, 91, 100, 105, 124, 192
destiny, divine, and Jewry 190
dhimmis, under Islam 214, 216
dialogue 217
diaspora, Jewish 14, 16ff., 20, 24, 26, 28, 39, 74, 80, 85, 165, 190, 194, 202
  mission in 32
  undoing 44, 45, 117
diaspora, Palestinian 20, 117, 128, 168f., 216, 224
  de-Palestinianization in 43, 44, 45
  and Zionism 148, 149, 188
disturbances (1920s) 134f.
dominion, human 207

election, Hebraic 14, 20, 47, 157, 188, 218
  renunciation of? 195
election, in Israel (1996) 63, 64, 71
enlandisement 20, 23, 79, 80
Enlightenment, the 26, 117, 189, 194, 197
enmity 90ff., 105, 208, 209
entry to Canaan 75
ethics, and 'holiness' 81ff.
  in conflict 75ff.
ethnicity 14, 21, 47, 105, 125, 166, 168, 188, 192
  and paganism 6
  and territory 8ff.
exceptionality 48, 75
  burden of 47, 105
  and moral standards 175, 176
exegesis of promises 78f., 87, 154
exile 20, 24, 73, 77, 78, 188
  Palestinian 117, 141, 176
existentialism 178
exodus 9, 75, 212
  and dispossession 81, 169, 170
exoneration, false 209

faiths, under test 204ff.
Al-Fatah 98, 106, 119, 138
  and violence 138
First World War 38, 39, 147, 149
fitnah 204ff., 213, 222
forgiveness 206, 208, 209
  Allah and 213
  and the Cross 222
  written on maps? 220

'Gentiles' 22, 46, 47, 48, 50, 73, 87,

'Gentiles' (*continued*)
    92, 103ff., 148, 163, 183, 188, 191,
      194
  avoidance of 29, 45
  idea of 21, 46, 221
  perpetual paradox in notion of 196, 200
ghetto 29, 41, 43, 47, 48, 96, 176, 188,
    194
God
  'God in Christ' 220, 221, 222, 223
  perception of 206
  and Torah 82
goyim 22, 48, 90, 194
guilt
  Cross and 221ff.
  evasion of 221

Hamas 65ff., 103, 142, 173, 205
  Islam in 211, 223
Hebrew, revival of 30, 44, 169
'Hebrew Canaanites' 45
Hebrew University 41, 125
'holiness' 21, 47, 153, 197
  anomaly of 71f.
  and place 21
Holocaust 18, 82, 89f., 97, 104, 127, 135,
    154, 207
  see also Shoah
Holocaust Memorial Museum, Washington
    154
'holy land', the 33, 47, 49, 71, 148, 175,
    188
  divisible 52, 115
  indivisible 52, 115
  Islam and 218
  never alienable 59
holy places 62, 70, 84, 85, 193, 194, 216
  museumization of 216
homogeneity, Jewish 58ff., 70, 93, 101,
    124, 192
'host nations' 26, 43, 80
  United States as 163

identity, preoccupation with 190
ideology, socialist 39, 40
imagery, poetic 178ff.
incompatibility 26, 91, 144, 153
innocence
  assumed 17, 26, 42, 55, 156
  myth of 208
  Palestinian, of the Shoah 90
Intifadah 64, 102, 128, 141, 160, 173, 179

graffiti during 75, 183
invasion of Lebanon 98ff., 123
  consequences in Israel 101
'iron in the soul' 168ff., 173
irony
  in Christian Zionism 154
  in Jerusalem and on Temple Mount 65,
    69, 193
  in Palestinianism 178
  in US/Israel relations 131f.
  in Zionism 37ff., 130, 144, 194, 217
Islam
  in minority condition 214
  in peace 212f.
  role of 204, 210f.
  'salvation' in 219, 220

Jewish Agency 36, 42, 92, 114, 166
  and the Mandate 54f., 114, 134
Jewish National Home 113, 133, 134
Jewish State 57, 68
  concept of 54f.
jihad 211, 212, 223
Judaicization of Jerusalem 65
Judaism 20, 31, 44, 68, 79, 130, 148,
    183, 220, 221
  betrayal of? 97
  concept of 'Gentiles' 104, 105
  futurism in 42
  as a 'nation' 38, 195
  politicization of 97, 176, 187, 191
  sacro egoismo 37
  and Zionism 187f., 191, 195, 198, 202,
    204
Judenstaat, Der 25, 26, 27, 33, 36, 169
justice, concept 206f., 217

Labour Party, in Israel 61
land, the 9, 16ff., 43, 81, 189, 190
  doctrine of 23, 24, 72ff.
  extent of 77
  privatized conceptually 28, 32, 199
  as sacramental 85, 190
  sale and purchase of 115, 135, 145
'land for peace' formula 59, 65, 68, 129
Likud Party 58, 64–5, 92, 103, 115, 143,
    160, 162, 172, 203
  and invasion of Lebanon 97ff.
literature
  in Israel 32, 44, 45, 169
  Palestinian 32, 45, 169ff., 178
location, Palestinian fate of 17ff., 127

Madrid Conference 103, 107, 131, 141,
   142, 160f.
   Palestinian statement at 128
Mandate
   French, in Lebanon and Syria 107, 113,
      121, 130, 145
   Palestinian 36, 38, 52, 55, 59, 61, 129,
      149, 150, 153
      Britain in 41, 69, 113, 114, 125,
         133ff., 154
Maronite Lebanese 98, 99, 121, 140, 145,
   174
   and Israeli intrigue 99, 100
Marxism, in Zionism 39, 40
   see also Borochov, Ber in Name index
Messiah 15, 49, 61, 70, 79
   and futurism 42, 61
monolatry 47, 198, 199
   statehood reverting back to 201
monotheism 47, 198, 201
   and Hanifs 67
   in Judaism 199
myth, and historicization 76

Al-Nakbah 59, 70, 115, 178
Name, taken in vain 81
Nasserism 110ff., 118, 122, 142, 211
'National Home' 27, 35, 53f.
nationalism 40, 42, 46, 49, 55, 108, 113,
   117, 133, 136, 149, 153, 157, 167,
   183, 189, 194f., 200f., 210
Nazism 89, 90, 94, 112, 125, 136, 152,
   189
negotiability 21, 52, 125, 141, 142, 144,
   173
   long Palestinian exclusion from 103,
      160, 183
   and forgiveness 220f.

Old Testament, in Palestinian Christianity
   217ff.
opportunism 52, 75ff., 187
   and scruple 75
Orient House, East Jerusalem 66
Oslo Accords, the 61–2, 63, 64, 65–8,
   70, 103, 110, 144, 146, 161, 178,
   192

Palestina capta 187
Palestine 8, 9, 10, 38, 71, 108
   Agonistes 1, 3, 8, 207
   Jewish use of the name 35, 37

political entity 130f.
   under Rome 10, 11, 35
Palestine Liberation Organization 13, 42,
   49, 59, 60, 74, 97, 98, 119, 120, 142
   avoidance of Islamicization 133, 136,
      142, 211
   Christians in 211
   decision of 1988 61, 70, 103, 141, 160,
      161
   formation 138
   and Islam 210f.
   and Jordan 159
      see also Black September
   in Lebanon 98ff., 121, 139, 140
   long non-recognition 103, 160, 183
   and Oslo 60ff., 66
   and Saddam Hussain 142
   'sole representative' issue 141
Palestine National Charter 49, 70, 107,
   146, 211, 223
Palestine National Council 62, 64, 70,
   107
Palestinianism 24, 25, 37, 48, 60, 221
   and Holocaust 82, 83, 127, 167
   identity in travail 127ff., 140ff., 168ff.
   impossible elimination 102
   as inconsequential 35ff.
   interior factions 173ff
   and Jordanian relations 158ff., 166, 167
   land love 23, 130, 169ff., 176
   miscalculations 52, 56, 106, 128ff., 136
   odds against 18, 127, 129, 143, 144
   post-1967 situation 58
   poetry 128, 176f.
   in self-statement at Madrid 128
   Zionist view 22, 36, 37 passim
Palestinians 68, 74, 88 passim
   diminishing numbers of Christians
      216ff.
   flight in 1948 and 1967 92, 117
   and forgiveness 208ff.
   incapacity for pragmatism 136, 144, 161
   and Islam 216ff.
   in Israel proper 139
   in Lebanon 98f.
   as 'Nazis' 60
   pain of 173, 174, 206, 207
   pawns of Arab powers 108ff., 116, 124,
      170, 177
   poetry among 45, 176ff.
   self-help alone availing 118ff.
   slow attrition of 125, 132, 161, 171

Palestinians (*continued*)
  status of refugees 106, 109, 112, 117,
    118, 137, 169, 170
  victimization 89ff., 140ff., 161, 177
  in Zionist eyes 37, 40ff.
paradox 10, 14, 20, 32, 37, 46, 66, 151,
    191, 194
  of place 29
  of statehood 48
particularity, Jewish 22, 30, 198
  and ethics 82
partition 22, 41, 52ff., 59, 93, 106, 114,
    115, 135, 144, 147, 153, 154, 183,
    192
patience 213
peace process
  bias in 58, 65, 66
  naive term 42
  ultimate peace-making 209ff.
Peel Commission 54, 114, 135, 136, 153,
    183
'people of the land' 14, 15, 83
perversity, human 209
Philistia, Philistines 1, 3, 13, 15, 47,
    71, 77, 81, 105, 130, 164, 217
pilgrimage, Christian 84, 217, 218,
    219
  and museumization 216
poetry, Palestinian 176ff.
political, the, limits of 219, 220
'promised land' 21, 71, 97, 199
  anomaly of 71f.
  meaning 75f., 154
  return to 24
prophets, Hebrew 10, 53, 80, 83, 85, 87,
    154, 164, 217, 221
  abeyance of 200

Qur'an 67, 183, 193, 209, 210, 212–14,
    216, 219, 221, 222, 223f.
  fitnah in 204, 205
  forgiveness in 213
  islam in 212, 223
  and peace equation 212f.
  sabr in 213
  sharh al-Sadr in 212, 223

recalcitrance, Arab 108ff., 118
reconciliation 219ff.
Reform Rabbis 65, 132
refugee issues for Palestinians 62, 137f.
repatriation

contention around 64, 106, 117, 121,
    137, 169, 170
  Israeli propaganda and 118, 170
repentance 208
resistance
  decision for 103, 114, 138
  literature of 45f., 168., 173
Resolution 242 (UNO) 60, 124, 126, 142,
    156, 166, 167, 183
retaliation 90, 92, 207, 208, 223
return, the
  doctrine of 49, 80, 152, 176
  prophecies and 77f.
Revisionism 38, 77, 192
rhetoric, Arabic 123, 126

sabr, in Qur'an 213
sacrament, Christian, of event and place
    190, 218ff.
Scriptures, Christian 19, 20
  exegesis 78ff., 217
Scriptures, Hebrew 9, 10, 16, 78ff., 96, 217
'sea peoples' 11, 16
secularity, and Muslims 210, 224
self-sufficiency, Israeli will to 91f.
Semitism 14, 44, 46, 47
separatism, Judaic 21, 22, 26, 28, 32, 43,
    45, 190, 191, 198
settlements, issue of 62, 65, 68, 160, 172,
    192, 196, 203, 223
Seventh Day, The 93, 97, 106
Shechinah, the 80
Shi'ah Muslims 99, 107
  and suffering 214, 215
shirk, in Islam 24
Shoah, the 14, 48, 89ff., 102, 152, 196, 197
  see also Holocaust
Six-Day War 58, 93, 97, 109ff., 125, 156,
    178
  Meccan sermon after 213, 223
  pre-emptive strike 111
'smiths', lack of in ancient Israel 13, 14
sovereignty
  divine 219
  issue in Jordan with PLO 98f., 139
  issue in Lebanon 99, 101, 121
  notion of 94, 131, 139, 144, 171
statehood in Zionism 54ff., 80, 144
  early view of 25
Sunni Islam 99, 214ff.

'uncircumcised', the 7, 11, 14

United Nations Organization 36, 52, 56,
    57, 58, 87, 93, 111, 115, 137, 152,
    162
  on Jerusalem 57, 193
  Partition vote in 56, 57, 115, 154, 155
  peace-keeping 104, 110
  'racist' vote in 157
United Nations Special Committee on
    Palestine 153, 155
United States of America 52, 67, 69, 70,
    110, 141
  aloofness from Palestinians 160f.
  arms to Israel 104, 107
  bias to Israel 125, 127, 147f., 160, 209
  as a 'chosen people' 73, 87
  Jewry in 40, 67, 115, 147ff., 153,
    162ff.
  oddhandedness 147f.
  pusillanimity 103, 147f., 173, 209
  Rabbinical Assembly 138, 146
  refusal of Mandate 149
  uneasy relations with UNO 158, 159,
    167

Versailles Conference 149, 151
vicariousness 91, 94, 153, 206ff., 210
victimization 89f., 123, 169, 177, 208
victory, tension in 94, 95
vindication of rights 208
violence
  and Islam 212, 213, 214
  and Israeli vigilantes 173
  strains of 138, 139, 140, 160, 173,
    188, 208, 209, 221
vulnerability 210ff., 219, 220
  of minorities 214
  in Shi'ah Islam 214, 215

Washington 18, 52, 62, 67, 156, 158,
    162
  Israeli nexus 144ff., 162
  Jewish lobby in 67, 147ff., 154, 162f.
Washington Holocaust Memorial 165,
    166
water factor 97, 111, 171

West Bank 32, 58, 60, 66, 68, 77, 98,
    111, 117, 158, 172, 179, 192
Western Wall 96
wilderness, theme of 20, 23, 33, 40, 83
Wisdom writings 200
wrong, when irreversible 206ff.

Yahweh, the divine Name 2, 16, 19ff.,
    47ff., 72, 76, 78, 80, 130, 186, 188,
    198, 199, 205
  house of 86
  and Samson 76

Zionism and Zionists 37, 43, 143, 187,
    217, passim
  agricultural 85, 131, 132
  and Arab identity 44, 45, 131
  bias 48, 154
  of the cheque-book 165
  Christian 154, 217
  Congresses 33
  contradictions 188ff., 194, 200, 217
  cost to all neighbours 97ff.
  and diaspora 109, 152, 189, 191
  early preference for British 150
  ethical conscience in 41, 42, 75ff., 82,
    88, 91, 100, 201
  extra-territorial in USA 148f.
  frustrations 119f.
  as a 'Gentile' thing 46, 194
  and 'the holy' 73ff., 84, 190
  and King–Crane Commission 151
  and the 'land' 14, 15, 17ff., 20, 31,
    176, 181
  language and 44
  opportunism 52ff., 75, 76, 110, 146
  personalities 52, 53, 69, 115, 156, 168,
    187
  positives of 197
  racism in 157, 192
  secularity in 79, 224
  socialism in 39, 40
  vengefulness of 89ff., 168, 169
  visionary quality of 17, 49, 52, 125,
    187, 189